not limited to the church), the changing definitions of love throughout a long marriage, and the achievement of personal success as a form of destiny. Readers will come away from *Unconverted* reassured that light—and lightness—can overcome any shadows or doubt cast by time or the uncertain heart."

—Gina Barreca, board of trustees distinguished professor of English literature at University of Connecticut and author of *They Used to Call Me Snow White But I Drifted* and *Babes in Boyland: A Personal History of Coeducation in the Ivy League*

Unconverted: Memoir of a Marriage ©2025

Release Date: June 17, 2025.

All Rights Reserved.

Printed in the USA.

Paperback ISBN: 978-1-57869-400-6

eBook ISBN: 978-1-57869-699-4

Library of Congress Control Number: 2025907383

Published by Rootstock Publishing

an imprint of Ziggy Media LLC

Montpelier, VT 05602

info@rootstockpublishing.com

www.rootstockpublishing.com

Book Design by Eddie Vincent, ENC Graphic Services.

Cover Art by A. Robert Hirschfeld ©2016, "Luminous Horizon," 12"x24" mixed media on canvas. Used by permission.

Author photo provided by the author.

The stories in this book reflect the author's recollection of events. Some names, locations, and identifying characteristics have been changed to protect the privacy of those depicted. Dialogue has been re-created from memory.

THE POEMS OF EMILY DICKINSON: VARIORUM EDITION, edited by Ralph W. Franklin, Cambridge, Mass.: The Belknap Press of Harvard University Press, Copyright ©1998 by the President and Fellows of Harvard College. Copyright ©1951, 1955 by the President and Fellows of Harvard College. Copyright © renewed 1979, 1983 by the President and Fellows of Harvard College. Copyright ©1914, 1918, 1919, 1924, 1929, 1930, 1932, 1935, 1937, 1942 by Martha Dickinson Bianchi. Copyright ©1952, 1957, 1958, 1963, 1965 by Mary L. Hampson. Used by permission. All rights reserved.

No AI training; no part of this book may be reproduced or transmitted in any form or by any means, electronic or mechanical, including photocopying, recording, or by an information storage and retrieval system (except by a journalist or reviewer who may quote brief passages in an academic or editorial review) without permission in writing.

For permissions, or to schedule a book club visit or reading, contact the author at pollyingraham2@gmail.com.

"With tender honesty and infectious humor, Polly Ingraham unfolds the story of her initial attraction to, longing for, and eventual enduring commitment to a man with whom she has so much in common; and with whom she has a very big difference. Polly is not religious. Her husband Rob is a devout bishop. We travel along with them, in both tender and ordinary moments, as they find mutual understanding and discover new depths within their own souls. This book will convince you of the power of love in a divided world. Love can weave different lives together in a bond that makes each of us more our true selves than we could ever have imagined. This is simply a must read."

—Jake Owensby, Bishop of Western Louisiana and author
A Full-Hearted Life and *Looking for God in Messy Places*

"Anyone who has felt the pressure to conform to other people's beliefs will recognize themselves in Ingraham's story of marriage, church, compromise, and resistance. *Unconverted: Memoir of a Marriage* follows one woman's quest for identity and community, and it wrestles with questions faced by many Americans who don't share the faith of their neighbors, or even their spouses. How much do you bend? How much do you reveal? When you love someone with beliefs different from yours, can you connect deeply and commit fully while preserving your sense of self?"

—Kate Cohen, *Washington Post* columnist and author of
We of Little Faith

"With brave, bold, and beautiful prose, Polly Ingraham effectively presents internal conflicts in a strong marriage defined by contrast—a wife without religious background and a husband called into the Episcopal priesthood who becomes a diocesan bishop. The author's determination to claim and proclaim her independent self is all the more moving and profound given her frequently uncomfortable immersion into church settings and her significant role in parenting and maintaining a household while advancing in her own career. The author's curiosity, her intellectual and even academic investigation into tenets of Christianity and the specific denomination to which her spouse has devoted himself, demonstrates her urge to understand without committing to incompatible beliefs. *Unconverted: Memoir of a Marriage* reveals in powerful ways that what melds and sustains this couple—love, passion, admiration, acceptance, parenthood, and individuality—is more essential than a shared faith."

—Margaret Porter, award-winning and bestselling author of fifteen historical and two contemporary novels

"Polly Ingraham's memoir is a refreshing, honest, and insightful look at the life of a marriage, specifically the blessings and challenges of a union between a deeply religious man and a secular woman. With humor and practicality, not flinching from self-examination, Ingraham explores what it takes to love someone despite opposite life choices, and how a couple sacrifices for that love, both in a literal and metaphorical way. I found the story moving way beyond any traditional clergy wife tale, asking deep questions about faith and commitment, and offering a hopefulness for the future of diversity."

—Mary Carroll Moore, bestselling author of *A Woman's Guide to Search & Rescue* and *Last Bets*

"Authentic on every page, Ingraham's *Unconverted* is funny, exuberant, astonishingly honest, tender, and brave as the author explores some of the deepest questions of marriage and love and living into her own fullness. A compelling and vivid memoir—as real as it gets!"

—Diane Les Becquets, award-winning and national bestselling author of *Breaking Wild* and *The Last Woman in The Forest*

"'Being married means, in part, being willing to move on in order to stay together,' Polly Ingraham reminds us in *Unconverted*, her joyful, nourishing feast of a memoir. In the unique position of being the wife of an Episcopal bishop who also happens to be the handsome, charming love of her life, Ingraham's thoroughly engaging first-person narrative confronts questions, familiar to many of us, concerning spirituality, the role of women in powerful institutions (including but

Unconverted

Polly Ingraham

Montpelier, VT

For Rob

Prologue

I walk past broken beer bottles and a person sprawled in an alley, toward the sound of clanging bells. The reddish-brown stone structure rises straight up at least a few stories high, commanding the block, with its much taller Gothic bell tower visible only from another angle. I had learned just a few days before where to find the heavy wooden doors that would grant admittance to this intimidating place where ancient rituals are performed. Still, about to enter all alone and feigning confidence, I wonder whether it is wise to continue.

It is a Sunday morning in late September. I am in New Haven, but considering all the daunting mysteries that I am about to face, I might as well have landed on another planet.

Fitzwilly's, the restaurant to my right as I reach Elm Street, is dormant after another rollicking Saturday night. The Yale Co-op, over on Broadway and brimming with brand-new textbooks on every possible subject, is also closed. No one under thirty years old stirs anywhere.

As I arrive at my destination, an usher in a blazer and striped tie bows slightly and hands me a bulletin, perhaps hoping that I am planning on becoming a new member of the congregation. "Good morning, and welcome to Christ Church!" I muster a smile and move in to find a seat amid the people, strangers to me, sprinkled around this cavernous space. I keep my eyes mostly down, my characteristic urge to wave tamped down.

Here they perform a "high church" brand of Anglicanism, the kind closest to traditional Roman Catholicism. Instead of pews, there is a collection of linked wooden chairs, with high backs and caned seats. They look like something out of Elizabethan England. Painted icons of saints in rich gold and red colors hang everywhere, elaborate engravings on each partition, and directly in front is a large wooden sculpture of an elongated Jesus on the cross: bearded long face, horrible nails, dangling feet, and the weight of his anguish. I sit down and gaze up, then down again, not sure where to look.

This is foreign territory; in fact, almost everything about the carefully designed interior makes me uneasy. I am here only because I am a clergyman's wife. The awkwardness of my first few Sundays at worship had made clear to me that I needed some kind of a game plan, a reliable way of behaving in this space.

In most work environments, people don't expect that an employee's spouse will show up on a regular basis. In fact, it's generally considered odd in offices or schools or auto body shops or laboratories for someone's partner to keep popping in. Not so in the world of religion; in this realm, it's the other way around. A spouse who participates in the life of the church is a value-added component. Their regular presence is considered good for business.

This kind of open invitation to join in can be construed as a kind of compliment or, if you're someone like me, an impossible thing to pull off: I am not one bit religious. Never mind the elephant in the room, what we have here is more like the mammoth in the marriage. The stakes are high: if I don't find an effective strategy soon, this woolly creature might cause the beautiful, but also fragile, love my husband and I had created to go extinct.

The service begins with my husband Rob and other people in silken white robes chanting as they walk. Our upstairs neighbor, Jay, swings a silver container of incense around creating a white mist. He does this with solemnity, no doubt aiming to set a mood of antiquity. In this setting, the occasional car horn or whoop of greeting between passers-by outside sounds especially crass.

I don't understand the order of service, the significance of each weighty gesture; I follow along in the hymnal as best I can, relying on my long-standing ability to read music and sing. Watching Rob up at the altar, I get the only reminder of why I am here. His physical presence sends a current right through me, and the rings on my finger say we are married. But I feel no satisfying connection between my entire earlier life—who I was shaped to be— and this moment.

Except for the handful of times that Rob had asked me to accompany him to services while we were dating, I had barely ever gone to a place of worship during my thirty-three years as a single person. Now, I watch Rob perform his duties, making gestures like crossing himself, bowing his head whenever the name of Jesus is mentioned, as if he'd been transported to some other sphere of reality.

I realize that, whatever he is doing and feeling, I need to be in charge of guarding my core self. Back in college, a professor of mine had said that "integrity" was one of my hallmarks. Now, past all the paper writing and thrust into this peculiar setting in the real world, I must grope for a way to maintain that quality. Sitting here, I wonder how to be honest about my identity, about what does and doesn't sustain me deep down, while also being true to my husband.

Especially when communion time comes.

This is the part of the service when differences between the truly faithful and the not-so-sure or the absolutely-nots are revealed. On each previous church morning, both when we were dating and in the early months of our marriage, I had wondered: Do I stand up and get in line for the wine and the wafer, essentially going through the motions under false pretenses? I'd opted to stay right in my seat and just watch the proceedings, as if I weren't getting on this particular train and maybe mine would be along soon. It was now becoming routine: each Sunday, I expect some people are noting my lack of participation, but I can't get myself to budge. Part of me *wants* to— for Rob, for our union—but a different part of me advocates staying put. I see no middle path.

Today, though, it's a new Sunday: now, I have a plan.

The night before, I experienced a breakthrough moment.

Over dinner, under the chandelier that looks both ancient and ridiculous, after I asked Rob something about which clergyman would be doing what part of the liturgy (a newly acquired word for me) at the next morning's service, he broached the topic of how I might comport myself. He did this in a sympathetic, not a didactic, way—aware that I'd been wrestling with the issue.

"You know, you don't have to take the wine and the wafer when you come up for communion."

Dropping my fork with a clatter I said, "I don't?"

"Nope. Crossing your arms in front of you is a sign that you would just like a blessing. The priest will put his hand on your head and say a few words."

"You're kidding me! How come you're just telling me this now?"

Rob and I had been married just a year ago, in September of 1990, right before he began his final two semesters at Berkeley Divinity School. At first, we'd rented a floor of a little pink house with a picket fence near the East Rock part of town. Once he started his first job as "Curate" (assistant to the "Rector"—head honcho) in August at Christ Church, we'd moved to a much bigger, older church-owned house a short walk from his new workplace. He'd tumbled down from a theological ivory tower to arrive at a fortress of religion, with me in tow.

I thought of the several times I'd accompanied him to church services before we were married, mostly at a granite, cloistered monastery in Cambridge, a place that intentionally set itself off from the hustle and bustle outside. These were unusual early dates. Those mornings of sitting side by side in a pew until he got up to go to the rail—not expecting me to go and then returning soon, hands clasped—were easy enough. I stayed still, observing. Once he changed positions, though, to be one of the hander-outers in front, it got trickier. While he was still in divinity school and assisted at a church in a prosperous suburban town, I drove down to visit on an occasional Sunday, feeling very much the guest rather than a part of the congregation, staying in my seat as I had done before. Now, though, he was in his first regular job, one that really mattered, providing us housing as part of the deal. I was making the two-block walk each Sunday, since not going at all seemed out of the question, but my keep-to-the-pew strategy was feeling more questionable.

Sitting across from me at the table, he shrugged. "Didn't think you'd be that interested."

The truth was, I hadn't up until then been that interested. This new option, though, might do even more than alleviate the loneliness of sitting on a kind of island during those long minutes: it could also help me fit in better and relieve some of Rob's own anxiety about my nonparticipation, which he was trying to keep under wraps. There might be some risk of appearing more devout than I really was—a kind of wannabe. I'd just have to see how it felt to take that walk, then reassess.

This morning, when the fateful time comes, I review in my mind how to proceed. I get up from the hard bench with filigreed back and walk toward the front of the church, hoping I won't make any missteps, certain that many eyes are following my progress. Click, click, click. I tell myself to just keep going and it will be over soon. I walk through the rood screen—an elaborately carved wooden structure that serves as a boundary between the congregation and the choir and high altar—and approach the rail to claim a spot. Here I am, next to all of these full-of-faith people, and there is Rob, the man who holds me tenderly at night, over on the other side, carrying a chalice filled with what he believes is the blood of Jesus.

I grab onto the smooth mahogany and kneel down on the red cushion. Then, remembering how I'd been coached to do this, I cross my arms over my chest with a quiet *thump*. They are now a little too close to my neck; I make sure I can still breathe.

Right now I feel as if one of us in this year-old marriage, I'm not sure which one, were emerging from a kind of jail cell to meet the other ever so briefly. Instead of being in harmony, merging in an embrace, we are on opposite sides of something that keeps us apart.

For a fleeting second, as Rob speaks quietly to the person with the bowed head next to me, I imagine what it would be like to hold both hands out and receive what my spouse is offering there—to see him as my priest. In a way, it wouldn't be so hard to put the chalice to my lips, place the feather-light disc on my tongue. But then, queasy at the thought, I realize that this act would transform me into someone other than who I really am, and other than who *we* really are, together. It wouldn't work.

Without making eye contact with me, Rob turns back to get more wafers, and into the vacuum looms his boss, a tall and angular man. He observes my crossed arms and, trying to smile, puts his large hand on my head and utters his blessing. I flinch, feeling no benefit whatsoever. Barely hearing what he says, I watch Rob and think how urgently I need to find a way to live—more than that, to flourish—in the marriage without looking over a chasm toward the man I love. If I am to continue coming to church, into a carefully delineated world that feels like his more than ours, I will need to be fortified with the knowledge that, in ways that matter most, we are bound together, and everything else could fall away without our noticing.

In the microcosm that is just the two of us, the rail must come down.

PART I

DISCOVERING

Chapter 1

Didn't Know What I Was Missing

When I was eight years old, in my prime tree-climbing and pony-riding time, someone named William Douglas published a book called *Ministers' Wives*. I learned about it some forty years later, when my husband brought it home to me one Saturday afternoon after a church rummage sale. "Here—you might be interested in this," he said casually, tossing it on the kitchen counter before going upstairs to change out of his black shirt and starched white collar. The front jacket described the book as "a path-breaking study of ministers' wives in more than 30 Protestant denominations . . . as wives, mothers, church-women, and members of their communities." Agog, I put aside whatever paperwork I was doing and dove in, starting with the mid-1960s publication date. In the same era that becoming a minister's wife was the furthest possible thing from my mind, it had been, in the society as a whole, apparently a topic worthy of some scrutiny.

In those days, with mainline church attendance surging, people must have wondered about the women who married the men in the pulpits. Douglas, a minister and also a professor, presided over a study supported by the Eli Lilly Endowment that surveyed more than five thousand wives of clergymen. Reading the blurb, I thought, *If back then I'd been exactly who I am now, would they have studied me, too? Could I have been a pebble to be counted?* The prospect of that was deliciously enticing: me—a deviant datum.

To find any real streak of religion in my family, you'd have to turn back the clock. My parents both sprang from a Methodist heritage, but the regular worshippers in that faith, on both my mother's and my father's side, lived a couple of generations ago. Indeed, my paternal grandfather, from Brooklyn, apparently turned away from religion because he had experienced it in his own childhood as unnecessarily harsh, with too many restricting rules to follow. He did not want his four children to live that way. When not at his law desk, he enjoyed ambling around outside, especially in his garden. My paternal grandmother, also from Brooklyn, was from a Quaker family. She was content to carry out some of those practices—going to meetings each Sunday and saying "thee" and "thou"—by herself without bringing her children into it, although later on she was happy whenever a grandchild would accompany her.

My mother, who grew up in a town just over the Vermont border in Quebec, lived across the street from the local Methodist church. Her widowed mother played the organ, with ramrod straight posture, and the minister often dropped in for a meal, but the faith never rooted in her or any of her four siblings. As children, they also looked with skepticism at the huge French Catholic churches displaying ornate everything while congregants struggled to make ends meet for their families. Trying to articulate this apparent inequity, Mom would scrunch up her face and say, "So much *gold*, Polly."

My mother and father were in certain ways very different from one another, but when they married on a cold February day in the McGill University chapel in Montreal, they must have had some understanding that their wedding would be the beginning and also the end of church for them. In about the only photograph we have from that day, they stand stiffly together, almost as if there were no underlying passion. The life they built together over the next fifty years demonstrated otherwise though. Maybe they were just uneasy about being in a chapel, or being photographed at all.

What I am certain about is that not only other people's marriages or past marriages, but even our own—the ones we live in day after day—remain filled with mystery.

By the time I came along, the fifth child and the first girl, my family's nonreligious way of life had been passed on and was well-established. On our hillside not far from beaches on the North Shore of Long Island, my brothers and I did outdoor chores and "roughhoused," had friends over for games, read in couch corners, listened to Motown records, practiced on instruments in little bedrooms with wood-paneled walls, told lots of stories, and laughed. Our prefabricated house was compact and all on one floor, but my parents had built it on fields surrounded by acres of woods owned by my grandparents. One of my brother's friends once said, "You mean you have this really long driveway and just this crummy house?" In a way, it *was* crummy, but it also buzzed with life.

My father had grown up with horses, and even though he commuted an hour and a half on the Long Island Rail Road to New York City each day, he wanted the same for us. And so there was Ranger, my brother Mike's Appaloosa; Baby, the Standardbred retired from the trotter track; Red, the Welsh pony, first my brother Sandy's and then passed on to me with a big red ribbon around his neck; and then finally Cody, the Quarter Horse who had competed in races, given to us by a friend. Their heads over the fence rails, watching our goings-on; their prancing in from a far corner of a field for feeding time; the desultory swishing of their tails at flies in summer; the growth of their long coats in winter; the tearing around their paddocks for sheer joy: all were key elements of my childhood. In similar fashion, my mother had a special fondness for Irish Setters; we had a string of those graceful, auburn-hued dogs because of her passion. She'd raised a litter before she was married, in that preamble time of life, and so she wanted to keep on being who she was, stroking the darling smooth heads and soft ears. We had Clancy, who grew old before I started school, and later Shanny, who used to run through the woods to the golf course and move players' balls. Momentarily irritated when she got a call to come pick him up, Mom was as attached to her dogs as Dad was to his horses. I absorbed both kinds of devotion.

None of us got dressed up on the weekends to go down to the churches on Main Street. Increasingly aware that other families—

mostly Catholic, in our town—did this, kept to a regular pattern of attendance, my brothers and I never asked to go on our own. It just wasn't discussed. When I look back on my childhood, this fact is astounding. How could my parents just ignore the whole, huge world of religion, a staple in the lives of so many good people? They never sat us down at the heavy oak table, gaining scratches each year and, glancing at each other for reinforcement, said, "You're probably wondering why we don't do what a lot of your friends do on Sunday." Then again, I can't recall ever seeking an explanation, either. They didn't look askance at our church-going friends, who numbered in the dozens, or criticize anyone else's parenting. We just lived without this particular chunk of life, whatever it was. And we still felt whole.

Sometimes, on Christmas Eve or Easter morning, I went with my across-the-street friend Lynn and her family down to the Episcopal church. These were photo opportunities—she and her sister in bright-colored dresses and patent leather shoes, her younger two brothers spruced up and sheepish about it. I remember the pews; the plush red velvet kneeler we put down at a certain point in the service; nothing about the sermons, except that, once back at home, everyone snickered about the clergyman who couldn't keep his conservative political stance out of the pulpit. It all felt so temporary; as a visitor, I could appreciate the novelty without delving into any big questions.

Dad's mother, whom we called "Gwy," gave me exposure to a faith tradition that was a kind of offshoot of mainline Christianity. For the colder months of the year, she lived in Brooklyn, but all summer she was in a house right down the road from ours. "Would thee like to come to meeting with me tomorrow morning?" was a question she regularly asked me and any of my brothers who might be around on a Saturday. She was a lifelong Quaker. As she got into her seventies and eighties, she knew it wasn't wise to drive alone, in her cream-colored Fury with the panel of buttons to the left of the steering wheel, the twenty miles over to the meeting house. I didn't mind going; the trips gave me my own special time with her, and making the turn off the busy highway into the tranquil grounds of the place always felt soothing. There was no liturgy (a word I hadn't learned yet), and I wasn't asked to do anything in particular. I listened to the breezes blowing in and the creaking sounds as people rose up from their seats to speak on a wide range of subjects: "I've been thinking about the end of the Vietnam War, and what it means for our country, and for our individual souls."

When I left for college, I didn't seek out the local Quaker meeting. I took one English course on the King James Bible (knowing at least that it was a very important book), but no religion. When I started working as a teacher, I had no inclination to add Sunday services of any kind to my long list of duties, returning to the Westbury location only for a memorial service for Gwy, who died in 1982. For five summers, I studied literature and earned a master's degree, staying in a secular lane. If I'd been asked, in my twenties, if I belonged to any church, I wouldn't have hesitated to shake my head, "Nope." Those early brushes with religion were just that—brushes.

When, in 1989, I met and then fell for my husband, I had already been through the rocky shoals of my twenties and was a couple of years into my thirties.

Practically an old maid by earlier standards, I had enjoyed stability in love and in work for a time, teaching for a string of years at a boarding school in Connecticut. In addition to having a steady boyfriend who was both smart and funny, I had a practically built-in group of friends. In one picture I've saved, eight of us are crowded happily on a couch with beers in hand and hats askew, one already married couple, but most of the rest of us showing the languor of being in comfortable, committed-enough relationships.

I caused my own problem when I dared to make a move into the unknown, feeling the pressing need to venture outside what felt too comfortable, too much like an extension of college. With a growing passion for animal rights, I thought that writing one grant proposal for the cause of "humane education" could be my ticket out of this privileged world, so I gave my notice that I wouldn't return for a sixth year as an English teacher.

Almost as soon as I left the protective embrace of the place, though,

I regretted it. "I've made the biggest mistake of my life!" I wailed, over and over again, finding myself stranded back in my old bedroom on Long Island with only my concerned parents for companions. No grant funding happened. I scrounged for a part-time teaching job at a commuter college, wishing desperately to turn back the clock. What had felt like a gleaming adventure waiting to launch became suddenly an unstructured mess of a life. My losses came pouring down all around me, palpable but irretrievable. If only I was back on that campus with all my friends, if only I hadn't been so naïve about life, if only I'd held onto what I had—the broken record kept playing. This was my first hard lesson in the phenomenon of personal overreach: tremendous security can lead to restlessness, to impractical thinking, and then, at least in this case, to a crash.

I had to start over again in a new place with temporary jobs and mostly unsuitable men. Moving to Boston in the mid 1980s, for no particular reason other than needing desperately to reset my life at age twenty-eight, I eventually made some stabs at dating again. I met a couple of guys through my college network and a couple of others in random ways: at a global relief organization where I worked, in my own apartment when the cable TV company arrived. This time was, in some ways, hazardous and definitely tough on the spirit, mostly serving to make my past existence glow ever brighter as it receded.

Gradually, though, I got stronger. While I wouldn't call it exactly "faith" that got me through, it was something akin to hope, or maybe just grit, an unwillingness to succumb to a lousy set of circumstances. I became immersed in a stimulating job with a nonprofit that brought Boston public school students into downtown companies for their first work experiences. In a position to help create opportunities for dozens of sweet and lively kids, I started shopping at Filene's for form-fitting suits and heels that clicked sharply as I walked down drab school hallways.

And then, thanks to a tip from mutual friends, I met Rob.

Chapter 2

Coming Together

On a January day in 1989, I picked up the phone in my apartment, the third floor of a white clapboard house near Porter Square in Somerville, a few T stops from downtown Boston. The smell of seafood wafted up from the fishmonger shop across the street, cars sped by, and the Christy's Market sign in the parking lot to the left was lit up, as always. It was a raw, sunless winter day. "Hi Pol," said Barbara. She and her husband, David, in their early forties, had stuck with me since I left my job at the boarding school where they still worked. They knew I was not fully content yet in my new urban existence, although recently I'd found more of a foothold. Having been high school sweethearts and wedded to each other and their steady jobs for more than a couple of decades, they must have thought I could use a little help.

"Do you happen to remember meeting a guy named Rob at Logan Munroe last summer, when you visited us? He was a teaching assistant then, also an alum from the school, graduated right before you started teaching here." Logan Munroe was the first dormitory I'd been assigned to; I had a tiny apartment smack in the middle of a long hallway where teenage boys returned from classes wanting to stir up some fun. Barb and David lived with their two sons in a house that was connected, through a study, to the dorm.

A memory of a dark-haired guy's T-shirted back flashed in my mind. "Hmm…kind of," I said, recalling sitting in their kitchen when he was heading out. He looked young and was, in fact, a full three and a half years my junior, still in his twenties. Fortunately we had not overlapped in residence at the school—he as student, me as teacher—but just missed one another coming and going. The memory of even seeing him walk across campus, with a backpack slung over his shoulder and shaggy dark hair, would have made me stop as I considered the possibility of meeting him *now*, when we were both beyond that place. Besides, if Barbara had recalled that we had first crossed paths this way, even if he hadn't sat in my classroom, she wouldn't have suggested that we go on a date.

"Well, he's actually working at a bank in Boston now, and David and I thought you two would enjoy meeting each other sometime. Can I give you his number?" She knew that I had enough gumption to make the first move. She also knew that Rob had already been married and divorced, and told me that, too, without emphasis.

I considered this suggestion. My dating life had actually picked up of late; for the past year, I had been seeing Matt, an upbeat guy originally from Arkansas, someone on fire for journalism. He had recently left for graduate school in South Carolina, but then had invited me to come down so he could give me a first look at the Gamecocks football stadium and then swaths of Mississippi and Alabama. We drove through torrential rain most of the time, windshield wipers working furiously, Smokey Robinson turned up loud. We laughed a lot. Afterward, though, neither one of us sensed any particular future for ourselves together. It was as if the road provided easy, paved traveling for a while, then gradually and gently dead-ended.

"Sure, but it might be a little weird for me to call him up cold. If you give me his address, I could drop him a line." I came from a family of people who wrote postcards easily. Getting out a colorful Flair pen a few days later, sitting at the card table I had set up for a desk in the tiny study adjoining my bedroom, I composed something jaunty, including my phone number.

Rob's response came swiftly, within the next week, so I wondered whether he might have remembered our brief encounter the summer before, glad for another opportunity. We were sure we'd recognize one another when we planned to meet, midweek, at a popular restaurant near my apartment.

I sat at a table first, and then he walked in, all business-like in a suit and tie and black overcoat. He wore no whiff of church whatsoever. More understated than effusive, he gave me just the hint of a smile. But he looked right into my eyes, and listened to my babbling. "I live with my roommate Katy just a few blocks from here." He didn't reveal much about himself, and I steered clear of the recovery from divorce issue. I learned that he was in the midst of training for the Boston Marathon with a college friend, he had several roommates in Brookline, and he had no car. He mentioned that he worked at Shawmut Bank, but that a big change—going to graduate school to finish a program he'd started several years back—was brewing. I found him intriguing. It was as if I were sitting across from a deep well that seemed to go down, past the light I was accustomed to, into some kind of compelling darkness.

About a month later, Bonnie Raitt's song "Nick of Time" was playing on the radio in my mustard-yellow Mazda hatchback when we lingered outside his apartment. That's just how finding him felt to me: I was moving into my thirties, and he was twenty-eight. Surely, my mistakes were behind me now. This guy was no fly-by-night casual kind of partner; he had some kind of inner heft.

He also had a specific plan for his own path into the future. One evening, when he knew his roommates would be out and we'd have his kitchen to ourselves for a cozy supper, he let me know that he'd been accepted by Yale Divinity School and would be moving to New Haven that summer.

"They took my credits from General." I knew by now that this was the school in New York City where he'd started before a major rupture in his life. "This means I can begin as a second year student, so I'll need to spend two years there, not three."

Although I was discovering that his face didn't often light up with joy, I could see that he was very happy about this.

"Oh wow! That's great!" I said, mind racing with what this change would mean for us. Before I met Rob, I'd applied to law school, prompted mostly by my passion for animal rights. I'd been accepted, but then turned down the offer, deciding that my job working with Boston teens was plenty fulfilling and I couldn't justify spending all that money, even though I knew my father—a lawyer himself—would have offered to help. Putting building blocks together toward the future wasn't exactly my specialty, even though I was the elder one here. "So two more years, and then you'll decide what actual occupation you'll choose?" I ventured.

"Oh, I thought I'd already made that part clear: I'm reentering a path that leads to becoming ordained as an Episcopal priest and serving in a church."

I'd heard him use the term "priest" before, each time conjuring a collared person in a black robe who moved his hands in the air and chanted in mysterious ways and definitely was *not* married. Could this guy I was falling for become that guy? If he did, what would he do with me? And would I need to change in some fundamental way in order to keep hanging out with him?

Daunting as those questions were as they fluttered by, I soothed myself with the fact that all of that was in the future. The here and now was good, mighty good. I felt pulled along, with the only right choice appearing in neon: JUMP ON THIS TRAIN BEFORE IT'S TOO LATE. It didn't matter to me whether he was going to be a truck driver or a corporate executive; he was the one. This wasn't exactly love at first sight, but just the next notch over.

As winter began melting into spring, we went out to art museums, jazz bars, and plays in small venues; Boston had plenty to offer us. Discovering that we each loved to read, we also found our conversations gained texture when he talked about George Herbert and W. H. Auden, poets I had missed in college, while I tried to articulate my devotion to Shakespeare and E. B. White. We inched closer to Big Beliefs this way, but for a while, we kept those at bay. Families, friends, jobs, travel—these were our first topics.

Gradually, I learned about his inner core. Early afternoon on Patriots' Day in mid-April, I was getting ready to leave my apartment to take the T over to Copley Square to meet Rob at the time he had suggested he'd likely be finished with the Marathon. I hadn't wanted to get wedged into the crowds lining the streets, and that was fine with him. In my usual way of trying to claim a kind of middle ground, I intended to be an enthusiastic greeter at the precise moment he made it in—to show up when it really counted.

The phone rang. "Hi, I'm done." His voice was calm, as if he were telling me he'd just finished a dentist appointment.

"Whaaaat, already?" It was a full forty-five minutes before he'd predicted.

"Yep, I guess we were a little faster than we thought—just under three and a half hours. I'm back in Brookline now. Still want to come over here?" If he was disappointed in me, he didn't let that show.

"Sure—I was just leaving. Wow, congratulations. How do you feel?"

"I'm fine. How about I make you chicken carbonara? Can you stop at the Star Market and get some eggs maybe?" Unbelievable—he'd just run twenty-six-and-a-half miles, for the first time ever, and he was thinking about making *me* dinner? When I arrived, he was ready with candles for the table.

Much later, when we both encountered *The Five Love Languages*, a book by Gary Chapman, I would come to understand that performing "acts of service" was Rob's specialty; when it came to love, he spoke mostly by doing.

By the end of that spring, after the flowering trees lining Boston's streets had settled into green, we started regularly coming back to my futon on the floor, lit all night by the orange glow of the Gulf sign in the Christy's parking lot outside. My hands on his shoulders, strong from pulling oars; his kisses long and tender; everything melting together in our silence as cars sped by outside. "Shhh . . .," he whispered to me as the shadows danced on the walls. "There's no need to talk."

Staying quiet wasn't my specialty, though. Feeling emboldened by the time summer arrived, when our daytime dates often took us away from the heat of the city to swim in Walden Pond, other twenty-somethings scattered in small clusters around the generous perimeter, I was ready to dive into the topic of religion. I knew I needed to choose the right moment—and it wasn't when we were doing anything athletic out in the sunshine.

I was no scientist, but it seemed like high time to haul our inner furniture out and examine the inventory. He hadn't wanted to be the first to broach the subject; the difference between us wasn't, at least at first, one bit sexy. The fact was, I was much more curious about the tables and chairs in *his* belief system than he was about *mine*, maybe because he could already sense that the décor in my particular soul had a haphazard quality: flashes of bright colors and cushions, some bookcases, but no real seating arrangement.

At the same time that I was dizzily falling for him, it was dawning on me that while we had full-on magnetism, I had nothing even remotely matching his deep faith in God, in the whole story of Jesus as Savior. I knew I wasn't completely lacking in good raw materials on the inside, but they weren't put together in any kind of intentional design.

Years later, he would tell me that, far from having everything figured out at this point, his belief system was more like a scaffolding than a completed house; he still felt very much under construction. But just the fact that he was working on this Very Big Project at all made me question whether I'd been doing a whole lot of dawdling, or whether just trying to rebuild myself had been sufficient.

In July, at a North End restaurant with tables spilling onto the sidewalk, I finally asked the question that had been buzzing around in me like a persistent fly from the start.

"So, you believe *what* exactly about the resurrection of Jesus?" I punched it out between mouthfuls of Bolognese. My tone was casual, not indicating that we were on the brink of something that could make or break us. Up until now, the story of the Son of God—crucifixion, certain death, then a miraculous rising up—had been only peripheral in my vision. Now it sat right on this table.

"That it changed everything. The women found the empty tomb, showing that he took on all of our humanity and dissolved the barrier between all of us and the Infinite." He looked straight at me, as if conscious that this was the heart of the matter, *his* matter, and my reaction would show just how much tenderness I had.

Taken aback by his absolute certainty about a series of miraculous events that had barely fluttered across my screen before and had definitely never stayed long enough to warrant serious confirmation, I could only ask another question. Looking back, I see why he might not have seen this as an especially sympathetic response.

"What exactly do you mean by redemption?" I'd heard the word, partly thanks to Bob Marley, but the concept was shaky. The red wine encouraged me to come clean, to shake out my ignorance as if it were a napkin.

"The process of being saved from death, from evil." He said it with complete assurance, as if he was telling me that he took the Green Line out to Brookline. Did he think this was actually possible? In my experience on the planet thus far, I saw about equal parts good and evil, life and death. When we hit a tough patch, we try to be brave and hope (some people pray) for a reprieve. Most of us get some small saves along the way, but an Ultimate Save? No one located in a body that wears out eventually can get that.

The waitress came to pour water from a pewter pitcher she held up high, asking in a sparkly voice, "Is everything all right here?" She was probably Catholic, knew all of this already.

"Wow . . . but we definitely all still die, don't we?" I was holding the table now, clinging to the literal, unable to fly into the ether of the spiritual.

"Yes, in a certain way, but when we know that we are all loved no matter what, that Jesus emptied himself so that we may more fully live, we gain a freedom that defies even the prison of death."

Again, he looked deep into my eyes, having placed his essence in front of me, waiting for my response. I was flummoxed. On the one hand, I knew that he was one of billions around the world who believed this; on the other hand, I couldn't pretend that I was one of them. The sweep of my past thirty years provided no such conviction. I had always *felt* loved; I just never associated that sense of security and acceptance with Jesus. For a moment, I flinched. "That must be an amazing feeling," I finally said, drawing upon my reliable supply of curiosity about what others believe without jumping in to swim in their particular pools myself.

The difference this time was that I was powerfully drawn to this man.

Watching from the edges, withholding my own endorsement, suddenly felt like going dangerously counter to giving myself over to love.

"It definitely is," he said quietly, candles flickering on the tiny table. "Can you possibly imagine it?"

I didn't answer, and was not able to imagine how resurrection actually happened. But I didn't have to imagine how my own life was getting more beautiful by the minute; that was an unmistakable fact.

I had a lot of questions about his faith; he had very few about whatever he thought I had that resembled faith. Or maybe he could tell it just wasn't there to investigate. Years later, he would explain this ongoing discrepancy by pointing out that I tend to release what's on my mind easily anyway, not waiting for an invitation. Practically drawing breath from a set of tenets that were so central to his identity, he tried to convey the depth of them to me in a few easy lessons, since I had asked.

I remember one conversation when he was ready to teach me about the overall rhythm of the Christian calendar—what comes before what and leads to what. He wondered out loud whether I was more of an "Incarnation" (the birth of Jesus as both divine and human) or a "Transfiguration" (Christ's appearance before his disciples in radiant glory) person and decided, maybe based on my mentioning that I liked the Christmas season best of all, that it was the former. Meanwhile, as soon as he uttered the word "Incarnation," my mind was going back to those packets of pale chocolate malt Carnation Instant Breakfast that my brothers and I once tore open on school mornings. My associations didn't quite click the way his did.

The more he brought out specific pieces of his faith, the more I was struck by both his own certitude and the implausibility of it all to me. We are all sinners, and sin is a form of death; Jesus died to take on our sins, to free us from them, as if we were peeling off one used-up skin and starting with another—over and over and over again, in an endless cycle. It wasn't that I disagreed with his way of seeing, exactly, but it all seemed too neat, like a wrapped up package, and definitely unscientific.

The chasm between us was, in many ways, vast. Sometimes, when I probed too much, I sensed that my voice sounded to him like I was shouting across the divide, a fruitless effort. "I just don't get how he could have *cured* lepers, with just a touch!" There was no easy bridge to walk across, but there was a kind of electric wire dangling there in space, and he knew it. "Look, Polly, no matter what I say, it won't sound rational to you, so can we just give it a rest?" Occasionally, his irritation level rose, and he snapped at me, or his head drooped momentarily, with disappointment.

And yet he stuck with me, either looking past my disbelief, or finding something else there, something that could stand in for faith. I began to wonder whether maybe he knew something about me that I didn't.

Rather than finding fault with me for not knowing people like Zacchaeus and Ruth, Leah and Luke, for not understanding what or who the Almighty could be, he said that he believed God had brought us together, and it was OK if I didn't see it that way. At first this image seemed weird, as if some unknown (to me, anyway) force was pulling strings, but then I decided to relax and hope that nobody messed with this amazing thing we had going. We each felt a magnetic pull that, he was convinced, was overseen by an Invisible Third Party and, I was equally convinced, had only to do with our own bodies and souls. I wouldn't have been able to say what a soul actually *was*, but I knew it was just as real as a beating heart.

For the first time in my life, though, I had to confront whether or not I could cobble together my own package of important beliefs, some structured way of seeing the world and human existence. Had I just been rolling around, more or less thoughtlessly, like I did when buffeted by the strong ocean waves on Long Island's South Shore, ending up with sand in my bathing suit, without any clear vision of what really mattered and why? Suddenly, I looked incompletely formed *to myself*. Not fully baked. Not autonomous enough. What could I do, short of adopting his particular Episcopalian frame of reference directly upon receiving it, to alleviate this imbalance? What did I have ready to toss into a spiritual bank account that our pooled resources might become?

Chapter 3

He Knew What He Needed

By the end of 1988, a few months before I met him, Rob had decided to leave his solid job in commercial banking, where he'd landed in a training program after spending a year in France, and enroll in divinity school, for the second time. Fellow young bankers must have thought it odd how he brought peanut butter and jelly sandwiches for lunch, saving money for tuition, instead of heading out with them. One of his colleagues said that it would have taken him "about a millisecond" to right himself from a weird decision like that. But Rob was sure: he was ready to resume a journey that had been previously interrupted.

The journey had started with a devastating accident. When he was in ninth grade, he broke his neck in a football game, actually walking off the field before being taken to the hospital. He lay in traction at home for months; friends came by for a while at first, then the visits tapered off. A Yale professor and Episcopal priest who did part-time work at the local church Rob's family attended visited regularly. Eventually, he introduced Rob, who was experiencing a whole new level of staring-at-the-ceiling boredom, to works of philosophy. I imagine them in that small upstairs bedroom, Rob flat on his back wearing glasses that kept his head immobile, taking turns reading Nietzsche, Kierkegaard, and Camus.

This kind of material would have been new to his family. Rob's dad, Bob, was a salesman, mostly of silverware. He loved meeting people and talked easily on a range of subjects. Growing up outside of Boston, he'd been a burly football player and served in the Korean War after college. His own father, Alfred (Rob's given first name), worked mostly as a security guard and also pumped gas on Commonwealth Avenue in Boston. He had a fiery temper and died young of a heart attack. Marie, Rob's mother, grew up on a small farm in Upstate New York; her father, Carl, did odd jobs. He had a midlife conversion experience that brought him to soup kitchen missions in Schenectady, but his spiritual reading was limited to the leather-bound King James Bible that ended up on Rob's desk. Showing an early ability for cooking through 4-H, Marie went on to college and then became a home economics teacher; later she would work in test kitchens and become a "food stylist"—a savvy career woman.

When Rob's parents married, they lived for a time in Minnesota. Rob was born first; soon after, his sister, Robin, arrived; then five years later, a brother, Mike. During these years, Bob traveled many miles through the upper Midwest, stopping mostly at hotels and restaurant supply showrooms, selling his wares. Once Rob asked to accompany him. He peered out the back seat window at plains filled with snow, found nothing much to like about the way of life he saw—men in bars, smoking and drinking. His dad's new job brought the family to central Connecticut when Rob was about ten; there they settled into a neighborhood that would provide some friendships, at least one bully, and multiple tragic stories of lives derailed or even ended. But this I would learn later.

After his accident and months lying dormant, with nothing but time to absorb new ideas, when Rob finally returned to high school and found the humdrum life there lacking, he asked his at first startled parents if he could go to a nearby boarding school. There he knew he'd find more stirring of the intellect, including a Department of Behavior and Ethics. Starting as a day student, driving back and forth, he would continue to explore big questions that were not, at first, necessarily ecclesiastical ones. He also decided to take up a new noncontact sport—rowing. Once in college, he kept reading deeply, but he felt no particular draw to church, until a kind of epiphany shone a light on the direction his life must take.

With the regular college crew season over, Rob decided early one November afternoon to head down to the Connecticut River on his own. He would take out the wooden scull that he had saved up to buy, from house painting and dishwashing jobs. He told no one his plan. Pushing off from the boathouse dock in rowing shorts and sweatshirt, he managed the two long spruce oars skillfully, so that the only sound was the rhythmic dipping of wood in water. The sky darkened, and snow flurries danced around him, disappearing when they reached the inky surface. Tall, straight evergreens stood sentinel on each bank. "You're at your most vulnerable when the oars are out of the water and you glide forward," he would tell me, years later. "It's a balancing act — the thing holding you is pencil thin, and the movement sends ripples raying out on either side." Hands getting raw, he suddenly felt that he was not alone, that there was a presence surrounding him, buoying him up, almost like he was being held. He was engulfed by warmth and recognized that this must be God. And he believes that, in this sliver of time, a kind of veil was lifted from the world, freeing him to be one with a fuller reality, to see, as Wordsworth described, "into the life of things."

It was this moment that propelled Rob soon after college toward getting the training he needed to become a religious leader. He enrolled in seminary in New York City at about the same time he married his college girlfriend, also a rower. But within a year and a half, after his wife's terrifying brush with cancer, the marriage crumbled, leaving him reeling, questioning everything, including God. He found himself paralyzed again—this time not physically, but emotionally and spiritually. Someone suggested a healing year away, in Paris, where he wore black turtlenecks, smoked, made new friends, and reassessed the direction of his life. Wanting to reinvent himself and make a new start, he decided to enroll in a training program at a big bank in Boston, to learn how to be a loan officer. There would be no philosophy or theology roaming these nicely carpeted halls, pondering life's largest issues, looking out the large glass windows at the cityscape. Maybe, he thought, he could keep healing there and gain some kind of certainty about the future.

Through his time of turmoil, his younger sister Robin—called Binny—was going through an ordeal of her own, one that would leave a deep imprint on him. Beginning when she was a teenager, lupus had been gradually breaking down the valves in her heart. She had already had surgeries, but by her midtwenties, the situation was growing dire. She was put on a list for a heart transplant—unusual for a young woman—and Rob, Mike, and their parents waited, fearful and hopeful at once.

Not long before I met Rob, he had been by her side in a Boston hospital room for many evenings while she lingered close to death. All through their childhood and adolescence and into their twenties, they had played and laughed together; she was the main person he turned to, for everything. Now her very being hung in the balance. At the end of each day filled with financial transactions, he would take the T and then the elevator up to her room and watch old episodes of *Star Trek* with her, or just be by her side, quietly. Finally, on a mid-December evening, a helicopter delivered what they had been waiting for: the promise of life, renewed. Another person's fatal accident resulted in the most tremendous gift Rob's family had ever had. Binny would go on to live almost another twenty years; she got married, gave birth to a son, and thrived in her job.

He emerged from the searing experience of the transplant with a conviction that he had a distinct calling: to be there for others, both in and out of hospitals, who were seeking to cross over into a kind of resurrected life of their own. This is what he must do.

Rowing alone on the river, being present with a beloved sister in a hospital room—both of these experiences pushed him toward starting and then resuming the training he needed to become a spiritual leader. He would reenroll in divinity school, a different one this time.

Chapter 4

Two Lovers, Three Mountains

In August of 1989, with Rob set to move to New Haven while I stayed in Boston, we felt the need to take our first trip together: hiking in the Tetons. The scenery on the two-hour drive to Jackson Hole, Wyoming, from my brother's home in Logan, Utah, was so spectacular that even I became speechless. The road twisted its way through Cache Valley, with trees hugging the steep cliffs on both sides. Emerging into the open, we stopped along a turquoise lake with mist rising up, to get the most delicious raspberry shakes ever concocted. Sipping the cold, thick, perfect pink with Rob's gaze on me, I felt a combined sense of peace and fulfillment, greater than any I'd ever known. "Hmmm...so good," I said to him, eyes closed. We savored this liquid ecstasy, sensing that the future held promise of many other kinds, although we hadn't made any promises to one another yet. Crossing the state line, we passed expansive green fields with horses grazing in the twilight, switching their tails.

Dropping our stuff in a wood-paneled motel room, we drove into tourist-filled Jackson Hole and headed into Billy's Burgers, where the only seats were at the counter. Without preamble, Rob took my hand, looked into my eyes and calmly said, "Polly, I want to be your husband. Will you marry me?" I felt the floor drop beneath me, but something prevented me from freefalling with it. Perhaps out of a misguided desire to appear more rational than passionate, perhaps keenly aware that we were in fact still getting to know one another, perhaps just not able to take in the enormity of his desire to be with me for eternity, not fully convinced of it, I responded with, "Wow... OK... We'll take it in stages, then." I was hedging my bets, sounding more like a schoolteacher than a woman in love, mouthing a kind of both-feet-on-the-ground caution that makes me shudder now. The sentence has lived on for decades.

Rob looked briefly crestfallen, but not really surprised. He didn't push me. I didn't do what I now wish I had: leap up off my vinyl-covered spinnable stool, with other customers in cowboy hats looking on, and throw my arms around him, saying, "Yes, yes, YES!" I was restrained without understanding why. The truth is, I still don't understand what piece of me felt the need to hold back, just a bit.

The fact that the Church would accompany us through our married life barely even registered, because I didn't yet have any idea what that would really mean. But I knew that I was still getting to know this man, and that he came with a kind of mysterious chaperone.

Rob sensed, fortunately, that the words I uttered while we sat on those counter stools belied my passion, that he was in fact nudging me to uncover it more fully. The three-day backpacking trip would be a turning point, because he'd made a bold move here. Waking up on the first morning out, we unzipped our green tent, damp with dew, to see three jagged peaks right in front of us, bathed in a rosy glow, presiding over complete silence. With no one else around, it felt as if we were the sole viewers of the most fabulous show in the world. I walked close to the edge of a ravine and stood in amazement; Rob came up and put his arm around my waist, saying nothing. The whole place rang out with the power of love when it's first fully realized. Here, Nature was the only backdrop, urging us on. We did not speak of beliefs, of differences; they would have been irrelevant. We absorbed only magnificence.

Sometime during the course of that day, my underwhelming response to his proposal the day before morphed into something more enthusiastic. *Yes I will marry you of course I will marry you because how could I not marry you?* According to Rob, I never came right out and said this; I remember that I must have, but maybe I just assumed he could tell I was all in.

By the third day, with the prospect of a whole life together stretching ahead like a forever trail, I felt a new round of questions start to bubble up. Putting aside for a time my ongoing uncertainty about Episcopalianism—filled in only partly through our dating conversations—I wanted to know about something more tangible, something that would surely impact me more substantially: church housing. With only a misty notion of the architecture of his faith, I shifted to the kind of topic—literally bricks and mortar—that would offer more concreteness to me. Situated completely in the secular world, I couldn't jump in his skin and imagine what it felt like for him to be leaving a bank office with floor-to-ceiling windows in order to reenter a spiritual realm where ancient theologians were floating around.

Lagging a few lengths behind him on the trail, not able to see his red cap over the tall block of pack, I piped up, "So how does the whole residence thing work with a clergy job?"

He turned around just enough to throw his voice back to me. "It depends on the church; often they provide a house, sometimes not."

Now I definitely wanted to pursue this topic, like a marmot with a mouse. "So you mean they just show us where we'll live? We don't get to choose? What if the place is too weird or dark or creaky or something?" I'd lived in boarding school housing fresh out of college, and it was fine then, but the prospect of this kind of automatic assignment happening in my thirties took me to another level of uncertainty, right alongside the murky matter of religion itself.

"Oh, the rectories are mostly pretty nice," he said. "And besides, we won't have to pay rent." I kept trudging along the path behind him, conscious that I had just learned a new word: rectory. His own confidence in the way of life that lay ahead of him—whether or not I chose to join him in all of these "stages"—was bolstering my confidence that we could do this into-the-church life together. *He* was the only magnet I needed, I thought. Whatever strangeness I might encounter in the world he was choosing to enter, even elements that might make me recoil, surely I could manage so long as our love stayed strong.

He'd asked me to marry him but he hadn't—yet, anyway—asked if I would be willing to become an Episcopalian. That would have been one step too far.

My eldest brother, Mike, and his wife back in Utah were the first people we told about our engagement. I took Maryann aside in their laundry room, eager to confide in a woman, and the blue eyes on her tanned face surrounded by brown curls widened with, "Oh wow, Polly, and you've only been dating for a few months, right? This is so exciting!" She wasn't far off with the time estimate: it was August now, and we'd first met in February. She had been raised strictly Catholic and took my nieces to church; they lived among Mormons and drove by temples that swelled with attendees every day, while my brother, a sports editor, stayed true to our nonreligious upbringing. Neither one of them saw any real difficulty for us in the fact that my fiancé was headed to divinity school—for the second time, determined to complete the degree and put a collar on, permanently. Or, if they did, they held back flickers of doubt.

When I told my mother by phone that Rob and I had just gotten engaged, she blurted out, in her usual light-hearted way, "But Polly, we're Methodist!" in a vain attempt to convince either one of us that there was even one square foot of religious ground under our feet. She and my father had only met Rob a couple of times, but they trusted both his dedication to his career path and his sincerity in loving me. Nobody in my family raised the issue of what kind of clergy wife I would be, whether I'd be happy in the role, and if my total lack of a faith life, let alone experience with church, would soon be put uncomfortably in the spotlight.

As far as I recalled, my parents hadn't pushed any advice through all the decisions my brothers had made (three of them were married at this point), and my mother didn't probe into anyone's activities, preferring to take a panoramic view of the family with, "We're all doing our different things." In retrospect, I think this restraint in voicing any opinions came from both a desire not to meddle and a feeling of having a full plate already. In any case, we five were fine with the we-support-you-as-you-need-us philosophy.

Not hearing any particular reactions but curious to get some feedback, I finally asked my brother Sandy, "Would you expect that after our wedding, I will become an Episcopalian to please Rob?" I was accustomed to soaking up input from my brothers as if I were a little sister sponge; they generally didn't pour it upon me, but I watched and listened intently, absorbing what I could from their broad experience. Sandy was a decade older, had studied British history, bombed around Europe on a motorcycle and worked on a Scottish sheep farm, taught in a school on Chicago's South Side and in another on an island in Lake Champlain before getting a second graduate degree to become a business professor. He didn't wait long before answering, "Heck, no, Pol. You don't just put on a religion like you put on a coat."

He didn't try to plumb the depths of how I felt, most likely because he thought he already knew. "It's a pretty big deal," he said, never having felt the urge to start practicing a faith but having observed others do it during the extra ten years he had on me. The getting dressed analogy made sense, especially because I thought I would have needed to feel chilly enough to *desire* that extra layer, that coat. Simply being married to someone who had always worn one didn't mean I would automatically go for the same look. But, on the other hand, beginning our engagement with an insistence on what I *wouldn't* do might spell its own kind of trouble ahead.

I was lucky, I realized, that Rob hadn't put me on the spot with this question; maybe I needn't worry about changing myself—committing to a set of beliefs—to please him. Wondering about the clergy domicile was pleasant enough, since I gave Rob the benefit of the doubt that some darling house with lovely flower beds and light streaming in would be in our future.

Then, a daunting new figure emerged—someone who already had partial control over Rob's life and therefore would also need to scrutinize me. He was The Bishop.

Chapter 5

Passing Muster

Having just restarted divinity school classes (second year) in New Haven, Rob casually mentioned while visiting me one weekend that we were now facing one very specific appointment. "Since we're officially engaged, The Bishop has asked for a meeting." This was a telling, not an asking. For now, I was willing to take the invitation as a compliment because it implied that, whatever anxiety he was feeling about introducing me to this person with authority, he was willing to take the risk.

I turned over on the futon, still on the floor after three years living next to Christy's Market, put my elbow down, and propped up my head. "Sure, I love meeting people. But does he actually have some say in the direction of our relationship?" I wasn't sure I really wanted to know, because this might take us into tricky territory.

"Well, kind of. Since I'm on my way to the priesthood, he needs to give his nod of approval, partly because I've already been married." Oh, right. Suddenly I realized that this personage had been tracking Rob through his ups and downs, that he'd known him longer and maybe in some ways better than I did. This was an uncomfortable thought. But still, here the two of us were, alone together in this apartment room with its tall ceiling and doors with perpetually loose knobs. There was likely a part of him that was wondering how I would present myself, whether I might even raise any red flags, or whether this meeting would be an easy win, but there was another part, at least I hoped there was, that was committed to standing by me, no matter what.

Looking back on it, I realize that this meeting represented the first of many times when my behavior—revealing as it might my stance toward the Church—could be a factor in Rob's devotion toward me. When he'd told me early on that he considered God a participant in our relationship, he wasn't kidding. Still, I needed to hold up my end.

A few days later, I called home. "Mom, guess what? I get to go meet The Bishop!" She fell silent for a moment, then, showing uncharacteristic and maybe even put-on anxiety, asked, "Oh Polly, what will you wear?" I could tell by her tone that she wasn't really worried, but rather excited at the prospect of my bringing our whole unchurched family into his office. Church, of any kind, even when it was right across the street, had always been a separate entity to her—the organ playing, the ornamental gold, the bowed heads—and she no doubt thought it would stay that way; but she also wanted peaceful coexistence. My new proximity to the whole domain meant the seven of us were about to be subjected to some close scrutiny, the exact nature of which was unclear.

Rob, normally a low-key person, had trouble tying his tie that morning in his Yale dorm room. He also showed concern about my dangling earrings and flouncy blue-jean skirt, checking me out thoroughly. "You're wearing *that*?" I flinched momentarily, thinking I looked plenty sharp, ready for any kind of appointment. Then it dawned on me that the meeting held higher stakes for him than it did for me. I had never seen him this nervous. Whatever this ancient hierarchy was that the Church was built upon, he bought into it. And, instead of encouraging me to just be myself, he wanted me to worry about making just the right impression. I said, "Oh, it'll be fine," but I was beginning to wonder. I had no playbook for what the "right impression" was in this context. Should I act demure? Indicate that I was ready to follow Rob anywhere the Church might lead? We hadn't done any rehearsal for this. All I knew was that I wanted to pass the audition.

When we arrived at the Diocesan House in Hartford, Bishop Headquarters, we had to wait for a while at the bottom of a grand staircase, with many previous Connecticut bishops, from their full-length oil portraits, peering down at us. Rob paced back and forth; for him, this place was all about power—the kind he needed to obey. I looked down at my skirt, which was above the knee but very full with folds of denim, and realized that it was also slightly tie-dyed.

After a long ten minutes, Bishop Walmsley appeared at the top of the stairs and gestured that he was ready to receive us.

At this point, I decided that only one of us could afford to be nervous, so I practically waltzed into the wood-paneled office in the big old Hartford mansion, relaxed and curious. Seeing a whole lot of framed pictures on his desk and also on the wall behind it—some of family but others of African travels—I went right over and started examining them. Later, Rob said, "Polly, you went behind his desk! You moved into his space!" Clearly, he viewed this man as a Very Big Deal, whereas I took the Regular Guy approach.

After a bit of small talk, whatever anxiety I had completely melted away. He was a kind man; his eyes showed that.

"Bishop, can you tell me why exactly we're here?" I was accustomed to being forthright, but this was taking it to a new level. I'd burst the dam.

Rob's expression told his thoughts: "Oh no, game over. He'll never go for this now."

But Bishop Walmsley stayed calm in his armchair, hands together, and said something like, "Well, I wanted to get to see you two together, get a sense of your commitment to one another." He didn't add "and also to the Church," but we knew that was implied.

I sensed Rob watching him watching me, hoping he wouldn't have to choose between the two of us.

Even though Bishop Walmsley hadn't conveyed displeasure at my question, there was a good chance he was sizing me up, assessing whether I had enough propriety with the right kind of spunk for the demands of the life ahead, when people would, like it or not, project their own images about clergy couples in our direction. None of this worried me then, since I felt my allegiance to Rob the person, not Rob the clergyman so much. But I would soon come to see that there would be no separating out these roles: package deal.

"I wish you both all the best in your life ahead together," he said as we were leaving. Rob breathed a sigh of relief as we walked down the winding staircase, looking at me as if we had just finished a grueling entrance exam. Now, he could have his profession and his love at the same time.

When we chose two sets of china for our wedding registry, Rob started calling the nicer set, the one with the thin line of gold all around the perimeter of the plates, "The Bishop's China," because he anticipated that we would call upon it only when his boss visited. I absorbed the fact that Bishop Walmsley's special powers, in Rob's eyes anyway, extended to ownership of some of our possessions.

In fact, we didn't host him at home at all during the busy child-rearing years; there would have been too many Legos on the floor. Much later, when we moved near where he had retired, the authority figure persona melted away and Arthur became a well-respected friend, looking on with interest as Rob began his own tenure as a bishop. When he died, his widow gifted to Rob many of his very fine clothes. But that would be much later.

Shortly after I had begun dating Rob, I learned for the first time that I actually had an ancestor on my father's side who had been a bishop in the Methodist church. Dad even had a small section of a slightly damaged, full portrait of this Bishop Andrews—his face with twinkling eyes and a smile, and flowing sideburns on either side. One day, Dad went into the closet in his home office, past the enormous law desk, and produced the piece of art, placing it thenceforth on display. This seventy-ish year-old man in the painting looked kind enough, but he was a complete stranger to all of us who, a few generations later, lived each day without any clearly drawn connection to the tenets of his faith. Maybe we had them without really being *aware* we had them; maybe the strands were there, reverberating like strings on an instrument, just without our making them out.

Familiar as I was with a general sense of doing-unto-others-as-you-would-have-them-do-unto-you, I still had only a foggy idea as to what distinguished an Episcopalian from a Congregationalist from a Baptist from a Lutheran. In my early view of our relationship, I thought it would be possible to put aside the whole business of what I believed or didn't believe and just concentrate on filling in blank areas of my education. I would play catch-up. Rob wasn't doing the same, because I hadn't presented any particular body of knowledge, except random things like reading music and riding horses, that was foreign to him. Maybe if I'd been bilingual, like my Dutch sister-in-law, he would have set himself to learning a smattering of my language, just to feel closer to my essence.

There's a good chance he also wouldn't have. I realize now, better than I did then, that he generally doesn't see the need to demonstrate his love by adopting any of my interests; so long as I'm happy doing what I'm doing, he wants me to keep on doing it, provided that we have enough quiet time at home together, with nothing scheduled.

I definitely wasn't going to convert lickety-split, most likely not at all, but I'd be damned if anyone would accuse me of *not even trying* to understand my husband's milieu. When I joined the local chapter of the Audubon Society back when I was fourteen, I was brimming over with an enthusiasm to keep a list of warblers in a spiral notebook, identifying as many new species as I could. Surely, I could apply that same investigative "I can find out more if I try" zest here.

Soon after we'd become engaged, I enrolled in a course, at Harvard no less, in Early Church History. The only credit would be credit from the man I wanted to please, even though he hadn't expressed any real displeasure at my ignorance in the first place—only occasional twinges of surprise and barely noticeable grimaces when I asked something like, "What exactly did Paul do to start Christianity?" It was the silence that followed the question that was most disquieting to me. I was sure he was saying to himself, "How can she possibly not know this and can I continue to stand it?" Unless I got smart quickly, maybe that dreamy look in his eyes would fade.

The course was taught by Reverend Peter Gomes, the highly esteemed minister of the solidly brick Memorial Church within Harvard Yard. His voice, trained in the American Baptist tradition, thundered through the lecture hall during our evening classes. Material that would have seemed intolerably dry to me a year before—the exploits of Emperor Constantine, for instance—now seemed, if not riveting, at least worth reading and discussing, because I knew that my husband-to-be had already studied it. Becoming acquainted with how Christianity began in the first place surely would help me in our conversations; it could be a kind of placeholder while I figured out what I would do about the heart of the matter: *being religious*. Rob was mildly amused, but not displeased, when I told him I'd enrolled. "Oh boy, you're in for it now," he said, predicting boredom.

Toward the end of the course, I asked for a private conference with Reverend Gomes in his study. This idea took shape gradually during his lectures. He kept encouraging us to come for office hours if we had additional questions, and so I figured I might as well try to get a little premarital counseling, just without my fiancé there. Besides, the other students looked content to take their notes and shuffle off afterward. I bet none of them were wondering about how to embark on a whole life journey with more Church, and not just the Early kind either, in it than they had ever thought possible. Skipping down the yellow brick road it would not be.

I brought my notebook with me as I walked down a wide marble staircase to find his office, but I nudged Constantine and all the other church fathers, whoever they were, aside at this moment. They were just history; my mission now was to see into the future. I took a deep breath before knocking on the heavy wooden door.

Having made it through the appointment at the Connecticut Diocese a few months before, I thought I had reason to be confident in meeting with another highly esteemed clergyman. Suddenly, though, I doubted whether this scholar and impassioned preacher would have the slightest interest in my plight.

"Come in, please," he said as I entered, getting up from his desk. We sat down in comfortable chairs facing one another several feet apart. The room was lined with bookshelves laden with volumes on ancient theology. He placed the palms of his hands next to one another, just under his nose, and settled in.

The last time I'd taken a seat in a highly respected faith leader's office, Rob had been there with me. Now, I was on my own.

I blurted out, "This doesn't really have to do with the course, Reverend Gomes, but it does have to do with my life. I'm engaged to someone who will soon be an Episcopal priest, and the thing is, everything about religion is new to me and I'm not at all sure I can participate in what he does or do what will be expected of me." I might as well have just thrust a tray crowded with plates and glasses filled to the brim right at him.

Gomes listened intently, moving his hands below his chin, nodding often as I continued to talk on the I-gotta-be-me-even-while-he's-him theme. His legs were crossed, and he bobbed one of his excellently made shoes up and down slightly. He was short in stature, mighty in gravity.

"Do you love this man?" his voice boomed out, even in a room so much smaller than a lecture hall.

Without hesitating, I said, "Yes, Reverend Gomes, I definitely do." I looked right at him, hoping for the wave of a magic wand.

"Well then! You're in for quite a time, especially if you choose to remain outside the church world. I can guarantee that if your husband dedicates himself to his congregations, the work will take enormous sacrifices."

Sacrifice. There was a loaded word. I saw Jesus hanging limp on the cross; then I saw Rob moving around his church, talking in hushed tones to people, willing to take on all their troubles. I thought how, on the one hand, I wanted very much to be with a man who *would* make sacrifices. That was exactly what my dad had been doing as a lawyer and sometimes as a neighbor, too, all his life. But at this moment, I got an inkling that a clergy spouse might not always be on the same side as those sacrifices, that he was referring to the prospect of opposing kinds of pulls creating real conflicts in a marriage.

His tone was sober, but he also smiled, as he sensed my earnestness in trying to bridge a wide distance appearing on the horizon of my life. He talked about a few of the challenges he had faced moving from a Baptist tradition up to New England, acknowledging that he'd never been married. "I wish you well in this excellent endeavor." Reverend Gomes was giving me credit for at least laying my cards right out on the table. Still, my disclosure only helped to illuminate a problem, not solve it.

"Thank you, sir, I appreciate your time." What did I think would come of this?

As I walked out into the cool hallway toward the empty staircase, I wondered when I would let go of the illusion that anyone else could take up the ribbons of our two souls, Rob's and mine, and tie them together in a perfect bow.

Chapter 6

Will You Cross Over?

Even though my own core beliefs hadn't yet bubbled up to the surface so I could collect them, having received both a nod from a bishop and a passing grade from an esteemed clergyman, I convinced myself that I was well on my way to legitimacy as a clergy spouse. Where there was a will, there would be a way.

Unbeknown to me, however, Rob had been harboring one particular worry that turned into a hurdle he hoped I might still clear: I had never been baptized.

For Episcopalians, the sacrament of baptism means having the priest sprinkle water from a font on usually (but not always) a baby's forehead to welcome them into the Christian life. It is understood to be an initiation into joining *Christ's body*, or the church itself. Babies in their parents' arms, carefully swaddled in white, eyes gazing up at the lights, don't have any choice in the matter; they are brought into whatever faith their families choose for them. I knew, without even asking my parents, that I, too, once had been in a different kind of no-choice situation: no church, no baptism.

I was a strong reader, an enthusiastic teacher, a pretty good friend, a passable pianist, and a lousy repair person, but the fact that I was *unbaptized* never even entered my consciousness. Suddenly, though, it became one of my most prominent features, like a large nose. I wondered whether my not getting baptized was like—to use a sports analogy that I grew up with—forgetting to step on the base way back there and therefore having the run not count. If so, my brothers were in the same possibly morally compromised situation, too, but they'd escaped notice, breezed through, were pronounced safe at home. None of my sisters-in-law (two of them raised Jewish) had needed to reckon with this issue. In my case, it was as if the umps had gone to the videotape and found me out. Change that scoreboard.

Rob first broached the topic of baptism when we were walking along the Charles River one fall evening, with the lights twinkling over on the Cambridge side. Our wedding date had been set for the following September, allowing ample time to plan. We were holding hands, not speaking of anything much. Then in came a torpedo.

"Look, I know and accept that you're not Episcopalian and am not about to try to convert you or anything. But there is something else that I've been wondering about."

We kept walking, but I braced myself. Maybe the gaps—where my missing pieces were—had finally been revealed to him.

"I know you've never had any interest in being baptized, and this might sound strange to say, but it would mean a lot to me. The process is not that big a deal, really, and doing this could bring us closer."

He got it all out in one fell swoop, then stopping to see my reaction, let go of my hand. The waves on the river were looking choppier now. I felt no buoying effect from God coming from out there; what I felt was rebellion.

"Closer, how exactly? I thought we were doing fine staying just who we are. I mean, I'm learning all I can about your world; isn't that enough?" My body stiffened, my inner core defending itself against assault.

"Yes, yes, I'm not trying to change you—this wouldn't change you, it would just create more of a shared experience between us. And, you may not see it this way, but baptism allows you to become one of God's own, always protected."

He beheld a perfect truth; what was crystal clear to him, though, was completely invisible to me.

With this, I realized that *he was actually worried about the state of my soul*, not just wanting me to be more like him. He believed he was standing in a beautiful room with a high ceiling and vases of flowers and colorful pillows and streams of light coming in, with a staircase leading up to an even more beautiful top floor. I, meanwhile, was outside on the porch, shivering but not even perceiving that I was cold. His eyes showed the tremendous longing that was in his heart, a longing to merge two parts of his life that he held most dear.

On the one hand, I had no doubt that he was, in his own way, looking out for my spiritual welfare, beckoning me to get safely inside because he knew the rains would come and the winds would blow. On the other hand, his anxiety, which he was trying to wear lightly, made me want to run. What was this? I was sure my parents had not skipped a key step, put me on an exposed cliff, and yet that is what he was suggesting. I felt suddenly enraged.

We were taking up the whole sidewalk now, people awkwardly passing on both sides, and the twinkling lights brought no comfort.

"Look, Rob, that may be true for YOU, but I've lived all this time as an unbaptized person—no, as just a person—and I refuse to accept that I am somehow lesser or unfinished or not quite right. Do you want me as I am or do you want a made-over version of me?" I spread my arms out wide. "And why have you not mentioned this until now?" I was quivering.

He didn't answer right away, gazing out at the river where, in the early mornings, he found peace in rowing. Sculling was a solitary activity; preparing for marriage, however, took two.

It just so happened that, during the December that followed, in 1989, Boston was reeling from a terrible crime: a pregnant white woman, Carol Stuart, was found murdered after a Lamaze class at Brigham and Women's Hospital. While a Black man came under suspicion and then was taken into custody for the crime, eventually, after he jumped to his death, it came to light that her own husband, Charles Stuart, had actually plotted to murder her, to get a hefty insurance payout. It was a horrific story.

I had a nightmare one night, seeing the grainy newspaper pictures of the smiling couple and then the dark-haired woman sprawled lifeless on the sidewalk. I woke up feeling that I, in some way, was also being attacked by the man I loved. The next day, I walked shakily toward the tall, red, airborne sculpture that marked my T stop, wondering whether this was a clear sign that I should heed or just a ridiculous exaggeration to be dismissed.

In divulging the nightmare to Rob that evening, I was not just trying to play my trump card; I was truly frightened for both of us. Maybe he *could* possibly wield his faith like a weapon; maybe I just didn't know him well enough to be sure he wouldn't inflict damage. Maybe, and this was hard even to admit to myself, my hesitation back at Billy's Burgers, my instinct to take things "in stages" actually had shown good sense.

After listening, he held his head in his hands and looked as if he'd been punched in the gut. "I hope you know that I would never hurt you," he said, no doubt reckoning with the fact that his fiancé's subconscious mind worked in such alarming ways, reeling from what felt like an accusation by association. Guiding me to the starting line of Christianity was, to him, all about enhancing my life, not threatening it.

After this, there was no more talk of baptism. Relieved, I tried to quell any flickering doubts about both the safety of my soul and the legitimacy of our union amid the thousand clear signs—the fireworks exploding in a rainbow of colors—that our love could and would go on flourishing.

The dream, though, was just enough to put me on guard for the future. It was ludicrous to think that my husband, who was on his way to becoming an ordained clergyman, a proclaimer of the Gospel, would lash out at me—at least not in this violent way. I shuddered at what my mind had concocted. And yet, I also sensed that I'd better not ignore a voice within me that was also perched high up on the mast of the ship we were sailing on—looking out for anything that might be surreptitiously approaching, even in broad daylight, to try to take a piece of myself away. I must guard against this kind of pirate attack, vigilantly.

He, no doubt, needed to do the same. He and his faith were wrapped up together, a whole package, and my love for him had to include it, too.

My slim knowledge of the Bible back then didn't include any exposure to 1 Corinthians, but much later Rob would show me how relevant a certain segment of that book was to our particular, and in some sense peculiar, relationship.

Back in the year 53 or 54 CE, when Christianity was just starting to take hold, Paul the Apostle wrote a letter that has stood the test of time. Addressing the people of Corinth, a cosmopolitan city in Greece, he tried to sort out some thorny issues, mostly relating to marriage, by offering rules of conduct. He took on sex—that timeless topic—because he granted, with a sigh, that celibacy was not for everyone; he also wrestled with the vexing question of whether unions between "believers" and "unbelievers" (because Christians and Jews and gentiles were mixed up together) can be legitimate.

Here's the segment that Rob remembers encountering during his second year of divinity school, right around the same time that we were taking that walk along the Charles.

> To the rest I say—I and not the Lord—that if any believer has a wife who is an unbeliever, and she consents to live with him, he should not divorce her. And if any woman has a husband who is an unbeliever, and he consents to live with her, she should not divorce him. For the unbelieving husband is made holy through his wife, and the unbelieving wife is made holy through her husband.... It is to peace that God has called you. Wife, for all you know, you might save your husband. Husband, for all you know, you might save your wife. (1 Corinthians 7: 12–16)

Much later, when he showed this to me, I understood better both why he would make a bid for my baptism, for my *joining him* in his faith, and also how he could—being turned down on that request—still stick with me. Even though Paul was referring here to couples who are already married, he was also sanctioning what we might now call "mixed" marriages; Paul was known for being a pragmatist more than an idealist. Had he advocated instead that a believer should in fact resort to divorce from a recalcitrant spouse, I shudder to think what impact that might have had on my fiancé, who had already established his commitment to the Church but hadn't quite sealed the deal with me yet.

If I had been the one studying this passage at the time, I would have taken issue with Paul's assumption that the spiritual benefits from one spouse to another flow only one way: from believer to nonbeliever. I'd want to ask him, "Is having a certain kind of faith the only criteria for lifting up the soul of a beloved?" Moving toward marriage with Rob, I wouldn't have been able to show any kind of creed card with a specific set of tenets on it. In lieu of that, I would have said *yes*, a thousand times, *yes*. I will give my whole self: everything I understand so far about cherishing goodness and beauty and what is right and true, along with all my flaws, to you.

Chapter 7

I Give You My Hand

Despite the fact that each of us had been shaken by this episode, the quality of our love took on a deeper hue in the months leading up to our wedding. We had gotten a glimpse of what could imperil us, and for the sake of nurturing all the other parts of our relationship, we became more determined not to let religion be the heavy.

On an unseasonably warm and foggy New Year's Eve, when we were staying with friends in a cabin in New Hampshire, Rob asked me to follow him a short distance into the woods, where he presented me with a sapphire and diamond engagement ring that he'd designed himself. By then, the hesitation, the excessive practicality that I'd expressed out in the Tetons, had evaporated. I was ready to marry him with all my heart.

Although he would have relished a church ceremony, Rob deferred to my preference for a very different venue. Now, I see that this must have felt like a concession to him, but he went right along with my wishes, voicing no objection.

We were married on the green blanket front field at my childhood home—the same field where countless games of neighborhood touch football and baseball as well as obstacle course competitions had taken place years before. I was feeling vigorous and calm at the same time, thanks to the infusion of endorphins from running an annual hometown race that morning with Jacquie, one of my bridesmaids. It was mid-September, and a rainy start made way for a blue and breezy afternoon, with clouds scuttling overhead. My mother, in a long turquoise dress she bought on a visit to my brother's family in Guadalajara, and my father, in a charcoal gray pinstripe suit, were so proud to welcome many of our neighbors who arrived on foot. They were parents of the now thirtysomething Freddy, Rip, Stan, Joey, Roger, and Tommy who had been regulars in games over the years. In a way, in fact, we *were* in a kind of church, if you considered the reverence and sense of community many of us felt on this grass.

In letting me choose to be here on this day, in not insisting that there be an altar and a rail and a cross nearby, Rob was acknowledging that we didn't need to be a fully Episcopalian couple from the get-go; we could just be bride and groom.

Getting dressed in my old bedroom, with the gnarled branches of the cherry visible through the windows, looking in the old wood-framed mirror over my dresser, putting on the pink sash over my layers-of-lace skirt with separate blouse showing a long row of buttons, I wondered if the rootedness I felt right here, in this place where I'd been encouraged to discover my true self, could be anything like a belief.

Fifty years before, my grandfather had planted the pine trees that had grown tall and now swayed all around us; the peach orchard that my parents had started together thirty years before was tangled with vines now, but it held memories of great abundance. Nearby was my mother's beloved laundry line, under which she always said she'd spent some of her happiest hours, generally with an Irish Setter nearby, while raising five children. Countless times I'd seen her walking jauntily back in sneakers, basket propped on her hip, catching a glimpse of herself in the window and smoothing down her hair.

The fact that my new husband, with a different set of memories and a whole other way of worshiping, was willing to join me on my home turf absent altar or pressed white linens or weighty cross, was just the sign I needed that he fully accepted me *as I was*. The way he looked deep into my eyes was evidence that he respected how I had been nourished and—at least for this day—found nothing wanting. In agreeing that Gregory, an Episcopal priest and Yale doctoral student he knew, could perform the ceremony, I had also agreed to a series of premarital conversations that had happened, smoothly enough, the preceding spring.

When this intellectual person, steeped in theology, arrived to perform his wedding day duty, it was reassuring to me that he was most concerned about getting to watch the Mets game on TV beforehand. For a little while, as he sat on the couch in our playroom, with my brothers coming in and out to catch some of the action, he fit right in.

Once the ceremony began, Gregory also understood that, in this setting, it made sense to go easy on references to a deity.

Our best man Ben, Rob's classmate, also on his way to priesthood, stood quietly by with folded hands, wearing a broad smile and sunglasses with a blue elastic to hold them, just as he did while cycling, until it was time to read his assigned lines from Walt Whitman's *Leaves of Grass*. My father, never one to hide his emotions, wept visibly for the beauty of the language, for our fellow Long Islander from the former century who had penned:

Allons! The road is before us!
It is safe—I have tried it—my own feet have tried it well—be not detain'd!
Let the paper remain on the desk unwritten, and the book on the shelf unopen'd!
Let the tools remain in the workshop! Let the money remain unearned!
Let the school stand! Mind not the cry of the teacher!
Let the preacher preach in his pulpit! Let the lawyer plead in the court, and the judge expound the law.

We stood there, Rob and I, listening to this persuasive call to leave the work-a-day world behind—even the teacher (had been me) and the preacher (would soon be him)—and set out on our own new journey, liberated from any prescribed roles. It felt as if Walt himself was with us, too, a crooked hat on his head. God? I couldn't see him, or her, anywhere. But I knew that Rob, with his belief in a communion of saints, did.

Camerado, I give you my hand!
I give you my love more precious than money.

I give you myself before preaching or law;
Will you give me yourself? Will you come travel with me?
Shall we stick by each other as long as we live?

The direct questions, the complete openness and acceptance, helped us feel that on this sparkling late September afternoon, we were all on the same page.

Yes, we shall stick by each other as long as we live.

With divinity school classes already underway, we could take only a few days out on the end of Long Island; no real honeymoon was possible. Riding around on rented bikes, we savored the beautiful end of summer air, seeing tiny insects and unidentifiable bits of matter floating in the rays of sunshine. I, too, was floating—in a new kind of happiness. Rob was now my husband, and I would accompany him on his final stage toward becoming an ordained clergyman. But did I have enough understanding of what this designation would ask of him, and of me too? Would he continue to be enthralled by the person I was? How closely would we, in fact, stick by each other? Those little particles dancing in the light, taking their sweet time to go anywhere in particular, looked so unbound.

Chapter 8

First Year, and the End Time

Over the preceding summer, Rob had found an apartment for us in the bottom floor of a pink house in New Haven, where he was finishing his last year at Yale Divinity School. Fortunately, I had landed a job with an urban school reform program that was showing good results around the country, so I felt something of a calling, too. It remained to be seen, though, if I could make the shift away from working directly with teenagers into an administrative role in which I mostly supported the higher-ups.

Rob, meanwhile, was continuing to swim in the study of theology, and he barely came up on the beach of secular life.

One day, when I got home from buying a dozen eggs down on State Street, I found him leaning back in his desk chair, pencil in mouth, gazing at the ceiling. No quotidian errands for him, only deep thought.

"What are you doing?" I asked, already sensing that he was in some place not easy for me to find.

"Waiting for the eschaton!" Beyond knowing that it must be very different from the postman who actually walks through the gate to our door every day, I had no idea what this was. But by even saying the word, he was trying to cast a line out to me, encouraging me to come closer.

"The what?" My response was automatic. We'd been here before; I didn't have the vocabulary.

"It means the end time, or the final judgment." The matter-of-fact way he said it made clear to me that he believed the prospect was real, as real as the Resurrection. Here we were again. The "end time" struck me as a pretty heavy thing to be pondering as we were just getting our coupledom started, living together for the first time.

Rather than ask more questions, I put the eggs in the refrigerator, preferring to brush off any unquiet thoughts about the turmoil that might lie ahead, either in our marriage or maybe just in his own mind. Rays of late morning sunshine were pouring into our kitchen, and I figured we'd probably get to have a few more breakfasts together, anyway. Looking back on the moment now, I see it as one of the first times when he was able to give me an inkling of the vastness of his imagination, of how—if I asked—he might be able to bring me part of the way with him.

I wasn't accustomed to this scale of "big picture" thinking, preferring to focus more on whether I should fry up some liver for him before his mother, an expert cook, found out he was low on iron; or when the next episode of *Thirtysomething* would come on. On Tuesday nights, my childhood friend Lynn, who now worked for a nonprofit organization near New Haven and happened to live a few blocks away, opened the white gate in the picket fence in the front of our house and joined Ben, who had arrived with screeching bike brakes, for what felt to me like a blessed hour of TV.

In *Ministers' Wives*—the book that Rob would find for me, years later, at a church sale—there is an entire section devoted to what wives of seminarians experience, or used to experience. Either my predecessors often had some real difficulty with this stage, or the people running the study chose to interpret their answers that way.

> As a result of all the pressures involved in seminary life, there may be a sense of growing apart from one another. The wife may feel cut off from the sources of her husband's intellectual and spiritual development. He is undergoing radical change; she tends to remain more static. There may be problems, therefore, in remaining a couple with shared commitments, beliefs, and practices, rather than two individuals with common housing and budget.

What? She's "cut off" as if she's some kind of removed branch? And while he undergoes all kinds of fascinating transformations, she stays sadly "static" like a member of some control group? This made my skin crawl, and I wanted to reach back to clasp hands in solidarity with my unknown sisterhood of clergy wives—ask them what was churning in their own lives, what kind of hurdles they were trying to clear when their husbands were imagining the end of the world.

While Rob dove into M/W/F "Liturgy" and T/Th "Patristics," I was going to a nine-to-five administrative job that both stretched my capacities and challenged my self-confidence. Staying static was not possible here; there were too many funding streams and interoffice relationships to manage. The organization itself was working toward an admirable mission in urban public education, but interactions between colleagues were sometimes testy, the issue of race was definitely in play, and it seemed to me that there might be some secret code I hadn't learned.

In particular, I was intimidated by a slightly older woman who was one minute my confidante and the next my accuser. "Let me tell you about the amazing movie I saw over the weekend" in a cozy tone was followed minutes later by a stern "Didn't you already make the hotel arrangements exactly the way he wanted them?" I never quite knew where I stood. Having for the most part received positive feedback in past jobs working with teens, by just following the beacon provided by my instincts, I was learning this time that I needed new tools, new strategies to thrive alongside colleagues who came with their own baggage. Maybe I lacked savvy in pleasing bosses, delivering the goods. Many days, I came home feeling small. Was this "development"? I wasn't sure, but something inside me was shifting.

Even in my early thirties, a full-fledged adult by any standard, I still needed to recognize and address my unfinished parts, which were more glaring to me than an incomplete set of beliefs.

Difficult as it was to begin discovering what didn't come easily to me, to accept the fact that I, like many other strivers my age, must tap into ways of gaining acumen in work skills, I wasn't pathetically stranded on shore, feeling estranged from the ministers-in-the-making sailing fleet. I didn't feel "cut off" from the sources of my husband's "intellectual and spiritual development" because I was experiencing *my own*. Going to work every day, trying to oversee grant budgets and make logistical arrangements for conferences while answering to a variety of higher-ups, I was grappling with challenges that nudged forward my understanding of both office politics and myself. My curiosity about what Rob was learning was still percolating, but I had no desire to be more involved in the content of his training than I was.

Furthermore, going back to the paragraph in the old book again, we didn't have a challenge "remaining a couple with shared commitments, beliefs, and practices" because we didn't start out with those in a nice neat bundle in the first place. Neither on our own nor within our premarital counseling sessions with Greogory did we create any big diagram showing that my CBPs—let's just call them that—matched up with his. We were winging it, starting to build a life together based simply on how drawn to one another we felt.

I learned early on that, while he was in seminary, Rob was actually on two paths at the same time: the academic and the ecclesiastical; the latter was the one dubbed being "in the process." Not everyone who goes to divinity school wants to become a minister or priest; if you do, then you need to answer both to your professors and to the larger church hierarchy who will, you hope, give all green lights once you finish your degree. That's a lot of people scrutinizing you at every turn. The event when Rob became one of them was called his "ordination" and it happened more than once: first to the "diaconate" (a level of service in its own right, for many people) and then a couple of years later to the full-fledged "priesthood." I kept lapping up new terms as best I could, constantly trying to gauge whether this process changing *him* was also changing *me*, too. If we were officially a pair now, did that mean that we shared each other's transformations?

In truth, I felt transformed just by the fact of being somebody's wife.

A few of my family members came to Rob's first ordination ceremony, which took place in June at the mighty cathedral in Hartford. We had been married for not quite a full year. As I sat down with my brother, his soon-to-be wife, and my mother, I felt our responses vibrating in synchrony: they took in the colorful robes swirling everywhere, the organ music ringing throughout the space, the gravity of each step each person took. I watched their necks turn and their eyes grow big as they followed the procession. I was the same as them, and yet not quite, anymore. After the service, amid all the pleasantries and multiple "That was *so* beautiful and you must be *so* proud!" comments, nobody asked any of us point-blank, "Are you Episcopalian?" I busied myself with making introductions, congratulating the other ordinands, meeting their family members.

Hosting my family members as outsiders, I became distinctly aware of my half-in, half-out quality. I was a creature who could try to blend in, maybe even take on some of the colors of my surroundings. The people who had known me all my life could see what I was trying to do; they understood. Now that I was Rob's wife, they counted on me to be as full a partner to him as I could reasonably be, confident that he would also try to be that for me.

Chapter 9

Unto Us a Child Is Given

I began my new life as a clergy spouse by going to church services about half the time. The hulking Christ Church in New Haven, where Rob began his first job after graduation and ordination both, was not an easy church for someone like me to slip into. It felt heavy, almost oppressive: the formality of every gesture, the bowed heads and solemn expressions, the jarring organ chords, the unyielding nature of the seats, the frequent references to death, the central presence of Jesus in agony on the cross. Adding to the lugubrious air, the priest in charge was a demanding taskmaster with a temper: I knew this from inside information. For a place that was supposed to be proclaiming "The Good News," it gave plenty of indication that we should instead be worried most of the time. I liked meeting people in the congregation—Betsy, the college librarian; Larry, the lawyer; Helen, the composer of operas; and Sid, the graduate student—but the overall aura at Christ Church was depressing, not uplifting.

With all my dating-era questions to Rob about the fulcrums of his faith, and my eager delving into how Christianity spread like wildfire in early centuries, I had been trying to inch closer to a friendliness toward, if not full embrace of, the Episcopal way.

But each time I walked into this particular place of worship, I felt a thickening of the border that separated my love for my husband from my discomfort with religion. When I was anywhere else, the difference between us felt almost invisible—like a fishing line that, while distinctly there, barely separates molecules in the vastness of air, yet when I entered into the space that was distinctly his and not at all mine, the solidity of the wooden rail at the front of the church transported itself right into my soul, where it expanded, like one of those little plastic creatures dropped into a glass of water. Except it wasn't playfully dancing around; it felt to me like a lead weight.

Him, I needed; all of this, I didn't.

Sometimes I was blatantly inconsiderate about what Rob might be experiencing at certain crucial times in the church calendar. A year and a half into our marriage, when he finally opened the heavy, front door of our house after a very long Good Friday, he was greeted by Bruce Springsteen's "Born in the U.S.A." turned up good and loud. I was in one of my ebullient moods, writing notes and putting away laundry and feeling mostly free of responsibility, despite the fact that it was the most somber day on the Christian calendar. He held back his criticism, just winced momentarily as he took off his jacket.

"How was it?" I asked, knowing even as I did that any answer he was able to give wouldn't go far toward delivering the essence of the three-hour service to me. It was his, not mine, and I couldn't make it otherwise right then.

"It's over," he said, and then approached me to offer a hug, his black shirt sweaty from spiritual exertions. "How are you?"

Once close to him again, absorbing some of his exhaustion, I knew to go over to the stereo and turn down the volume. I wasn't sure if I'd done any real damage by not anticipating his homecoming with more thoughtfulness; it was only that initial wince I saw, but it was entirely possible that he'd registered the hurt I inflicted, stored it away somewhere.

I was finding that marriage was often about trying to make that bold leap to what may seem like the other side, putting yourself in the mystery land of your loved one's head to make a thing of timeless beauty: a true connection. Could I extend myself more, reach farther? If I had this particular day to do over again, I would have at least chosen a more somber track for him to come home to, or better yet, been waiting for him outside the church when he emerged, giving a sign that I understood just how much he had gone through, putting myself aside for a time, the better to receive what he was bringing.

In the first months of being a wife to a curate, I learned a central tenet of clergy life: Rob was there for people in his congregation always, and most particularly, when people were suffering. By transference, this became a dominant fact of life in our marriage, too, continuing through to the present. Except when he is on vacation, Rob is forever on call for distress. People generally don't ring up to say that they've just had a wonderful new job offer, that their kids are turning out very nicely, or that they have seen the glory of the Lord. They call when they are struggling to cope, when a spouse has left, when someone has fallen ill, or, and this especially, when death is near. Bad news always seems to have the upper hand.

Frankly, this aspect of Rob's work has never stopped being a hard thing to witness. I keep thinking that, overall, there must be at least as much happiness out there as sadness; as much kindness as cruelty; as much heroism as cowardice; as much goodness as sinfulness. If Jesus and his apostles performed miracles, then shouldn't church life provide ongoing demonstrations of joy? The music, especially when strings or brass are involved, comes closest to doing this for me, but still the overall tone feels *heavy*. I'm not irrational or heartless enough to expect that people could try harder to curb their misfortunes; each time someone suffers a loss, I feel the blow, too. Collectively speaking, though, I can't help but wish my husband's world might have a more generous dose of high spirits sprinkled in. Then maybe I wouldn't seem quite so irreverent by contrast.

I've come to see that, in marriage, it's as if both partners were holding ice cream cones: one partner's black raspberry dribbles over onto the other person's maple walnut, and the other way around. That way, you get splotches of life in an unaccustomed flavor. Sometimes the new taste makes you want to try more, sometimes, not so much.

While I was intrigued, to some extent, by Rob's experiences at church, I was beginning to realize that what intrigued me the most was not so much what happened there and what it all meant, but rather *the interaction between whatever it was and his essential self.* He—flesh, blood, mind, and soul—was the one who made my heart leap up. And, concurrently, as he began to spend so much time with the people in the congregation, being drawn in to their issues, I sensed my own need to make sure I had a unique place in his life, not to lose any of his attentiveness—to the hills and valleys of my physical landscape as well as to the psychic and spiritual ones, which were not always, I was beginning to sense, so reliably appealing.

In our new spacious home, I lapped up the bands of sunshine that fell on the wooden floor in our bedroom each morning, and I loved the dew on the grass in our tiny backyard, the smell of the grapes over the terrace where we sometimes sat with our upstairs neighbors, even the blaring horns and sirens of the surrounding city.

And, amid the bounty of a New England autumn, I got pregnant.

Influenced by Rob's perspective on our marriage, I continued trying to decipher what God, if he/she existed, was or wasn't doing in our lives, whether the marriage was running fully on its own two wheels or if there could be an invisible driver. With Rob so sure about the presence of this other power, I wondered if I should just stop fretting about my inability—if that's what it was—to be in on the arrangement and do my best to be the kind of wife who was still the woman he'd fallen for in the first place, not the kind of wife who was missing a connection to the Almighty. And besides, the fact that I was getting noticeably larger with a new life, beginning to feel stirrings of little limbs, made the presence or absence of God less pressing, by comparison.

Giving birth to a baby boy on a still July day, not quite two years after we were married, felt like an achievement that was just ours—Rob's and mine—alone.

Ahead of his arrival, we got some indication that the stars might be aligned in our favor. After a rigorous hike with friends around the time of my due date, I woke up in the night to discover a gush of clear liquid. My water had broken! Or, as Rob exclaimed, "You've lost your mucous plug!" This was a brand-new, strange and damp, biological fact to absorb. Reassured by the nurse on call that we did not need to come into the hospital right away and I could start the early labor on my own, we kept busy by going to a shoreline town to conclude our baby-friendly Subaru station wagon shopping. When I asked for a bathroom at one stop, I was informed, "No, sorry, not here, but you can find one next door at the Breakwater Café." I stared at her, incredulous, still leaking. Wait a minute—could this be a God thing? No, no, it had to be just a surprising gift, the kind life had offered up many times before, whenever a moment became a gem.

Rarely have I felt such a sense of certainty about my way forward. As we drove back to New Haven in the brilliant, teal-colored car with rich tan upholstery, my sense of purpose and readiness made me the equal of any bold fighter among the ranks conjured in the hymn "Onward, Christian Soldiers." I may not have been a fully stamped Christian, but I was ready to summon all my strength for a cause. Now, my belief system didn't matter nearly as much as my determination, my physical stamina.

With the support of a midwife near my rocking chair, sending me occasionally to the shower, and Rob always nearby, I labored in the hospital for twelve straight hours before delivering William James. When, after a blurry hour of recovery, I called my mother, she went right to a superlative. "This is the happiest phone call I've ever had!" As I was growing up, she'd never conveyed a whole lot of specialness to me just because I was her only daughter; this moment, though, rang out differently. No doubt retaining memories of her own five deliveries, feeling the joy beyond any other kind of joy each time, she was so proud of me. Through my exhaustion, I was, too; and ready to fall into a deep sleep.

During the early days of his life, as I watched my baby respond to all kinds of sensations, just *being* in this new world, everything having to do with religion felt more distant—as if the rituals people continued to engage in were going on somewhere behind a soundproof glass window. In the afternoons, I wheeled the royal blue baby carriage, an item passed down by grandparents, around the quads of the Yale campus, watching the pigeons rise up ahead. The whooshing birds, the high branches on the mighty oaks, the college students striding in twos and threes and laughing on street corners all created a scene of pulsing life. Rob, meanwhile, was able to move between his two worlds gracefully; he'd been getting accustomed to being called "Father" by certain people in the congregation, but this wriggly creature at home needed both his mother and his father, the people to whom he was genetically linked, in a whole new way.

The fact that, during our premarital counseling sessions, I'd gone along with the plan of having any children we were going to have raised in the Episcopal faith didn't loom large to me during Willie's infancy. As Rob began to speak about plans for a baptism, I could see how much this would mean to him; just because my parents had opted out of the rite for me didn't mean I needed to continue that tradition now. I wasn't sure what appointing a "godmother" and a "godfather" would mean for the future—the terms sounded slightly suspicious to me—but I trusted Rob to make this kind of decision keeping the well-being of our child front and center. He was clearly energized by the process, eyes lighting up as he proposed candidates to me.

When our baby got old enough to get laced into a "Jolly Jumper," strings hanging down from a secure clamp in a doorway into a little harness, and he bounced bounced bounced, touching his little bare toes to the floor while he gnawed gently on his hand, I was held spellbound. The physicality, the sense of discovery, the energy, the *realness*—all of it resonated within me, like a perfect chord.

Rob, too, enjoyed watching him jump, saying, "Look at how he works those legs, developing the kind of strength that will help him be an oarsman one day!" Just when I had grasped that everything he saw was imbued with some kind of religious hue, he'd go and surprise me by talking about his favorite sport. Then I remembered his story about the epiphany he'd had while rowing alone on the Connecticut River in college, how it changed the whole course of his life. Even athletics, his kind anyway, had God in the mix.

Chapter 10

The Way Someone Disappears and Also Doesn't

In a few short months, though, our happiness had to make room for something else entirely.

I wanted to have at least a part-time job along with being a new mother, to provide me with some outside world contact, so I started teaching one composition course at a nearby commuter university. One Tuesday afternoon in early October, with the leaves just starting to change, I pulled the car back into the garage as usual. The string of bells on the back door sounded my arrival, and then I entered the next door into our oblong kitchen. Rob had been with Willie during my couple of hours away, but now he would be more than ready to hand him over to be nursed. This was the best part of the day for me: I owned the mild satisfaction of having been effective in the classroom, interacting with a batch of twenty-year-olds who needed the credit; then I got to make what felt like, each time, a triumphant return to my baby, center of my world.

Something was different when I got home this time, though. I saw it on Rob's face as soon as I climbed past the leaded window with many rectangular panes, like a cousin of the stained glass ones at the church, and reached the top of the stairs.

"I'm afraid I have some bad news," he said, holding our almost-three-month-old with a pale blue receiving blanket draped over him. "Come in here and sit down." He lifted his chin in the direction of the study, a room with windows looking out on a couple of tall trees near the front sidewalk. The early afternoon light poured in through the leaves.

I sat in the desk chair, breasts stone hard with milk, yearning for my child, but now with heart racing.

"Your mother called to say that your dad died this morning."

Died? In an instant, everything went dark.

"She found him collapsed in the bedroom, called 911, and the ambulance took him to the Veteran's hospital, but he was already gone when they arrived. It must have been heart failure. He had already been so weak."

I said nothing, and Rob let there be silence for a few huge moments. Not knowing what to do, with nothing making sense, I got up and enveloped myself within the physicality of my husband and son, who was breathing softly. Anytime before this, I would have thought that Shadowy Death lurked around the cold, gray building down the block and was a force that made Rob get dressed in heavy robes on an occasional regular weekday. Now, though, it was palpably here—not in its churchy form, either—right in this sunlit room, socking me broadside and making me dizzy. I couldn't conceive of a world without my father.

I'd been aware of Dad's decline over the summer. A decade before, he'd fallen into a crushing depression. Calling from the airport, on my way to Costa Rica with my close friend Jacquie, I absorbed my mother's effort at mild reporting, an understatement that rang in my ears long afterward. "Dad's not feeling so well."

His near immobilization lasted through much of my twenties. The twinkle that he had in his eye, the over-the-top optimism and limitless graciousness at the time of our wedding had been brought about at least in part by successful electroconvulsive therapy treatments, something he'd resisted hard at first. In fact, I watched my brother Sandy ultimately force him to get in the car toward the psychiatric help that brought our father back to us, albeit in a slightly changed form.

When Rob entered my life, I hoped that the two of them would have enough opportunity to recognize some of the traits they shared: intellectual depth, a capacity to listen, and a "Do unto others as you would have them do unto you" philosophy. Dad, I knew, wouldn't choose to talk about religion, since it wasn't familiar terrain to him, but he'd convey a sense of respect for Rob's studies.

There was precious little time for any bonding, however. During my pregnancy, Dad slipped away into remoteness again. Back came the pained demeanor, loss of appetite, and lethargy we'd hoped had been banished. When my mother came up to help us after Willie's birth, she looked drained by more than just the heat. And when we brought our baby down to Long Island later that summer, Dad tried so hard to summon any sense of connection. A photo from that visit shows him looking frail and taut, sitting in the same gold armchair by the fireplace where he'd sat before, through too many still afternoon hours, with a grandson on his lap who gazed up at the expressionless face of a man who had given me everything.

I remember one particular morning when I was about eight. It was winter, the sky was sparkling blue; Dad was dressed up in his suit, overcoat, and hat and on his way to the shed. It was too low a building, melting into its surroundings, to be called a "barn." When I heard him get ready to go, from my bedroom down the hall from my parents' room, I decided to follow his feet crunching on the driveway stones for the short trip out to see the horses who had been in their stalls all the cold night. Noticing that he had left his briefcase in the freezer room, on the way out the door, I knew that soon he'd be gone for another long day of law work in the city. Maybe, this way, I could get a few moments alone with him, feel the glow of being his only daughter.

Watching from the wide doorway to the shed, I saw him dig into the metal container holding the grain. He scooped out the rich brown concoction of oats and sticky molasses, never too much, sliding the wooden door that opened first into Baby's stall, then Red's—each time bringing an eagerly nodding head and appreciative knickers from the other side. The grain fell into a built-in wooden tray that Dad had constructed alongside the larger slatted bins for hay.

"Hey, Red boy," he'd said softly, reaching through to give the pony's neck a pat. Sometimes, when Red found a break in a fence and got out to graze on the lawn, Dad called him "that rascal," but he loved him deeply, as he'd loved all of the horses he'd ever had, stretching back to when he'd been a boy. I heard the sounds of both animals chomping, then using their thick tongues to get every last bit of the precious stuff. I felt no immediate need to reveal myself, preferring just to observe my dad doing his usual morning task of devotion.

Inside the house, he rarely served meals—Mom did all of that—but he always showed tenderness in the way he spoke, listened to our tales and our music, and responded to an array of needs. With no fanfare, he would pay for five of us, in a fourteen-year span of ages, to go to college, and a few of us to graduate school, too. He was the Quiet Provider and also Believer In Us Without Judgment.

I watched him shake out a few sections of baled hay, reach in again to make a delivery in each stall, brush off remnants from his clothes. Finally, spotting me nearby in my robe, he startled at first, then said, "Mornin' Pol. It's a little chilly out here! You warm enough?" He came right over and leaned down to give me a hug, and I smelled the distinctive, slightly musty scent that always accompanied him.

As we walked back to the house together, my rubber boots slipping on the ice, he found out a little about the third-grade day I had ahead of me. "Do you think you could let the horses out after you have your breakfast?" he asked. He'd picked up his briefcase, put on his hat, and gave me a peck on the cheek. I wouldn't see him again until around 8 P.M., when the boys and I would be back in our own rooms, doing homework. I was proud that he'd trusted me with this important task, glad for the prospect of going back out there to watch Baby and Red step gingerly out of their stalls.

He never explained *why* having horses was important to him, just like he never explained why we didn't go to church, but we knew that our father's feeling for these animals as well as for what he called "keeping up the place"—chopping wood, building fences, mowing, fiddling with the tractor—was part of his own particular code, a full version of which could be translated into a solid set of beliefs.

Now, I often wish that Dad had offered more explanations, like crumbs on a trail for me to follow, so that it would be easier to preserve his essence during all the decades I'd go on living without him. But instead I recall the swirls of dust in the air after we cantered together on the hard dirt of the Long Island Lighting Company lines—me, now about ten, on Red; he on Baby. Dad leaned back, with one hand on Baby's rump, and said, "Look at the tops of the trees up ahead, Pol, swaying against the bright color of the sky." I recall my pony's thick mane as he gathered up the strength in his neck, the yellow part of his eyes when he pushed his head toward the sky. Tapping back to the feistiness of Red takes me directly to the steadiness of my father.

Ten years later, at twenty, I was close to graduating from college. When my parents came up to visit once, Dad and I took a drive together. More or less out of the blue, I confided in him about the anxieties I'd been having. "Sometimes I don't feel comfortable with myself, and I'm not sure which people I most want to be with, either." My self-doubts all came tumbling out, as the Connecticut River flowed gently by, just beyond the road that hugs its banks. Dad probably didn't feel equipped to delve into this knot of issues with me, his youngest child. He didn't ask for more details. Looking at me with the gray eyes that I hadn't inherited, and waving one hand in my direction for emphasis, he said quietly, "Just be yourself, Pol; that will always be enough." It was too pat of an answer, maddeningly incomplete. But once again, I absorbed his belief in me, the fact that he was always standing by.

The remembrance of my father's life was not a "service" but a "gathering." My mother used the term first, taking it from the Quakers, although she had never been to a Quaker meeting with my father's mother. What she wanted, what we all wanted, was a time to come together in our own living room; there was nowhere else we could possibly go. We invited friends and family, as many as might be able to crowd into the space. They parked in the side field, just as they had when they had come to Rob's and my wedding a couple of years before, then greeted by an ebullient father of the bride.

The pebbles on the driveway still crunched as the five of us, each with our own families now, approached the familiar back door. The same pine trees loomed overhead; the low-lying shed melted just a little more into the earth out back. Our house remained simple, sitting close to the ground, with no upstairs or downstairs. As my mother used to say, proudly, to anyone who wondered, "It all came on one truck!" Knowing they would be able to build something on what used to be a potato field above my grandparents' house, my parents went and looked at some models and readily chose one.

The design couldn't have been more basic: a kitchen and living room in the middle, bedrooms on either side. The entryway was through what we called the "freezer room" (to store the harvest of peaches that came in for a number of years) and then a kind of playroom or den, where my brothers, on a couple of cast-off couches, watched games, and I practiced on an upright piano. When I was about ten, we discovered that termites had infested the wall separating the kitchen and the living room; after it came down, the greater openness was a big benefit to the liveliness and reach of our conversations.

Built-in orange couches were in an "L" formation in the center of the living room, with bookcases up above and also on either side of the fireplace. A few comfortable armchairs rounded out the circle, each with a reading lamp, and colorful oriental rugs lay on the floor. Dog hair was on any surface that accepted it. During my childhood, the space was empty during the day, but every evening we converged there, in stages. First my parents had their cocktail hour; Dad usually had a manhattan with a cherry, sometimes a martini with an olive; Mom sipped bourbon mixed with fruit juice. My brothers remember this early evening time as having a kind of sacred quality: do not disturb. They were often off in their rooms, doing homework or practicing instruments. Later on at least a few of us brought books and settled in, with our choice of reading lights.

When invited guests came for a meal, the room took on an added dimension. Dad enjoyed getting a fire crackling, then being in the background, setting the stage for a lively combination of voices. He went back and forth to the kitchen, passing plates of cheese and crackers and checking on drinks, letting the stories being told be the main offering. As my brothers grew up, they brought home tales from the Peace Corps in Peru and Nepal, teaching in Washington, DC, going to law school, being at protest marches, coaching hockey. And their friends who had once played games outside came back, too, with their own accounts of life after high school. After time moved on and all these guys came less frequently, my twenty-something friends dropped in, one at a time, for visits. Each time, Dad was so pleased to wait on them, as if they were princesses.

At the memorial gathering, Rob accepted the role of master-of-ceremonies. On this afternoon, he would not be a priest, although it was precisely this training that informed how he was able to set a tone for grief. Handsome in his suit, he stood by the fireplace, where my father had also stood countless times; he held no Prayer Book. "We are here to remember Hank," he said quietly. I sat just a few feet away, with our three-month-old son on my lap. There were no rails, no rituals. Rob must have felt the formlessness of it all, the lack of scaffolding, but he was once again in my family's space now. By going to church services, I had regularly traveled to *him*; now he was traveling to *me*.

Married just two years, I sensed how crucial this kind of movement was for us. Amid my grief, I was also flooded with a new level of confidence that my husband could in fact put his own faith, the faith that dominated his life every day, on a polite hold while he answered another call relating to the kind of life, faithless in a certain narrow sense of the word, that I had always known. This felt like a love that was soaring on its own power.

One by one, my four brothers got up to speak, each one unable to get through their words without weeping. Dad had done nothing less than show them what it was to be a man—never directing the choices they made; always setting an example by how he lived, demonstrating assiduity and kindness. When it was my turn, I said that Dad had always referred to me as his "perfect daughter," believing that a father was entitled to use hyperbole. He made me feel special, every single day. Other people spoke, some standing way back in the kitchen doorway, describing gestures large and small that had impacted them: the way he stopped when he saw someone stranded by the side of the road; the way he volunteered his law expertise over many evenings to fight a company threatening to bulldoze acres of land in our town; the way he made valuable introductions for a young person starting out in a career.

We all knew that his self-effacement, his proclivity to feel guilt about any undone task, mostly law work for his clients, also brought costs, to him and to our mother. We wished he had been less self-sacrificing, been able to enjoy life into his eighties; we wished that his heart hadn't given out.

In those bewildering days after my father's death, I stumbled around mentally, wondering where and how I could continue to find him. Then, taking myself over to nearby Sagamore Hill, homestead of Teddy Roosevelt and a place Dad had always loved for its echoes of a rollicking family life, I looked up high at some branches with October leaves quivering. In one piercing moment, I realized that Dad would continue to be *actually everywhere*, like Whitman. The mere action of my looking at things imbued them with his spirit. This revelation has, in fact, continued—more fully than almost anything else I have predicted. I don't believe in the afterlife or reincarnation; I don't believe that Dad is in heaven or still living somewhere in another form. I do believe, however, that all the different sides of him—the gentle guide, the tireless provider, and the father who disappeared into despair—stay within me forever.

Chapter 11

In the Garden

Two of my favorite early books, both read to me by my mother who had first encountered them with her mother, were by Frances Hodgson Burnett. What I remember best about *A Little Princess* was how completely absorbed in the tale my mother was. She must have been so glad to have a daughter after all those boys, partly because she could revisit this book again. I was about six when she read it to me. The protagonist Sara Crewe, the little girl who came to a British boarding school from India, was at first surrounded by wealth provided by her father. Then, with his sudden death, she lost all her possessions and had to move into a bare attic. She bore up, making friends with servants she never would have known had she stayed at her high station. The dreadful headmistress Miss Minchin cared nothing for her pain. Tears streamed down my mother's face as she read through this section, replaced by delight when a secret benefactor—the mysteriously generous Ram Dass—transformed Sara's dank chamber into a comfortable and beautiful place. Goodness prevailed; patience and kindness were rewarded.

I knew nothing about resurrection then; but as my mother sat on the edge of my bed holding that dark blue book with the gold lettering, I learned how life can be reaffirmed, even reclaimed.

A year later, knowing I was at just the right age for this author, she introduced me to the other Burnett novel, *A Secret Garden*. This book full of mystery traces the relationship between a cranky girl named Mary and Colin, a sickly boy who cries out repeatedly from some other distant wing of the mansion. We learn that he is not only physically unwell but also spiritually hindered by his chronic self-centeredness. Eventually, with the help of Dickon, a boy who is very much one with the natural world, Mary is able to wheel Colin outside and through a forbidden door to the walled-in garden. A place that had been off-limits for years after Colin's mother's death becomes a place of rejuvenation for all.

I, too, had a kind of secret garden. It was tucked away down the hill from our house, not walled in and forbidden, but also not easily accessible to the outside world. Going there, most often when I was around thirteen, was what I imagined going to church was like for other people: a place apart, a place for reflection, a place to sense a larger spirit, or what Ralph Waldo Emerson called the "Over-Soul." But the congregation consisted only of me, myself, and I.

While a garden can be any tiny plot of earth that is cultivated, this one was generous and gemlike at the same time: a green clearing in the woods with about a dozen flowerbeds. It had been my grandfather's world, and though in the half dozen years since he died everything had become wilder, the outlines of what once was a carefully tended green space were still clear. Granddad had always been a multifaceted individual—a lawyer, a writer, a trout stream fisherman, an amateur ecologist and painter, and as he himself wrote when the census taker came around, a farmer. He and my grandmother lived in Brooklyn most of the time, but they, being fortunate and escaping the worst of the Depression, acquired a home on Long Island during the early years of the twentieth century. He took to tending roses as, I was told, a peaceful antidote to the rush-rush of their city life. And, perhaps, to have some quiet moments away from a wife who could be formidable.

Enhancing the magical feel of the place was the presence of a small house perched on a slight hill overlooking the garden. Built originally as a honeymoon cabin for my Aunt Winifred and her husband, Harold, in the late 1930s, as the decades progressed it became more of a nuisance building—attracting hooligans who hiked in off the back road to drink and smoke. Although years later my father would make the sensible decision to take it down, it held for me as a young girl a kind of mystique, if not allure. People had lived there, at least for a time, and they enjoyed complete seclusion, having only flowers and trees and birds for companions.

Some rich red roses still emerged each spring during my youth, despite having lost the dedicated hands that used to care for them. On the other side of the garden from the house rose a huge weeping willow tree, with cascades of small green leaves, like a girl whose hair was too bountiful to be controlled. And beyond that was the small pond, silent except for the occasional quack of visiting ducks, and almost completely hidden by the dense growth all around it. I knew from experience where to find the narrow path that led past a tall patch of bamboo making a wonderful whispering sound on one side, and a couple of intentionally planted and thriving holly trees on the other side, to a small wooden dam between two cement blocks. The sound of the trickle of water running over that dam is among my most vivid childhood memories; it was not a particularly dramatic spot, but it was a tremendous focal point. From there, I could look right, to see ever-shifting reflections and colorful leaves drifting in the pond, and left, to what we called "the swamp" where herons and turtles and muskrats had their own mysterious domain. It felt magical, a place where startling things could happen at any moment. Everything would be still, and then—look!—ripples in the water showed a swimming creature, oblivious to my presence.

Now, I realize that these moments probably provided me with my first "spiritual" experiences. The jumping up of something in my core, the sense of connection with everything not-me, the looking forward to more life unfolding ahead: except for the fact that I didn't feel accompanied by any deity, I felt most everything else I'd hear churchgoers mention years later.

Throughout my elementary school years, as she had done for my brothers, my mother volunteered to host every single class picnic at our house. After the field games and the watermelon pit fights were over, we all tore off down the hill, on what we called "Emil's Path" (so named for the man who had worked for Granddad) to see, and when teachers weren't looking, actually go right into, the luscious black slime. When the obligatory thank-you letters from the kids arrived in a rubber-banded pack a week or so later, one mentioned how the "squish, squash" sound of his footsteps was a favorite highlight. To this day, my classmates still recall these forays. I was so proud to show everybody my special places. Once, on somebody's dare in seventh grade, a few of us agreed to meet right at the little dam for a day of playing hooky. That was a strange experience for someone like me, who rarely transgressed, but in a way it was necessary: my version of what my brothers occasionally did when the ice was especially perfect at a nearby skating spot.

While I sometimes enjoyed sharing this spot with friends, primarily it was a place where I could be sure of being alone for long stretches of time. When I was around eight or nine, I would write my innermost thoughts, confident that no one would ask to read them. In my early teenage years, partly following the example of a couple of great-aunts and one great-uncle I hadn't even known, I became interested in ornithology. That propelled me to head down to the garden daily during prime migration times, with binoculars and spiral notebook in hand, searching for fluttering warblers making buzzy sounds up high in the trees. When I reached my twenties, a serious boyfriend who grew up in a city would say to me, incredulously, "Wow, you're the first person I've ever even *met* who watched birds."

I had no Bible, I had no idea what went on in Sunday school, but I was without a doubt getting a kind of spiritual education here. In me was an emergent sense that I was a unique individual, alone where it most counted, holding some kind of reins. I had a physical being as well as a mental and emotional one, and I was in charge of my own self-integration. Around the age of ten, I had moments of being thunderstruck, even frightened, by this simple yet also complex realization. The responsibility of steering my own thoughts and actions felt both empowering and staggering; I pinched myself, trying to figure out which part of me—soul or body—was the *real* me.

Sometimes—especially when I scurried high up in a pine tree, mindless of the real danger of dead branches cracking and sending me down, down, down, with no one having any idea where I was, and I looked out to see the deep cobalt blue line of Long Island Sound—I knew I was as fully alive and sentient and capable as anybody in the world. And that it was entirely up to me how I would choose to engage with everyone out there—which qualities I would cultivate as I grew up. As I touched a splotch of pine pitch on the trunk of the tree, the kind that always left stubborn, sticky, brown marks later on, marriage was not even on the periphery of my mind. Eventually, though, I would discover that I had plenty of my childhood self still with me when I vowed to be true to another person.

PART II

SETTLING

Chapter 12

Going to the Chapel

When it was time to push off from New Haven, a place both gritty and like an Ivory Tower at the same time, we were three: Rob, me, and one-year-old William James. He had just learned to walk on our cracked driveway, next to the leaded windows that we cranked opened with difficulty. Actually we were four—if you count the Church as a kind of constant presence, and I do. We were leaving the hulk of gray building on the edge of a bustling urban campus and heading for a newer, wooden, A-frame chapel on the edge of a more bucolic one. There would be grazing animals and long barns right across the road from a collection of no-nonsense, brick buildings and a sign that said, "Flagship Campus: The University of Connecticut."

For most clergy families, each church provides the base of operations, sets the tone for the whole way of life. But a peculiar spouse like me, who doesn't naturally fold right into a given congregation like an egg gets mixed into cake batter, also needs something else: a neighborhood, a town, a strong secular pulse. And most of all I craved the warmth that comes with human connection. What I wasn't sure of, during this next move, was how much I would need to start mixing things using a made-up recipe.

Much as I value lightheartedness and try to espouse it, I've never been one to leap easily into major changes, to push past boundaries. I'm still bothered by the fact that, when I lived for a semester in Toulouse with a French mother who wagged her finger at me each morning with a variety of warnings about whom to avoid, I never even pushed my way over the Pyrenees to see Spain. Now, this seems pathetic, something like the way a wilted flower looks. I still don't know what was holding me back, but I fear it's connected somehow to my "We'll take it in stages" response to Rob's proposal. This is not a trait I'm proud of, but it also may partly explain why I couldn't slip right into my husband's faith when I married him. Big shifts felt big.

And while I hadn't become particularly attached to our huge, take-me-seriously starter house in New Haven, I wasn't so eager for a different church to assign a much more modest domicile, either. "Oh, the rectories are mostly pretty nice," Rob had assured me, as we walked in the Tetons. Now we were about to see.

When we made the drive from New Haven up to Storrs and saw the house that came with Rob's first real job as priest-in-charge of a church, I cried. It was a split-level, unappealing-looking place on a quiet dead-end street: charmless. With a child to tend to and no paying job of my own in this region of the state known as the "Quiet Corner," I cared plenty about our actual center of operations, and this didn't feel promising. We met no one on that first trip; everything was too still, and so I was free to conclude that I was bound to be lonely. "Is it really that bad?" Rob asked, trying to be both upbeat and tender, anticipating at least a short drive to church.

The couple who had lived there before, we had heard, were very much partners in their commitment to a religious way of life. The former vicar—that's the term used for a priest at a church not fully operating on its own engine—was also an accomplished composer of hymns. He and his wife went to church camps together, I'd been told. Never having gone to camp and only recently to church, I conjured a vague image of the two of them sitting at a picnic table, crosses on pieces of rawhide dangling around their necks, somebody strumming a guitar. I didn't hear through the grapevine that she had been involved in anything *other than church*; for instance, that she sold insurance or waitressed at the local dive or went scuba-diving. No, the woman who had lived there before me was a complete clergy spouse, and that had been enough for her.

Following in her footsteps I would not be, but it remained to be seen how this new place would take to my particular brand.

In his first post Rob was a curate at his job out of divinity school, and I had had some leeway in my role. He wasn't full-fledged yet, and neither was I as his spouse: sometimes I would be in church, but more often I found ways of avoiding that too-heavy cloak around my shoulders. Once he accepted his first full-time position leading a congregation, however, I began to get the impression that there was some aura of expectation, almost like a certain chair waiting for me. The fact that we had a toddler made my going to church each Sunday both more and less appealing: on the one hand, I craved companionship and appreciated the warm welcome we got; on the other hand, sometimes just the packing up and getting there at a certain time to hope that my son would either enjoy playing in the nursery or not squirm too much on my lap in the pew while I listened to Rob's sermon felt like a tall order.

The design of the church itself was completely different from the one we had come from. It was a modern A-frame structure, allowing natural light to pour onto the large cross and altar below. On weekdays, the eighty-five-year-old organist practiced upon her instrument with a determination that resulted in a swelling sound on Sundays. It was a small congregation, but there were a number of families with young children, and soon it became clear how tightly knit they had become to one another. Each Sunday that he presided, Rob sensed a greater feeling of intimacy in the church. Going with that intuition, he initiated changes up at the altar, including reducing the prominence of the communion rail; instead of making a box shape all around where he stood, it would now be in two shortened segments, leaving a wide opening. "After Christ Church," he told me, "I'm ready to bring down the barriers." Maybe some of my dislikes were rubbing off on him.

It would not be easy, let alone polite, for me to be standoffish here. And besides, Rob and I wanted to have another child. Once, with any luck, I became pregnant again, I would become physically more pronounced as a clergy spouse. What I did or didn't believe—though still vexing, like some kind of itch I couldn't quite reach, although I was starting to try—took a backseat in my mind. It wasn't relevant to my daily life as a wife and mother. I was part of the fabric of a tapestry that was much larger than just myself. Surely, I could bring my own colors, the ones that appeared without any coaxing or analyzing, and just melt in somehow.

Just shy of Willie's second birthday, baby Cora was born. For the rest of that summer, she slept deeply during much of the day, often in a seat under the small apple tree on our front lawn. While her brother played with his toys, I'd glance outside to see a mop of dark hair, one tiny hand frozen in midair, fingers separated as if she were in midsentence.

When fall came, I was reliably bringing them both to church.

Once he was released from his car seat, Willie ran happily toward the glass door at the lower level of the church building. With all his might, he pulled it open so he could sprint down the hallway and try to find his friend Simon in the carpeted common room before Sunday school started in the smaller chambers where kids were assigned by age group. I carried Cora, all bundled up in a fleecy blue zip-up suit, her round dark eyes peering out. Linda, Mary, and Sherry were already there—coats off—organizing arts and crafts materials on tables before distributing them to the several small classes, where kids would color and paste and construct decorations, some Christmas-tree worthy, to accompany the Bible lessons for that day.

"Hey, everybody," I said breezily, trying not to draw too much attention to myself as I paused to extricate Cora from her wrap and then walk across the room to the stairs that led up to the main part of the church, where I planned to feel marginally more at ease seated in a pew with my baby.

"Good morning, Polly," they said warmly, looking up from their tasks, "And we're glad to have Willie this morning, too. Bet he'll like the activity about Jonah and the whale that we have planned." Part of me was sure that my overall reputation as a mother slipped a notch each time I did not participate in Christian education at the church where my husband worked; another part of me was just as sure that any attempt to teach kids about Bible verses that I never learned myself would feel disingenuous. Who was Jonah, why did he go in the whale, and what exactly was the takeaway?

On some Sunday mornings, what I was missing in my background felt about as vast as the ocean. I considered trying to swim with a stronger stroke and do what Rob often suggested, ever since we met, with a weary voice, whenever I asked a question related to Scripture: "Polly, just read the Bible." This would mean essentially summoning, and maintaining, the same inquisitive spirit that got me enrolled in the Harvard course. Or I could try to rest assured that, no matter where I was on either the knowledge or the belief scale in this particular area, I was still fully capable of showering my children with all the love and support that they would need to rise up and flourish. I already had what it took. Yes, I convinced myself, this option was probably the one to stick with, the one that would have a steady source of sustenance deep within me, like a reliable stream making its way over rocks to feed into a river.

"Yes, I really appreciate all the work you've put into this," I said to the women, glancing back to make sure that Willie was being shepherded in with the rest of the two- and three-year-olds. Climbing the stairs with baby on my hip, hearing the opening hymn up above, I wondered whether, if you're fully invested in a marriage, you're supposed to undergo a range of interior changes—slight ones, but still perceptible, like the phases of the moon except not returning ever to exactly the same shape. I saw myself, at this moment, as someone content to be taking my place in a sun-bathed pew, glancing up at my husband who spotted us with pleasure, or maybe just relief.

Still, I decided to keep my seat at communion time. The rail here was not as intimidating as the one in New Haven, and I had learned the strategy of crossing my arms and bowing my head. And yet, with a baby on my lap, and my own little rivulet now trickling positively in my head, it was really just simpler to stay put. *Don't look down*, either, as if I was vaguely guilty of something; *look up and smile* as people moved up and down the center aisle, on their very important mission, eyes straight ahead.

Chapter 13

Riding, Past and Present

As Rob started tending his flock, I discovered other kinds of flocks—the animal kind—nearby.

The University of Connecticut began as an agricultural school. While other academic programs and big time Division One sports were in many ways eclipsing that old identity, the "Ag School" was in fact still going strong, especially for the core cadre of students who came to Storrs for the range of specialized occupational training they could get there.

Partly because it reminded me of where I grew up, I loved the whole area called Horsebarn Hill. On the opposite side of Route 195 from the main part of campus, there is a driving loop, and—depending on which end you start from—you'll see either the horse barns or the chicken barns first; then, in between, there are the pigs and the cows and the sheep, and rolling green fields. If you take a short hike up to the top of the main hill, as we did so many times, often with friends, you get a wonderful view of the whole bustling campus nearby. The silver dome of Gampel Pavilion, which takes in thousands of basketball fans on game nights, gleams prominently; but for a few moments anyway, as the soft breezes blow, you're glad to have your feet on the grass, taking in the quiet.

This part of campus satisfied my soul. Indeed, it reminded me that I had a soul. The whole farm-ness of it soothed me, provided a fountain of renewal. There was no altar to approach, and yet each time I took myself over there it felt like I was cupping my two open hands together, *receiving*, taking in sustenance that fortified my entire being.

I brought our kids to see the animals often, sometimes putting the bikes in the car so they could ride all the way around the loop. Walking behind them as they sped ahead, watching the sheep cavort in the field next to us, I knew fulfillment. In the winter, bundled up, we piled in the car as a family, joining many others in the community, to go sledding on the big hill opposite the horse barns. The space was wide open; no trees to provide the possibility of a sickening, concussive *thwack* as they had on either side of our narrow Emil's Path during my childhood. But it was steep enough to send some young bodies hurtling off their sleds, sometimes with serious consequences. It wasn't unusual for an ambulance to be called. "Woah, look at that!" Rob said, holding wide-eyed baby Cora close to him as he watched the aftermath of another wipeout. "Polly, don't take Willie down that way—stay over on this part of the hill." When we were together, and he was looking out for us, just us, everything felt right.

We'd lived in Storrs for six years when Henry arrived as our third child, in the heart of winter. I was just a couple of years older than my mother had been when she'd had me, her fifth child. That spring, instead of staying for the whole church service as I had done before, I started heading over to the Horsebarn loop, somewhat surreptitiously, on Sunday mornings. First dropping off the older two for Sunday school, I knew exactly how much in-between time I had to stay outside to walk with the baby in the backpack and our black Lab, Zeke, by my side, through long grass with dew still sparkling on it.

Thirsting for a more established way to become a legitimate denizen of Horsebarn Hill, and not yet back to regular employment apart from the kids, I registered for an "Introduction to Farm Animals" course through the School of Agriculture. I was only an auditor, but if I could have earned credits from enthusiasm, they would have stacked up. Leaving the kids with Rob for brief periods, I attended classes with undergraduates less than half my age, almost pretending that I might be headed, like many of them, toward veterinary school. Although I had earned a public school teaching certificate to go with my previous boarding school experience and might have just focused on getting back to a path in education, full-time work with two toddlers and now a newborn was too daunting. Plus, something in me felt unfinished, uncolored-in, and it wasn't exactly my lack of a faith tradition.

All the back-and-forths to the new church accentuated the fact that Rob had his occupation and spiritual center all wrapped up in one. It was as if he went out each morning to hoist up his flag, always the same flag, one that surmounted all boundaries between countries, so it could blow in the wind, the long strings bouncing against the metal pole, reminding him what he stood for. Comforted as I was by a feeling of some kind of energy moving vigorously within me, I needed to find my banner, too. It would have animals on it.

It was a Tuesday morning in crisp fall, and I was relishing the pocket of time I had away from the house that had been, of late, feeling more cramped. Sitting in the steeply banked lecture hall with rows of folded wooden seats that made a sharp slapping sound when they were shut, I lapped up how different both the students and the subject matter were from my last foray into academia. Here, most everyone wore hooded sweatshirts and boots that clomped. They brushed remnants of hay from their pants as they greeted each other, digging out notebooks from their backpacks and slumping down in their uncomfortable chairs. I wondered what they'd make of ancient theologians, but all those names I'd taken notes about had now faded from my mind.

Up on the huge white screen, we looked at diagrams of bovine anatomy, jotting down distinctions between the various stomachs cows have. Our professor—who I later would learn was a devout Mormon, a fact that never entered his lectures—dug his hands into his jeans and paced back and forth, occasionally tapping his pointer up at a segment of the animal. "Now if any of you have ever worked around cows, you know that they chew and chew and chew."

I didn't really know cows, only horses, but my older brother Sandy had swung his life in their direction, working alongside a partly blind dairy farmer up on the Quebec border who was something of a tragic Ahab figure, while keeping his main profession as a teacher. Almost a decade earlier, when I listened to Professor Gomes describe the conversion of Constantine and the rapid-fire spread of Christianity, I had a very particular purpose: learn a little bit of what my husband was steeped in so that we could be closer. It was ludicrous, in a way—trying to be more like him. He knew he didn't need to do anything like that for *me*. Marriage is not a profession you prepare for by studying up. It's love itself that must carry you through, like a wave that two people ride together.

Now, in this brightly lit amphitheater, I was striking out in a new direction that actually felt old, but a different kind of old than ancient theology—old within me. Ever since I read *Charlotte's Web* and E. B. White's essays about farm life, moving on to James Herriot's *All Creatures Great and Small* and then Farley Mowat's haunting *Never Cry Wolf*, all the while spending hours outdoors with my own horses and dogs, I developed a conviction about the value of our relationship to animals. Unlike my classmates here, I was not taking stepping stones toward a career in animal husbandry so much as heeding some kind of inner voice encouraging me to stick with what I loved then, what I had always loved, what filled me out as a person.

Up front, the professor was checking his notes, about to move on to a new segment. He changed his slide, scanned the room, spotting at least a couple of students with heads back, tuned out. Oh good, I said to myself, it's time for pigs.

"So, do we have anybody here who hangs out in the pig barn?" He was walking around now, waiting.

There were some guffaws from the audience but also a few raised hands. He pointed at one of them and asked, "What's the biggest misconception most people have about pigs?"

"That they're dirty," came the reply from a guy with outstretched legs in the aisle. "Also that they're stupid."

"How do you know they're not either of those things?" the professor went on, smiling now.

"Because I have a job taking care of them, and they are definitely an underrated species. They do like to roll in the mud, sure, but they're also wicked smaht." More guffaws, but people were sitting up to look at this guy now.

An idea started to form in my head, an idea that connected various strands in my life. Like Charlotte in the corner of the pig barn, I could spin a web.

After class, emboldened by my acceptance or at least quasi acceptance here, instead of heading up the steps, which some of the guys took two at once, I decided to approach the professor down front. Even though we were about the same age, and I knew his name was Ken, I didn't get that familiar.

"Hi Professor. I wonder if I could ask you about a project I have in mind?"

"Sure," he said, leaning on the black island that sat in front of the screen, with rolled up sleeves.

"As you can tell, I'm a little older than most of your students; I live a few miles away and I bring my kids—they're little—here all the time to see the animals. I think slightly older kids from the community would really benefit from coming here, too, especially if they could also get to meet some college students." I was all bubbly now, the way I could get—more sure of myself in new terrain, tapping into an old part of me, than I had reason to be.

He let me go on and then said, "Sounds like you're interested in making a 4-H club? Have you done one of those before?" He didn't think I was way out of line here; maybe my idea could take on legitimacy by fitting in a traditional category.

"No, but I've definitely heard about them," I said, as if that made me qualified. "4-H" had an old-fashioned ring to it, like something out of an old TV show, but if I was trying to create a new little community that included animals, this might be the way to go.

Amazingly, he agreed to become a faculty advisor and instructed me on how I should proceed, through various levels of State University clearances. Clipboard in hand, I started scurrying around to the appropriate offices, also to the schools, talking it up to my friends whom I saw at Montessori pickup. Key to the program's success would be persuading Ag School college students that they must be missing children in their lives and here was their chance to give back to their community! Amid a flurry of permission slips and clarification of rules, I planned a schedule of events: a series of regular after-school visits to the various barns around the loop, combining the two age groups into matched pairs.

Without aiming for a program that would fit within religious life, I was, in a way, setting up another kind of service, an alternative means of worship.

Whatever unease I felt when faced with the realities of Sunday school could be alleviated, I discovered, by watching a fourth-grader race toward a field shouting "Look, the sheep are running so fast!" and then a nineteen-year-old leaning down to try to explain what might have gotten those sheep going, and in the process paying close attention to whatever the child was wondering. This kind of moment of interchange represented a *communion* I understood; I could vouch for it. Chances were that the lives of these two people would be slightly changed. Here, there were fences to climb up on, but no real barriers.

The 4-H club was fine as far as it went, but the restlessness I had with my own identity in these days would soon find another outlet in an activity that allowed me to wield a mallet. One day, packing up from a session, I saw a sign that said, "Come and Learn to Play Polo! Six Weeks of Lessons for Beginners Starting Soon!" Suddenly in my mind a new persona of "Polly the Polo Player" emerged, almost as if I could become Rocky's Adrienne, taking the reins of my own transformation by shedding glasses and releasing my hair. In my case, it would be getting on a two-thousand-pound beautiful animal who turned on a dime. I could in fact be a *better* clergy wife, I reasoned, more content with the packing of diaper bags and the mundane back and forth from vicarage to church, if I broke free from the dull stereotype that still lingered around my shoulders—even if it had just been me placing it there in the first place—and did something on the wild side.

I wouldn't exactly be starting from scratch, since I had been lucky enough to grow up riding horses throughout my childhood. Jumping up on a horse's back had been one of my main activities during all those churchless weekends. In deciding to sign up for polo lessons in my forties, I was partly trying to stoke the embers of a youthful pastime and partly trying to follow in the hoofsteps of both my father and the aunt for whom I'd been named; I was trying to conjure them in some way.

When two people marry, each of them brings along boxes of possessions—material ones, of course, like yearbooks, some cookware, and old record albums. These generally get pooled in the mishmash of setting up a joint household. But also, there are the individuals in the wings who have shaped and will continue to shape each person's identity, people who have left a deep imprint.

Back at the house, amid the weighty photo albums I'd been trying to maintain as our kids grew, I found a much smaller one, with just a handful of black-and-white pictures giving separate glimpses of my mother and father in their youth, before they ever imagined one another. For the umpteenth time, I gazed at a startlingly clear image of my Aunt Polly, at the age of ten, and my dad, two years younger, with their Shetland pony, named Circus. Or maybe it was Wedding Bells, the other pony I'd heard about from those days. Dark-haired Polly was riding, legs dangling down and garters visible; my father was on the ground, holding the lead rope. It must have been about 1920. We know from all the stories passed down that the four of them spent a lot of time together, romping around my grandparents' place. Although they looked very serious here, these two siblings were avid and often mischievous riders in childhood.

Aunt Polly was the bolder of the two, at least when it came to hatching ideas and satisfying her ever-burning curiosity. One day when she was nine years old and alone in the house, she saw Wedding Bells peering in from the field and, deciding that the pony looked lonely, invited her inside. The four-footed creature readily clomped up the stairs to check out the bedrooms, but, legend has it, she didn't want to go downstairs again. Polly had to summon a local farmer, who in turn rounded up a few other men to help. Four men, one for each leg, picked the pony up and brought her back outside. My grandparents were probably distraught when they found out. Many decades later, when Polly's adult reputation for figuring ways out of all kinds of fixes had been firmly established, imagining her as a girl, flummoxed and needing help after a foolish decision, became reassuring to me. She was never perfect, after all; she got herself into jams.

I studied the photograph for any signs of who each of these siblings would become. They looked back at me, calmly, divulging nothing. But I knew that the years stretching ahead would include more riding for both of them, that they would maintain a devotion to this activity, almost as if it were a way of exercising their particular kind of faith. And I knew that my urge to carry on some of what they did was akin to why people so often continue to worship at the same kind of church their ancestors attended. A way of life is illuminated for us, and liking it well enough and not seeing any other that looks more compelling, we follow the lampposts right along.

By any account, Mary Ingraham Bunting Smith led a remarkable twentieth-century life. Staying home from school for large hunks of her youth because of various illnesses, she read voraciously, largely educating herself. Without attending any church, she set out to learn as much as she could about various religions. By age twelve, for instance, she'd read the entire Quran. And, despite unsteady health, she rode voraciously, too. Wanting to try polo as a teenager, she hid her hair under a helmet so she could sneak onto a men's team. Women were not allowed to play.

Known mostly for having been president of Radcliffe College during the entire decade of the sixties, she was also a microbiologist and the first woman to serve on the Atomic Energy Commission. Gifted with an enormous curiosity and determination, she was a true visionary who worked tirelessly to advance the cause of women everywhere. The front flap of Elaine Yaffe's biography of my aunt, published in 2005, includes this description: "Above all, she is important because she was one of the first to perceive, and come up with remedies for, the ways in which American society was stifling women's aspirations and thwarting their achievements." In addition to earning a PhD and then excelling in her career, she was an accomplished farmer and homesteader. She and her husband, Henry, a pathologist, lived with their four children in a basement in rural Connecticut while they built a house. Not long afterward, she became a single parent when Henry died way too young. She kept bees while she was a college president, sometimes excusing herself from meetings to go tend them.

Knowing that I had been named for this remarkable person was a complicated legacy. My father respected her enormously; we all did. There was nothing about how she carried her accomplishments that made her intimidating, mostly because she was always down to earth, with tremendous good humor, too. Many of the women I knew during childhood—like my own mother and other aunts—were plucky and resourceful. Polly was unusual, though, in that in addition to having a full and rich home life with children and always animals, too, she had also become a higher education leader with a national reputation.

Fortunately I was not foolish enough to try to measure up to her. During my freshman year of college, when emboldened by my high school success in advanced placement biology, I chose to tackle genetics. I was in for a rude awakening. Sitting in the big lecture hall, watching the huge screen with detailed diagrams of cellular material, the professor with his pointer and his explanations that barreled forward, I felt that somehow, I'd missed a few crucial steps. I can still see the "C-" glaring out at me from my term report card, and it stung.

I would not go on to become a microbiologist like her (although I redeemed my pride somewhat by doing a bit better in other science courses). But my own brief resumption of being on horseback in the Storrs arena—trying to learn how to manage the long mallet while giving my mount just the right signals with legs and hands, and doing reasonably well—provided a reminder of who my aunt used to be, and the kind of person I still wanted to be, too.

About a decade before I took up the polo mallet in Storrs, months before I started dating Rob, she also quite literally took me in when I was in my Adrift Stage. Trying to tap into my college alumni network for job leads, I met with a banker or some smug guy behind a desk who leaned back in his chair, and said, "Oh as a Dartmouth alum you really shouldn't have any problem." A lot he knew. I signed on with a temporary agency and realized that I would have to slog through this mess for a while. It was really the first time in my life that I learned the cruel truth about young adulthood: you can screw up and it's nobody's job to bail you out. Somehow, you've got to find a way through what feels like an impenetrable thicket.

Aunt Polly didn't ask a lot of questions; she just understood. As soon as she got wind of my difficulties, she offered me a place to live in the top floor of the house in Cambridge she had moved into after marrying her later-in-life husband, Clem, a retired doctor. "You can live in our attic," she said, "where medical students used to stay." As a college president, she had no doubt seen her share of young women in various stages of upheaval or collapse even. During her tenure, her habit of leaving the porch light on to indicate that she was still up and it was fine to come and knock, just to talk, seems unbelievable decades later.

When I pulled into the narrow driveway with a tightly packed mustard hatchback Mazda and saw where the back stairs were, I knew that this tall yellow colonial could be only a short-term place to lick my wounds and sing a mournful song. I needed to get myself together and chart a course. Following years of being steadily with people my own age, having regular suppers with two people over seventy-five felt weird and, at first, exacerbated my feeling that I'd veered off from where I was supposed to be. It felt like one small step away from being back home, with my parents, a bleak predicament I'd only recently escaped. It was entirely possible, I thought, that my aloneness would stretch on and on in perpetuity.

And yet, a couple of months into my residence there, I began to notice a shimmering quality that, I sensed, could help me on my way, propel me forward toward a fuller life. I would first need to let go of the idea that something that was by its very nature *temporary*—a two-week job, a month's room rental in someone's house, or even a morose state of mind—would get calcified into something hard and permanent. I would have to be gentler to myself, in one way, and also tougher on myself, in another. Just a couple of years before, at school with a plethora of friends close by, I'd known happiness. I needed to believe that happiness, maybe a slightly different kind, was attainable again, and that this time—more than before when the ingredients had been dished out for me—I'd actively need to create it, on my own.

One evening, after yet another drab day at a Back Bay office where I took messages on pink slips and was hardly spoken to, another T ride followed by a long walk past homes aglow with family warmth, another climb up two flights to my chamber, I came back downstairs to find Aunt Polly moving about the kitchen quietly, slightly bent over. Dressed in slacks and a brightly colored cardigan sweater, she'd already set three places at the little, rickety metal table by the windows. I was feeling forlorn but trying to put on a brave face. *Things will get better, you'll feel like you belong somewhere again soon, just hang in there.*

"Anything I can do to help?" I asked my aunt, who was now peering into the oven with potholders ready. "Well, hellooo," she said, looking over her shoulder to greet me with a smile. "Glad to see you!" I wasn't anonymous to her, anyway.

Clem came into the room, dressed as usual in a three-piece suit, tie, and white sneakers. For most of his career at Boston Children's Hospital, he had helped to launch the field of neonatology, furthering understanding about premature babies. Over the mantel in the living room hung a large, framed rendition of a tree with many branches, given to him upon his retirement; it depicted how his protégés had brought this new area of medicine to various continents. Now, he had more time to indulge in his other passion: Wordsworth's poetry. At almost every one of our meals together, he would look up at the ceiling while summoning his memory and then recite some lines.

He moved right over to Aunt Polly, in his usual stiff gait, saying something close to her ear that I could not hear. She looked puzzled for a moment, then her face lit up. Taking the casserole out of the oven, she brought it to the counter, still grinning widely. "What was that, Clem? You want a Michelob? Oh, for a moment I thought you said, 'Want to make love?' I was about to say that would be very nice, but maybe not right now, before supper." Wearing her broad smile, she gasped for breath, the way she did when she found something hilarious.

I blushed with embarrassment, but quickly realized how congruous this actually was with what I had seen going on between them on a daily basis. They were two people who had come together for the final chapter of their lives, pooling their resources of experiences, children, and grandchildren, and exploring a range of topics, while also feeling physically drawn to one another, just in a calmer way than when they'd been my age. Even though, to all appearances, they were eminently *successful* people, even tops in their respective fields, they had not lived without pain, without setbacks. After losing their spouses in midlife, each of them had known loneliness.

We took our seats, lit the candle in the center. Nobody said grace or anything much to punctuate the beginning of the meal. The table was so small that we had to avoid bumping elbows. As darkness fell and our conversation roamed, I summoned a little bit of faith that I would in fact have a future.

Soon afterward, Aunt Polly gave me some furniture to help me move into my own apartment a few miles away. "This will be just dandy," she said, looking around my new living room that overlooked the garish convenience store sign, with Boston's tall buildings in the distance. It wasn't dandy right away, but soon enough I felt relaunched. With roommates and jobs, life began to pick up, one notch at a time. When the call came, I would be ready to meet the man who brought his deep and mysterious faith, like a fascinating new animal on a leash, with him into the restaurant.

Chapter 14

Love Thy Neighbor

If Horsebarn Hill was where I placed one flag, our neighborhood gradually became even more my spiritual center. Here I was planted and began to grow; here I moved confidently, knowing my role.

Over the course of just a few years, the same split-level house that had put me in tears became a home with rays of connection spreading in all directions, up and down the street. There was Sammy, the girl just Willie's age directly across from us; Julia, Becky, and Tara—the group of sisters who eagerly walked up to be mother's helpers; Alex, the boy without siblings who had a tremendous array of toys and could play equally well with Cora or Willie. The fact that the road wasn't too short (about a quarter of a mile) and, just above our house, started a gradual downhill slope that ended in a cul-de-sac meant it was perfect for kids learning to ride bikes. And perfect for meeting neighbors, too. Once we got to the bottom circle, generously wide and devoid of any cars, our kids and any others we picked up along the way could tear around and around, pausing to go explore the stream that was a short walk through the brush. The houses that held strangers were the exception.

My mother used to tell the story of how my brother Rob, at about age eight or so, came running up our long driveway after discovering that a family was moving in up the still sparsely populated street. "We live in a neighborhood now!" he proclaimed, elated. Our fields and woods were great, but having kids to play with was even better. That's how I came to feel on Ellise Road, after a time. The design of the house itself became inconsequential. What mattered was we were surrounded by friends, and there was a kind of porousness in the walls of our homes as we went in and out, mingling our kids and our lives.

In many respects, my husband Rob's first neighborhood was his church congregation. It didn't really matter how far-flung people were geographically; once they got to church, they became all one big family, under the same tent. He was just as glad to let me take the lead in forging our on-the-street relationships; being essentially an introvert, he didn't have a whole lot of excess energy for meeting additional waves of people, though he was glad for me to do so. As a result, between the two of us, we developed an extensive network that came most to fruition during birthday-party-time in July. Since both Willie and Cora were summer babies, born one year and 356 days apart, we generally planned back-to-back extravaganzas at our house. We didn't scrimp on the efforts, either, working on equal footing for the common cause of entertaining children.

When Cora turned six, we had a standout one. It was the final hour before guests started pulling up, and the clock was ticking. Rob and I walked together across the parched grass past the blue-and-yellow swing set to string up a clothesline between two trees. There we would hang pieces of oak tag on which, last night, I had written individual kids' names boldly with magic marker. As we positioned ourselves on either side of this farthest patch of backyard, I glanced over to Rob in his green T-shirt and felt our marital connection crackle. Here we were not clergyman and wife but husband and wife, father and mother. We had created this child together, and we were about to celebrate the ongoing triumph of her life by providing a series of activities—first they'll do this, then that—for eager soon-to-be first-graders.

This kind of togetherness felt so similar to when we were strapping Willie into his Jolly Jumper, knowing he would bounce, bounce, bounce for sheer pleasure and we would revel in his joy.

The Bible has a lot to say on the subject of hospitality as a Christian virtue. But I didn't need to know any of that on this day. I had my own memories of how my big brother Rob once planned my August birthday parties, relieving my mother of the duty and making sure that any child who arrived would have a sense of belonging, of fun, while running down the lawn with an egg in a spoon or hopping in a burlap bag. In my mind, celebrations like these constituted life achievements because they resulted in a frothing over of happiness that would live on in memory. And at this moment, Rob and I were allied forces, piloting our planes in tandem through blue skies, on a mission to bring about as much childhood joy as we could. Suffering, loss, death—they had no place here, for the time being anyway. Even the patch of woods behind our backyard could engulf us in darkness if we ventured there; but on this day, we didn't.

With the length of rope secured on either end, we attached the rectangles of oak tag with clothespins at regular intervals; Rob was willing to follow my lead on how far apart they should be. I appreciated feeling a surge of confidence that I had, in fact, done enough preparation to make way for a successful party.

"Where did you say you wanted this banner?"

Rob hadn't been involved in designing the brightly colored letters spelling out "WELCOME TO CORA'S FIELD OF DREAMS PARTY!" on a big swath of white paper, but he was available for posting it up, knowing that adults and children together would be ringing the doorbell soon. I had a partner in this effort, and we were on common ground. For the rest of the afternoon, putting forth the best possible welcome on home turf would be our shared goal.

For a moment, I considered that Rob probably felt very much this same way whenever he was at church before a service. I had heard him describe a morning of multiple baptisms as "really fun." This startled me at first, until I realized that my own various definitions of fun spring from one particular brook of experience. He had his own brook. During the course of our union so far, there had been a trickling in from one to another, but I was beginning to see that the merging process might never be complete, that some parts of each one of us would remain independent rivulets.

And maybe complete merging didn't have to be the only way to a happy marriage.

"I thought right at the top of this hill would be good, by the garden. Can you find a place to attach it?"

He considered my expectation, but then had his own idea. "I think it'll be better around the garage, so people can see it right when they arrive." Without waiting for a confirmation, he headed down there. Oh, good point, I thought. Marriage is so much about moments like this—the give and take, the tossing back and forth of perspectives, the sometimes digging in and the more frequently letting go, the occasional magical convergence.

Soon, our yard was full of kids tearing all over. We sent them racing back to the clothesline to find their own rectangles, then directed them to the picnic table where—with an array of doodads—they sat quietly for a while to make their own baseball stadiums, in keeping with the hit movie *Field of Dreams*. The parents who stayed past the drop-off (most of them) stood behind their kids, occasionally leaning in and exclaiming, "Oh wow, that is so great!" and talking about nothing much. We were all together, crowded around a table. Rob relaxed, knowing that there was no need for any lexicon, order of service. I stayed a tad anxious about things going according to plan; he was not at all. Just let the kids play.

Ten and then again twenty years later, I would look back on these pictures, missing everyone, most especially the two adults—mother and father of the boy from farther down the street, both Medieval scholars, oozing kindness—who died within a couple of years of one another, after we had packed up and moved away. We returned to walk stiffly into the Catholic church and then up to the gravesites, twice, unbelievingly.

After the presentation of a cake thick with icing, on top of which I'd drawn a wobbly green and purple baseball diamond, it was back to ten kids tearing around. They rocked the play set with their reach-for-the-sky swinging, lined up in bathing suits for the Slip 'N Slide. The trio of sisters from down the street helped wherever they were needed. Our place was a hive of activity.

I looked around and spotted Rob engrossed in conversation with a couple of fathers. When I saw the heads of the other two go back in laughter, I surmised that Rob was giving them a good story. My heart fluttered just as it did when we first met; once again, I was admiring him in a comfortable pair of old jeans. Maybe he was telling the one about the time when, growing up in Minnesota, he actually found another boy's *finger* at the bus stop when the spring thaw came—a result of a midwinter mishap with a Toro snowblower—and just put it in his lunchbox, to show off at school. Or maybe it was the one about when, fed up with in an act of teenage rebellion at the age of fifteen, he packed a few things, took a candy bar for sustenance, and headed down to the bus station, buying a ticket to make his way back to the Midwest, where he and his sister used to have so much fun playing in endless snow tunnels.

He has always told me he likes it when I express appreciation for his sermons, saying that my thumbs-up for his hard work matters to him more than the approval of all his parishioners. This is sweet, and I'm trying to do better when I have the opportunity, but I sometimes have trouble jumping on what I perceive to be this particular bandwagon of praise, even though he insists it doesn't really exist. I can't count the times people have told me, "That was such a good sermon your husband gave!" The fact that my opinion arrives on a different plane, carries its own special cachet, allows the glow that he has rightfully earned, each time, to be transferred, at least a bit, over to me. Insofar as it's possible for one spouse to observe another in their work, it's lovely and right for compliments to flow. Still, some of the most powerful moments in marriage are when you witness your beloved doing something without an audience, or at least without the audience seeing them the way you do.

He's a gifted preacher, and I am always proud when I hear him speak in a formal setting. Seeing him as a regular guy in the neighborhood, though, brings its own kind of thrill.

Chapter 15

The Power of the Pavilion

When my father called home jubilantly from the hospital with the news that I had been born—finally a girl after four boys—my ten-year-old brother Sandy didn't exactly share the joy. "Oh no, now we can't have a good basketball team!" he said. To him, there was nothing more satisfying than getting good air and jamming a ball home, in the company of other like-minded individuals. Many years later, this same brother would make a court inside his huge Vermont barn, and the piled high hay bales would provide a perfect narrow opening for players to enter, amid the imagined din of the crowd.

Satisfied by horseback riding and playing tennis in my youth, I never took up the sport myself, but it came roaring back when our son, Willie, discovered the wonders of dribbling, passing, and shooting.

Probably in large part due to the fact that he spent the first part of his childhood near the campus of the University of Connecticut, Willie developed an early passion for the game. Our town was so completely dominated by the Huskies that there might as well have been a huge dog's head in the sky every day, watching over us. This was rural life only in part; the Division One status of our teams propelled us all to the national stage.

When he was eight, Willie attended a weeklong basketball camp sponsored by the famous UConn coach, Jim Calhoun. He loved every minute of it, especially brushing shoulders with some of the players. I remember one night when I went to pick him up; it was about 10 P.M., and he was the lone day camper still shooting baskets on the main floor of Gampel Pavilion, with a few relaxed counselors in their enormous shorts encouraging him, rebounding any shot that might happen to make it all the way up and in. Among them was an incoming freshman who would go on to NBA fame.

Looking down on that shiny and perfect floor, past the rows of empty seats, I saw my son in his own kind of heaven. Whether or not he would become a standout player in the years ahead didn't matter; he was on a path of striving with all of his might, finding a reason to practice, practice, practice until he tasted the fruit of success.

The chapel was at the edge of the university, right near the Catholic and the Congregational churches as well as the Jewish synagogue that also served students and faculty. A ten-minute walk away, in the heart of the campus, loomed the tremendous Gampel, a gleaming silver dome with a patchwork of squares that shouted out, "I'm what's really important here now! What else can compare to my splendor?" It was obnoxious in one way, exciting in another, and I was mostly a sucker for it.

Once, friends of ours with three daughters, a clergy family from another town, provided us with a rare treasure: tickets for the whole family. We parked at the quiet chapel, where a huge cross overlooked its wooden pews and the renowned organ waited for Sunday's services, and walked past big brick buildings to the jam-packed crowd and the jubilant sound of the band. Another kind of worship, stretching the term only slightly, was about to get underway. It wasn't a heavenly light people were after here, but rather the glow of a very earthly kind of glimmering success.

Walking in those doors, trying to keep hold of my kids' hands, I absorbed the contrast, and the odd similarity, too. If people go to church to be part of something larger than themselves, to move beyond their individuality in some way, to let go of their sins alongside others doing the same, it is also true that sports fans go to arenas to feel the throbbing excitement of a contest that, at least for a time, allows them to release the cares in their regular lives.

Are they seeking something ultimately insignificant, even perhaps a mirage? Or are they experiencing a kind of—that word I never used to say—communion? When I wondered about this aloud once, Rob taught me that the original Greek word is "koinonia." In the Christian tradition, it means "fellowship, sharing in common." Walking up to the rail for members of the congregation is, I was learning, at once a very personal but also a very collective experience. Attending a game with thousands of others, on the other hand, heightens the group bonding to such a degree that the individual is just about subsumed; it allows fans to both cheer their team and actually be swept up into *becoming* their team, too.

When I glanced at Rob's face as we climbed high up in the bleachers, with the clanging sounds our feet made on the metal steps amid the growing din of the crowd on every level, I saw that giving himself over to this kind of frenzy wouldn't be happening. He looked subdued, as if he'd tolerate more than enjoy the experience. Instead of saying, "Wow, this is amazing!" and thereby demonstrating my full allegiance here, I offered a more muted and empathetic, "How're you doing?" I felt obliged to check in with whatever his inner life was doing. Not wanting me to pay him any mind, to call attention to himself, he said only, "I'm OK." Once we got seated, he tried to give himself over to the blaring nature of it all, go with the kids' enthusiasm for everything pouring into their senses, knowing that the kind of glory sought in this place couldn't be the kind that caused his heartstrings to reverberate. In fact, in those early years of his ministry, it was hard for him to experience pure joy. Some years later, he would write about this time; but that would be his own story.

Chapter 16

The Upheaval

When we first arrived in Storrs, somewhere at the back of my mind floated an understanding that my husband's first run in charge of a church would be just that—his first. After all, he needed to keep growing in his vocation or, to use a term common in secular professions, one that he himself sometimes used, partly tongue-in-cheek: "advance." He'd get stale, surely, staying under the same steeple for too long. But here we land on a common challenge in marriage, at least in our particular marriage. Because of how my childhood played out, I'm someone who, when a few years go by, begins to send down roots deep into the earth, gets comfortable, nestles in for a long stay alongside my companions. Here is where we are, I tell myself, and so let's do some flourishing. The future? That's off in the mist somewhere.

This "love-the-ones-you're-with" approach is sensible enough in a clergy family, until a certain gong from somewhere offstage sounds, signaling "It's Time to Move!" Then, suddenly, the sweet little church on the edge of campus becomes more like one little planet within a huge universe that is The Entire Church, and leaving the neighborhood becomes a kind of casualty, like collateral damage. Spaceships, it turned out, were available for us. Rob always knew this, knew that his adult life would consist of strapping in for takeoffs and unbuckling for arrivals. From his perspective, everywhere he'd land would be, in some way, familiar. It would be up to me to find the best approach to getting on board.

Back when we were sitting across from one another in a North End restaurant or hiking in the Tetons, when he with a kind of flashlight illuminated elements of his faith and then more practical issues of church housing, we delved into plenty of key topics. But neither one of us knew then how important the matter of *moving* would be to our marriage. Or, more specifically, the matter of how each one of us would respond so differently to a move. If Rob had asked me back before we were married, "So how do you think you will feel when we've been in one place for a while and then I get a new job somewhere else?" I probably would have shrugged and said, "No big deal." I would not have wanted to anticipate myself being anyone other than a get-along-go-along spouse. Once I became a mother, though, the stakes were raised considerably. Then, my own childhood memories of the way an extended community can just keep getting stronger, the way you can practically know a whole town if you stay long enough, came rushing back to me. I wanted my children to be wrapped in the same kind of security blanket I remembered having.

After Rob began sending out his materials, it wasn't long before he got some nibbles. He had a few phone interviews, taking them in our downstairs study with the door shut. Soon, one particular church in another state became very interested, and he reciprocated the interest. Off he went for a day of interviews, and he came back cautiously enthusiastic. The next step, I learned, would be for *me* to go: to check them out and be checked out in return. Rob wasn't laughing this time.

We had been married for almost ten years, and I'd joined him frequently at his place of work, but now I would be presenting myself as part of the package for people who were looking us over, considering a purchase. And, to compound the difference, I would be going alone to a set of appointments in this potential new community. The stage was set: they already knew they wanted my husband, and he was pretty sure he wanted them, too. Even before I got in the car, the deck felt stacked. Not exactly *against me*, but stacked nonetheless. There were a whole lot of them, only one of me, and I wasn't sure I understood how much real me to bring to this appointment.

On the way up to the town in New Hampshire, I wondered how it would feel different if I'd been a full-fledged Episcopalian. I wasn't a complete outsider because I regularly came in the closest possible contact to the guy they wanted to be their leader. And yet, I wasn't an *insider* either. That same odd mix again. What I felt, driving on the quiet roads strewn with colorful leaves after a rain, was a sudden allegiance to spouses everywhere—in the current age and stretching back through the centuries, too—who felt they were supposed to fall in step somehow, fit in with the program, complete the picture. Even when they were not at all sure they wanted to.

It was almost as if doe-eyed Princess Diana were seated right next to me in the car, letting me know in her dulcet tones how impossible it had been for her to be true to herself and to please the royal family, as well. "Much of the time I felt that I was supposed to adorn and adore Charles without speaking out too much about anything. The trouble was, I really *cared* about a lot of stuff." Then from the backseat, Rosalynn Carter spoke softly in her Southern drawl: "When Jimmy told me he wanted to run for president, I didn't think it was a good idea to leave our farm." Mary Todd Lincoln piped up about how it was all well and good that her husband saved the Union, but their way of life sure brought with it a tremendous cost to her mental health. She stared stonily in front of her, tears streaming down her face. Within just a few moments, it got very crowded in my car, and the windows all steamed up.

I couldn't recall any other time in my life when I had been the guest of honor, except maybe those birthday parties my brother Rob planned; but this afternoon would be exactly that. The whole setup promoted me to Queen for a Day, but with a catch. Some of the church women had gotten together to put on a lovely lunch—"luncheon" actually, to use a term I recalled from the Nancy Drew mysteries I used to devour—in someone's home.

Finding the right driveway, the one with many cars already parked in it, I found the space they had apparently left for me and then walked down a few steps from the side entrance of this house into an expansive living room. I was greeted by plenty of light, flowers, and eager faces. Clearly, our hostess was accustomed to entertaining. The dozen or so women were already chatting, about their kids and goings-on in town. They struck me as a kind of adult sorority, accustomed to mingling with one another. Their laughter rippled out, combining with the clinking of the sparkling punch glasses. I was the object of their interest today, the new recruit they wanted to woo.

One neatly coiffed woman with a green blazer and gold earrings, about my age, leaned in, "So, tell us about your kids. You have three, right?" This was an automatic way to get a mother talking, and so I did. But as I moved around the room, lapping up the interest everyone showed, smiling, and making eye contact, I remained conscious of the fact that it was really *my husband* they wanted in the pulpit of their church. I was, to be blunt, not so much a full person as a crucial piece of furniture that needed to be carried across the threshold. They knew that he wouldn't come without me. Perhaps, I couldn't help thinking to myself, mischievously, I could be the kind of sofa with arms just wide enough to make getting through a doorway a little tricky.

Afterward, three women took me on a tour of the town, which on this fall afternoon was as bustling and appealing as any New England location could be. Our first stop was the church itself. The stained glass windows looked stunning; the rows of pews went on and on; the pulpit commanded attention, even when empty. Most likely, my guides were still not aware that I would once again be deciding for myself how much time I would be spending here. Nobody directly asked me, "Are you religious?" or "How do you like coming to church?" Everything in the way they spoke to me suggested that I was considered His Other Half, cut from the same cloth.

A short walk down a cobblestone sidewalk was the rectory, where we would live, and my companions were very eager to take me there. It was a nineteenth-century white clapboard place, well maintained and spacious. We entered through a gate and made our way through a warren of empty rooms. There was nothing lacking here, except that the house was right up against a busy street, with a very small yard, and my mind quickly leaped to the issue of where I would take Zeke, our black Lab, for his exercise. To me, this was not just a side issue—it was central to my life. Probably any number of other clergy wives would have been more interested in kitchen counters or closet space. "I'm wondering about where I would walk our dog," I ventured. Shelley jumped in, enthusiastically. "Oh, there are some wonderful trails a short distance from here, maybe a half mile in the car. We'd be happy to show you if you'd like?" While not wanting to appear ungracious, I made a mental note of how the space-for-dog question stood up to be noticed. Living here would mean such an easy walk for Rob; he would probably go back and forth a half dozen times a day. It would be old-fashioned in a charmingly British kind of way, that gate opening and closing all the time. But something in me felt friction with the whole presentation. And I could tell they were watching my every expression.

"So now how about we show you the elementary school? Here, we can take my car." Jane, the main spokesperson among my guides, was still chipper, and I buckled in next to her while Shelley and Susan got in the backseat for a short drive across town. They wanted to come, too, even though they waited out the actual dip into the building they already knew so well. After the school security process and name stickers at the Main Office, we started a walk-through, meeting any staff people who happened to be traveling through the halls. Jane took each opportunity to introduce me. "This is Polly, and we're very much hoping that her husband will soon be our new rector. Her kids would be second- and fourth-graders here if they come, so we're just giving her a look at the school." She never stopped smiling.

"Oh, how nice to meet you! You'll really love it here," said a woman who resembled Ms. Frizzle from *The Magic School Bus*, carrying an armload of books.

During a lull in the greetings, one of the church ladies said, "My own kids went to this school, and they loved it. They're both in college now—how fast the years go!"

I was thinking about Goodwin Elementary, back home, the building on the wooded road that we would be leaving behind. It had been everything I had hoped a community school could be, a gathering place for Suzuki concerts and all-school assemblies with a wise and warm principal. Friendliness was already in the air on the walk from the parking lot to the front door. And we were only getting started there, with a firmly planted third-grader, a child in first grade, and a toddler yet to begin. How could any other place be better?

As we strolled back to the car, Shelley and Susan reappeared from a bench, and Jane said, "So, now that we've seen all of that, let's talk a bit about what *you* might like to do here! We've done a little homework on that, too." They formed a kind of circle around me.

With Church, Home, and School—three main pillars of the new life awaiting me—identified, my guides thoughtfully turned their attention to the kind of employment I might want to seek. This, presumably, could be my fourth pillar: Job. They knew that I'd been working to help welfare recipients become self-sufficient, so they were ready with suggestions of organizations I might try to contact to get set up in that same field. "So-and-so in the church works at such-and-such, and she'd be very glad to speak with you about how to start networking." They genuinely wanted to help me, and I was duly impressed by their research, but at the same time I couldn't let go of the fact that their motivation was springing from what *they* wanted: my husband as their priest. And that, in turn, might have been a good thing—for him, in isolation, as a clergyman. But we were married and must make big decisions together. It felt complicated, as if I had to see my way clearly through a process of weighing what had real value and what did not. That afternoon, I had, in a way, been watching one long commercial, preparing to discuss with Rob later whether or not we, as a couple, should decide to buy.

"I think I can research some of those organizations once I get back home," I said on the drive back to where my own car was parked. "Thank you all so much for the hospitality; it's been quite overwhelming." And that was the truth.

When I got back in the car, I felt unsettled. Inside me, the weather was humid and stuffy, and storm clouds were rumbling off in the distance.

On the one hand, I'd been given a kind of red-carpet treatment, been the center of attention all afternoon; anything I uttered was deemed important. On the other hand, I was being shown all the elements of a potential life I hadn't had any role in creating. There was a kind of automatic fit mentality. People might as well have said, "We think we understand what you care about, and look—it's all provided, right here!" Oddly, it didn't really matter if each individual piece they showed me gleamed adequately, leaving nothing to be desired. The whole process hollowed me out. I'd done too much *worldbuilding* in the place where we lived to let go of it easily and start over. With two kids happy at their sweet school, a toddler beginning to make friends at play groups, a part-time job that suited me, the vistas of Horsebarn Hill, *and* a close-knit neighborhood, I felt that I had climbed a kind of tree, branch by branch, achieving a perch that I was in no hurry to relinquish.

Recalling how it felt to be eight and gazing out over a swath of green toward a blue expanse of glimmering water, I knew that some of the treasures we earn we must try to keep.

Gripping the steering wheel, almost as if it stood in for Ellise Road with the cul-de-sac where bikes go round and round at the bottom, not yet ready to turn on the ignition, my head was spinning, with my key roles—wife, mother, working woman, friend—colliding. I tried to listen carefully for the clearest voice inside myself, but it was garbled. Part of me said, "It's just a move—what's the big deal? You've moved before." And another part said, vehemently, "Shouldn't it feel mostly right, somewhere inside me?" There it was again, that feeling of trying to access my own soul, what they talked about in church. I tried to recall what it felt like when Rob and I set out for Storrs in the first place, how I cried when I saw the house, how I evolved soon afterward, how resistance to change in and of itself was an unhealthy trait I did not want to maintain, how being a clergy spouse demanded a receptivity to starting new chapters with new congregations.

Last time, though, we were so clearly making progress—leaving a post that had run dry for Rob, going forward to more responsibility, with one baby who had not yet forged his own bonds to anyone else but us. This time, there were five lives to consider—even if I didn't count the dog. The ante had been upped. My role felt different now: I had to be a kind of lookout for all of us, trying to anticipate the gains and the losses within the whole family while Rob moved on the urge, the *need* really, to spread his wings in a larger venue.

I understand now, years later, that on this particular day something crucial was revealed to me: if I acted as if it were my duty as a wife to move through a kind of receiving line, shaking hands and greeting people, without understanding what it was I most needed for my own happiness, it would be at my—and perhaps also my family's—peril. It's one thing to be gracious; it's another to err by wanting to please others too much.

I had to locate myself somehow. My life felt like it was on a kind of precipice, even though the road home that evening was level all the way. Yes, I had a husband who was gaining stature in a Church with tendrils stretching all around the country, and together we had three young children. But I was also in fact a person in my own right and could not be swallowed up or even, strangely enough, prematurely embraced by well-meaning individuals I didn't know. If changes were inevitable out there in the landscape of my life yet to be lived, I'd better take a whole wide look at the view and determine which way held the most promise of a rich and bountiful existence—for us all. Coming into my mid-forties, I sensed there wasn't time to be just going through the motions.

Turning on the ignition, I made certain that all my own hunches, as real as jabbering children in the backseat, were present and accounted for before I headed home. I was not about to leave them anywhere.

Chapter 17

At the Piano

It was the time of spring when the white cherry blossoms on the old tree next to my childhood bedroom were most fragrant. I'd sent out invitations, written in careful cursive, that said: "If you aren't gardening or going to the beach or playing tennis or doing some other fun thing on Sunday, May 31st at 2 p.m., please come to my Senior Piano Recital!"

It was 1975, and I was just shy of eighteen. In those days, I didn't usually refrain from using exclamation points.

I was of two minds about this event, to be held in the community room of our town's local public library. Part of me was proud and ready, since I had been practicing the pieces in my program for about three hours a day for weeks. The other part of me, though, was both terrified and embarrassed. Who was I to be summoning people to get in their cars on what would probably be a beautiful sunny day to sit in hard chairs to hear me try to play and probably mess up? Even in writing the invitations, I slipped into my accustomed "don't go to any trouble for me" mode, something that I'd inherited from my father.

Wearing the same long, pumpkin-colored dress I wore to my brother's wedding on a Florida beach a couple of months before, I got there early to warm up on the huge instrument, which I'd played only once, a week before. More than fifty chairs had been set up, with an aisle in between. All around the perimeter of the room, recessed lighting set an artistic tone. I sat on the shiny black bench and took a few deep breaths, heart already pounding. I had chosen to be here; nobody made me come. The reward or the penalty would be mine alone to claim.

My piano at home was a serviceable upright, nestled in a corner of the playroom, in between my father's study and the TV viewing circle. On the wood-paneled wall above hung a bright red, woven rug with several colorful South American birds—an item brought back by Mike, my first brother to do Peace Corps. On the piano itself, a tall pitcher filled with what my mother called "silver dollars," beige-colored discs on slender stalks, had stood motionless for years, a thin layer of dust on each surface. I was the only child left at home now, all brothers off, so I didn't disturb anyone's sleeping in the morning. Over and over and over again, I played my warm-up Hanon exercises from the yellow book, my Bach prelude and fugue from the blue book, my Beethoven sonata from the bigger blue book, my Chopin ballade from the off-white book with orange lettering.

Each time I made the half-hour drive to my teacher's house for a lesson, I knew I could demonstrate some progress: greater facility with measures dense with notes and more depth of feeling, too. As the recital date drew closer, Mrs. Johnson—hair dyed red but everything else about her so true—started standing over me and saying calmly during our hours together, "So now I'm going to take the book, and you'll play it on your own." Gradually, I memorized each piece, freeing myself from those pages, aloft with the music for long stretches of flow. When I slipped up, hands suddenly in midair with no clear destination, I glanced over at her, and she said firmly, "Just start back in wherever you can; keep going." I learned that playing an F-sharp for an F or a few moments of silence could be forgiven; a momentary dissonance can almost evaporate if the air around it is capacious enough, if you are ready to offer up something else that's right.

Mrs. Johnson and her husband, a musicologist, were coming down the staircase now, finding the community room. She waved to me but didn't approach, murmuring quietly to her husband as both of them looked around the room, estimating the acoustics. She believed in me, or at least that's what she conveyed. My parents were right behind them, and my mother grasped Mrs. Johnson's hand warmly while my father introduced himself to Mr. Johnson. As other guests started to appear and began reading the one-page program I had typed up and copied, I got up off the bench and retreated to the back, feeling very alone, looking for my courage.

Starting piano lessons in the fourth grade, I had done not much more than follow the rules for the next half a dozen years. My brother Rob, who sometimes went out in our side field to play "Taps" on his trumpet, teased me about the countless times I launched into the unceasingly cheerful and thus soon irritating song called "The Joyous Peasant." Conveniently, it was a short walk from my junior high school to Mrs. Krueger's home, where I entered from the back, down the steps into her basement studio, complete with a waiting area and magazines for thirteen-year-olds. With hair done up in a swirl on her head and cardigan over her shoulder, she looked almost glamorous for a middle-aged woman with four kids. Knowing that her range extended from beginner to intermediate, she recommended that I move on to Mrs. Johnson, who took on more advanced students, when I showed signs of hanging in there. I had no particular reason either to quit or to make piano any more important than anything else in my life, and my mother was pleased that I was picking up a skill that she lacked, a skill that brought some of her own mother back to her, so I agreed to keep going. Accustomed to plodding along in the humdrum town of sheet music for kids, I entered a more mature Classical Land, with a higher canopy, lusher trees, steeds holding their heads high amid the whispering of secrets.

One day at Mrs. Johnson's piano, with volumes of music in neat piles nearby, I played the Brahms "Intermezzo, Opus 118, Number 2 in G Major" and felt my life shift. This was a piece that sounded achingly beautiful when my teacher had first dangled it in front of me, and I recognized it as the same piece my brother's college girlfriend, a go-getter who loved Irish Setters, had played once at our home. Suddenly, months later, I heard my own fingers achieve almost this same level of beauty, able to articulate first that simple theme—like a tender thought worth sharing—followed by the cascade of notes showing the dramatic impact of that one thought. I could join myself to this work of art and fly; I could do it whenever I wanted, too, for no particular reason other than it made me feel more alive, enchanted, moved. I said nothing special to my teacher on that day, but I knew that I now possessed the power to thrive as a pianist. Practicing took on a whole new purpose: I wanted that feeling *for myself*; performing for others would be secondary.

It was a little bit like the epiphany Rob had on the water, rowing, except without God.

As I got started with the Bach prelude and fugue, I tried to overcome the jittery knees and shaky fingers I always had during recitals. "C'mon, Polly . . . you know this music. Just share it." One knee was in fact quivering, but I tried to ignore it and pressed on through the few slipups, the packed measures that I couldn't see but had to feel, arriving at the end of the first piece to encouraging applause. Out there were a sprinkling of relatives, many neighbors, high school teachers, and a varied bunch of friends: Lynn, my across-the-street pal; Florence, politically active and wearing overalls; and then Cristy, with a sparkling smile and unflagging devotion. They were pulling for me. My four brothers were elsewhere, in their own lives. I started to relax with the opening calm chords of the Beethoven sonata, fingers recalling just how often they had practiced this. Lulled for a time into complacency, I made one major gaffe along the way, pausing for an eternity before diving back onto the keys. By the time I reached the Chopin ballade, though, I was willing to go for broke, savoring the quiet opening—a tale told by an old man, Mrs. Johnson had said—and then tearing through the "presto" section, caution to the wind.

After it was all over, I saw my mother's glowing face as she clapped enthusiastically. Dad, too, was beaming. They were glad, no doubt, that the risk I took in trying to do this paid off—that I had held firm in myself. The Johnsons gave me a bouquet of flowers, knowing that custom from many concerts. Before heading back up our driveway, I stopped at our neighbor's house at the bottom of the road. Mary Ellen couldn't come because she was dying, wasting away with cancer. Her husband Jack, an artist, was jovial as he puffed on his pipe, still working in his studio when he could, despite circulation problems that made moving around challenging. Something deep within him told him to keep painting.

Mine had been an imperfect but also a bold performance. I had gone for it. From then on, I knew that relying on having the music always in front of me on the stand would be insufficient. Memorizing adeptly also wouldn't be enough. Soon, I would need to learn how to improvise, taking what I could from the masters whom I had studied. I must feel in my own fingers that I had agency, and then I must use it.

PART III

REBUILDING

Chapter 18

Finding Grace

We bypassed one move, but soon settled on another. Rob reluctantly accepted my balking at the first Possibly Perfect Place. "OK, then," he shrugged, loading the dishwasher that evening after my return, catching my eye long enough to convey his disappointment but not outright disapproval. "We'll just have to keep looking." He didn't push or try to convince me that my doubts were insubstantial. But St. Mark's Chapel was, for him, becoming a set of church clothes that no longer fit. He began chafing at certain limitations—the number of people the place could accommodate, for one; the breadth of issues that the church might take on, for another; the fact that we were living in a house chosen for us that was becoming too small. To make a sleeping space for our third child, Henry, we removed our closet door and put his blue bassinet right in the alcove a few feet from our bed. That actually worked fine when he was a newborn, gazing up at the twirling black-and-white mobile, but the writing was on the three walls he would soon be able to reach out and touch. Our family was expanding, and Rob's aspirations were, too.

My husband was on a forward trajectory in a craft with jet-propulsion engines, to another part of the Universe that was the Church. I could see the longing in his eyes, almost the same kind I'd seen when he was falling in love with me. Back then, when we stood together in awe of those Tetons, he'd reached out to pull me close. Now, he wanted me to strap in beside him, with excitement, as we took off together.

I sensed that those jabbering hunches that had accompanied me on the ride back from the New Hampshire town, filling the car with their squirming, had to be quieted somehow so that this marital journey, the one that had started with a series of vows, could continue. The problem was that my secular roots were sinking deeper in right on the dead end street where we lived. In theory, I knew it was healthy and right not only to *move on* in life but also sometimes to *move* in a physical sense. People did it all the time, unstrapping themselves.

What kind of good bargain could we make at this juncture?

Once my parents, with three little boys, had settled into their prefabricated house on what used to be a potato field above my grandparents' home, they never budged. In fact, each of them would actually *die*—fourteen years apart—right in that house, which itself had stayed the same over forty years except for an added-on screened porch and study for my father. During school years, I knew a few families who moved. When my good friend Lizzie from junior high disappeared, it felt like a kick in the gut, even while I stayed put. My family settled deeper and deeper into a patch of soil, entrenched. On the shelves above the refrigerator, two small glass jars labeled "Paprika" and "Oregano" sat idle for years, the red or green remnants clinging to the sides.

But Rob's childhood had been different. His father's profession as a salesman of silverware required several moves in the Midwest before they finally came to the middle of Connecticut, when Rob was about ten. His nostalgia for those early times in Minnesota never left him. But mostly Rob had developed a sense of fluidity about where *home* was. And, as he became more closely aligned with the Church, it in fact took on some of the meaning of the word "home." A house and yard were not unimportant, exactly, but they needed to work in tandem with the place of worship. Now, he had his sights set on a new one of those; it must have been already gleaming in his mind.

With his name and updated "profile" out there, Rob continued getting nibbles from other churches regularly. Both of us were still recovering from our division over the last episode, and we sensed how fortifying it would be to feel like a united front. He enjoyed reporting back to me about some early exchanges, so that we could happily agree on what was clearly ridiculous. One church, for instance, revealed its internal squabbles over liturgy: "We should probably tell you that some of us will just not let go of the previous version of *The Book of Common Prayer*, and there are schisms here." Red flag.

In another phone conversation, he was asked, "Will your wife be attending church?" He didn't hesitate to reply, "Well, most likely only occasionally. She's not Episcopalian." Thud. A long silence on the other end was followed by this plaintive question: "But will she at least come to our ham and bean suppers?" We laughed, in full harmony, in easy agreement that we didn't need to contort ourselves in any particular way for people we didn't know. In principle, I don't mind ham and bean suppers at all; in fact, the two probably go very nicely together, with the rich brown sauce of the beans seeping into the saltiness of the pink ham, the whole combination making even a hardy paper plate sag. But there was a crucial difference between my perhaps *wanting* to go when the time came and being *expected* to go. The fact that Rob now got it felt like a triumph.

Plummeting back to the 1950s momentarily, with women in flouncy skirts and cinched belts cheerily carrying casseroles and quieting the children while the men were in charge, we both regained our footing where we actually were, in the closing years of the twentieth century, when for the most part husbands and wives merged at home in the evenings but went to their own distinct jobs each day. It was fine for the Church to maintain ancient rituals during a service, but dictating a clergy spouse's role surely was a remnant of a past age that had to go.

If, underneath this agreement, Rob was also beginning to get uneasy about my fitting in somewhere, about whether I might possibly hold him back by his white collar, he withheld that anxiety. "There are more openings coming up. We'll just keep looking."

Buoyed by his understanding, I began to think we could make the next move fully together, in step. Remembering how it felt under the tent, on the dance floor at our wedding, when each brush of my cheek against his made sparks; how when I held onto his strong shoulder I could hardly believe this was happening; I wanted it just like that.

When you take the back road route, the crossover from Connecticut to Massachusetts is barely noticeable, marked by a simple sign that speaks in a whisper. Grace Episcopal Church in Amherst, at first glance, looked like everything that a thriving church could be—an elegant, gray stone building that had seen plenty of history, smack dab in the town center, with an array of colleges nearby. After New Haven and Storrs, we both knew that the stimulation provided by academic towns was a big plus. The flip side of that coin, we also knew, would almost certainly be the plethora of people in the pews who would not take everything the preacher had to say just sitting down. Opinions would fly like arrows, everywhere.

Plus, thrown in for good measure, the Emily Dickinson homestead was right down the street from the church, occupying about the same substantial amount of real estate. For me especially, this was a good sign—a link to literary history and also to my own extended family. Sensing that this time our stars might be aligned, after his first couple of interviews, Rob suggested I head back up there with him for the third. "I bet my mother can be with the kids for an overnight." He was revving up his engine. Especially considering our persistent divergence when it came to matters of faith, or lack of faith in my case, this was a precious opportunity for synchrony.

It was the spring of 2001, and the movie *Memento* had just come out and was playing in an old, classic theater right near our bed and breakfast in Greenfield—a town on Route 2 about fifteen miles north of Amherst. Dizzy with the intoxication of being away from three children, we grabbed the chance to see any passable film and walked down the broad sidewalk amid the scent of blooming magnolia trees, their pale pink petals tossing in the breeze. With just a sprinkling of people munching on popcorn in the cool darkness, we had our choice of seats. There, we formed our own little world. A kind of psychological thriller featuring a murder, the film moved simultaneously in two directions in time: in black and white we saw the regular, forward story; interspersed in color, the narrative went the complete opposite way. It was confusing, but also tantalizing, and it held our attention completely. Only at the end did the two strands come together in a way that made any sense.

"Wow, that was amazing. Did you get it all?" I was eager to connect verbally, a filly bursting out of the gate at the racetrack.

"I'm not sure. Let's wait to talk about it later, after it's settled a while." Typical Rob, restrained about attaching too much meaning to anything too quickly, wanting to let it all brew—drip, drip, drip. "C'mon, let's enjoy the walk back." We held hands, once again in the fragrant evening. I tried to tuck away my abundant thoughts for when he'd be ready to embrace them, offering his own as companions. It occurred to me that *his* internal movie could be playing in black and white, *mine* in color, or maybe the reverse. Marriage feels like this sometimes, and it can be startling, even unnerving.

What mattered most, though, was splicing together whatever our two reels were, without any words.

Life lurches forward in only one direction. Events unfold, we make choices large and small, and we're hurtled relentlessly into the future. Apart from wonderful moments of replenishment, the kind my mother read to me about in *A Little Princess*, there is no turning back the clock to live in a previous time. What's done is done; what's gone is gone. The whole premise of *Memento* was, in a way, absurd. And yet, we do arrive often at one station or another, look around and ask ourselves, "Which train brought me here and did I choose to get on it?" And when you are married, you learn to make choices alongside someone else, a person who is also making choices, often with uncertainty. Sometimes you defer, sometimes you lead, sometimes you compromise. And you hope.

The next day, after he had one more icing-on-the-cake interview, we walked through the compact but vibrant downtown of Amherst. Compared to Storrs it felt practically like an urban center. It was late spring, so the college students had cleared out, but still the streets were full of activity. We saw people sitting close together at little tables in restaurants, hurrying to their appointments, selling jewelry on the sidewalks, and dropping money in the guitar case of a performing musician.

There must have been other churches in this town, but the one reaching out to claim my husband occupied a place of particular prominence. Anyone just passing through, parking in one of the spaces made available within the town green, would see the gray spire reaching upward. Coming inside, especially in summer, they would be greeted by rich, red carpeting and a cool expansiveness; a beckoning toward the altar; stained glass windows in blues and reds and greens and yellows, each telling a story.

Soon enough, I knew, if this all worked out, Rob's name would be put on a piece of wood that slid into place right underneath the title "Rector." In an important way, I would belong here, too, thanks to the bridge of marriage—the plank of wood that either one of us traverses whenever we are *going somewhere*, either physically or spiritually, mostly to accompany the other one. On that bridge, we move beyond our premarital terrain, take a new trail and gain a new vista, sometimes after some initial jitters.

If we (because it would take both of us) chose to accept this position, I knew that Rob would practically take up residence here. For me, though, it would be different: each time I entered, there would be that little daypack I'd carried around since we were married, with a voice inside that said, "Look around you, see where you are; every window and candelabra and hard wooden pew is a direct result of that guy who brings the leaping feeling to your heart. It's OK that you've agreed to come, more than OK; you're becoming larger than what you were before, extending yourself to go beyond what you were."

But that alone wouldn't be enough. The voice continued, "You will also need your own places—probably more than one, because the one he has is so large—places that draw you in immediately. You will feel like a moth drawn to bright outdoor bulbs on a humid night."

I found one good prospect that same day, a beacon of light, worth my fluttering toward.

On our way out of town, following up on a suggestion from a vestry member, we stopped at Mill River Recreation Area, where the town's baseball fields were. There was plenty of parking surrounding an enclosed pool, a couple of tennis courts, grills and picnic tables protected by a roof, and three emerald green fields, regal in their blanket of silence on this June early afternoon. *Now we're talking*, I thought. Rob took in the way I hurried out of the car, eager to witness my joy. He joined me in my lifted spirits, saying, "So Eleanor said this is where the Little League plays games? That'll be next spring for Willie, right?"

For him, these were points of information—significant, but dwarfed by his larger sense of being drawn to the church a couple of miles away. For me, the fields expanded into much more, a destination with its own kind of integrity.

"Yep," I said, inserting my fingers into the individual diamond-shaped spaces of the first metal backstop we came to and leaning against it. "This place looks great." Gazing through the crisscrossed pattern to a square, beige, stiff cushion, hardly distinguishable from the dirt around it a few yards away, I felt right at home.

What I remember about baseball from my childhood is how constant it was. I was too young to recall my brothers going off to Little League games, but they all did, and the games were just a couple of miles away. We also had a makeshift backstop, made with old shingles, in our field that had witnessed many pickup games before my time. I'd heard about them so often, absorbed the history as if it were my own, so that when I got to know Freddy, Rip, Stan, and Roger as older teenagers, I also knew how, years before, they'd done plenty of arguing and taunting and storming off. Sometimes, and I wasn't supposed to bring this up in their presence, there had even been tears.

Well into their twenties, on visits home, my brothers would get mitts and bats out from the big wooden crate in the freezer room. "C'mon Sand, let's see what you got!" Steve would say as he dug deep to find the well-worn glove he'd left there before college. I joined them, too, even though nobody really asked me; I was still the tagalong sister, the one they enjoyed having around, just not right in the heart of a contest. This didn't much matter to me; I had gotten accustomed to being the little one, on the periphery. And despite not being invited, I didn't feel neglected; when I asked to be shown how to throw far or hold the bat, they'd always comply. "Here you go, Pol, try it." These were their beloved rituals.

The question of who had the best arm (or "whip" as Dad called it) was often raised, with real tests to find out. My brothers would line up by the elm tree near the house and then, on command one at a time, lean back and hurl a baseball to the other end of the lawn, near the peach trees. Rob, the youngest, would often be asked to judge, lifting his arm up and yelling, reluctantly because he knew there would be an aftermath: "That time it was definitely Steve, by a few feet," whereupon Steve—never one to contain his pride—would start strutting around until Sandy tackled him in frustration.

Dad wasn't directly involved in these turn-back-the-clock contests; he was usually on the fringes, doing work on his Farmall tractor, sweaty cap on his bald head. He had never been a ball player, but he got a kick out of seeing his young adult sons fool around this way, much as they had done years before, when I'd been learning to walk. He demonstrated his faith in these rowdy events mostly by taking pride in maintaining the grounds. Years later, after my brother Rob moved into what had been our grandparents' house down the hill, he set out to make a real baseball field for impromptu games in what had been a horse pasture, and named it, with a simple wooden plaque, "Hank's Field." On opening day, neighbors and friends from around town came to celebrate. Then, when my brothers and I gathered with our own kids to play, once a summer usually, we would carry on a system of *belief*—that's how I now dared to see it, steeped as I was becoming in my husband's world where creeds were recited—that included grass, family, athletics, and laughter.

So deeply was a love of baseball ingrained in me, that it figured in the naming of our first child. Once Rob and I had decided on the name "William James," I thought that while it was nice to give a nod to the bearded nineteenth-century philosopher, author of *The Varieties of Religious Experience*, our son would be called "Willie" after the great Mays.

I returned from my reverie to see Rob walking down the first base line, toward the bank of the stream that we couldn't quite see yet. Wherever there might be any moving water, he would find it. "Hey, wait up!" I said, releasing my fingers from the backstop so quickly that it vibrated. Together, we imbibed the coolness in the shade of the trees clutching the edges, watching the black flies circulate inches over the liquid surface. For me, there would still be a cluster of doubts hovering around the communion rail: how often I would go near it, how at ease I would be in its vicinity, how far around it Rob could come, and how frequently, to meet me in the plain world. At a bigger church, the demands for his time surely would increase, and the communion rail itself would loom larger. Out of the corner of my eye, standing near the grills that people used for cookouts on weekends, I still saw its gleaming mahogany. But right at that moment, near the sun-bathed, emerald fields, there was just a leafy canopy and blue sky. We were fully together, fully safe. I said nothing, not wanting to spoil the moment.

I felt the beneficence of Nature, aligned here with the goodness of baseball, washing over me, almost as if I were being baptized. I thought it best to keep that to myself.

Soon, Grace Church made its offer, and we accepted.

This time, there would be no crying from initial disappointment about the provided raised ranch, because we could find our own place to live, like regular people. "You go ahead and start looking," Rob offered. "I'll come back up when you've got some possibilities." I felt a surge of something like power, until I remembered that it came only at the cost of leaving our beloved neighborhood, where the house itself had become almost unimportant. Even though I more fully saw and felt what we were going toward, the grief over what we were parting from—all that we had built up over time, with people who had embraced the arrival of each of our children—started taking on the heavy weight of storm clouds. There was no avoiding this part.

And then, there would be the inevitable opinions of others, the weighing in. At the first realtor's office, a woman who had just heard a quick profile of our family said, "I definitely see you in such-and-such a location," specifying a certain section of town, new sprawling houses and manicured lawns, that was in a very high price range. Here it went again—well-meaning strangers presuming to know what would be best. In the way she nodded at me knowingly, eager to convey her own conviction about where we belonged, I was brought right back to my solo drive to a town where everyone was cheering for me to take my assigned place. A drained-of-color version of myself would have performed better, perhaps; or a cutout paper doll of a clergy wife. Maybe I was abnormally sensitive to other people projecting their own vision of a good life. Like an animal sensing danger and pricking up ears, I felt a need to sniff my own way forward at my own pace.

Sally, the realtor I settled with, was different. It helped that she reminded me of a former childhood neighbor and longtime family friend who was also a famous Broadway actress. Sally, too, was an actress—in local regional theater—and she had a kind of inherent warmth and vivacity about her. She was also a grandmother who pulled off wearing natural looking, dirty blonde hair in fetching, slightly unruly ringlets, along with bright red lipstick. We connected immediately. Soon she was calling me "Honey," and I saw no reason to hold back on the jumble of feelings that were bubbling up.

Setting out from her downtown office, we drove all over, up to and down from the adjoining hill towns. One thing I was certain about: I absolutely did not want to live a few blocks away from the church (as we'd learned from the last round of interviews) even though Rob would have been content with that arrangement. His place of worship, I understood by now, was an extension of his very being. The new office was located in a building that looked exactly like a house, and it was attached to the church by something cleverly called the "Connector." Anyone could tell that this structure had at one time been the rectory, where Reverend So-and-So's tots had probably learned to walk. This fact *used to* be charming, for other clergy families. For me, having my husband serve in a church was fine, distinguished even; but folding the family into the place on a daily basis, almost as if he wore a cloak that swept everyone up in it, would be suffocating.

What I was looking for was some demarcation, matching the kind that existed in our individual selves.

Eventually, in one of the hill towns, a solid fifteen-minute drive from the church, Sally brought me to a brick red Colonial that sat up tall and proud. On the way there, she offered some assurance that we wouldn't be too far out in the sticks, even though that wasn't at all my worry. "Oh, there's plenty of town and plenty of gown out here, too." I didn't ask, but she must have meant academic types, the plethora of people who worked for one of the five colleges in this region. The patch of level green lawn in front looked to be awaiting games, a basketball hoop was already there, and the tall pine trees all around, branches waving in the breeze, were reminiscent of my own childhood landscape. A fenced-in garden hadn't been recently tended, but the roses climbing around the outside of it spoke a lush language.

If we moved here, I thought hopefully, I could probably replant myself and grow—the way I had learned to do in the last place. But would there be any neighborhood? This house was on a main road, and the cars whizzed by, heading downhill. It was the kind of street with no shoulder that parents might forbid their kids from riding bikes on, actually. It wasn't at all the same as where we lived now, I told myself, but that was the whole point of moving: change. Trying to replicate whatever we had before would be an exercise in frustration.

Right down the road was the town's small elementary school, which had a quirky reputation. "A lot of 'project-based learning' here, I've heard," Sally told me, using two fingers to show quotation marks, being careful not to be overly enthusiastic. Still tied by my heartstrings to Goodwin Elementary, I looked at the low-lying building with the circular driveway and got no particular vibe. It was an open question whether our three kids would thrive when they started walking through those doors, but at least I wasn't surrounded by a few people whose own wishes for me to like it were so transparent as to be unsettling. I felt some autonomy here, some wiggle room. Choosing this little community—reached on one side by climbing a series of "S" curves, on the other side by a gradual and mostly straight up, up, up—meant establishing a whole hunk of life that could stay separate from church. "Hmm," I said to Sally. "I'll try to find out more about it by calling around."

Imagining the pieces of our life felt a little bit like keeping the items on a dinner plate distinct: the peas and the mashed potatoes would get all mixed together eventually, but the meal looked more appetizing when I could behold each item with its own distinct qualities, and balance out the colors.

Sometime during the summer before we actually moved in, Mary Jo, a woman down the road who had filled me in on the elementary school by phone, invited me to come over for a visit. Parking in the half-circle driveway, I walked over an entryway terrace with a riot of perennials and herbs in all the crevices, giving a European flavor. Her little dog—so different from our big black Lab—yipped furiously at first, but she quickly quieted him. Over her long kitchen counter sat a long column of glass jars, fruit preserves she'd put by after hours of picking and boiling and pouring and gelling. We sat at her light-filled, circular table, a simple vase holding fuchsia dahlias in the center. I knew from our previous conversations that her son was the exact same age as Willie, her daughter a year younger than Cora; they hadn't met yet. She related some elements of her own challenging move from Ohio a few years before, including how hard it had been to leave the garden she had worked so hard on there. Then she said, "You're really lucky, coming here as a pastor's wife. You'll get a head start in getting to know people because the congregation will naturally want to welcome you based on your husband's position." A lifelong Catholic, she was confident in her reasoning even though she hadn't ever gotten chummy with a priest's significant other from her own churchgoing past.

"You really think so?" I said, startled and flattered both, almost as if she'd just complimented my appearance.

Maybe she was right; maybe it was high time that I pushed aside any internal quibbles about *being religious* and just made the most of all the factors working in my favor here. Church didn't need to be a stumbling block; in fact it might become a large hunk of goodness, a fundamental piece of a flourishing life in a new place. I could try looking at this in a whole new way. Gazing again at all those jars on the counter, I knew that the goal was getting to abundance. For that, I needed to make sure of all the resources I had.

Mary Jo—with her good sense, school savvy, and green thumb—became my very first friend there. With her house just a couple of level miles away in this mostly hilly town, she fit right into my hope for at least the *possibility* of building a new community not based in any one building, no matter how spacious. Bolstered by her encouragement, with the beginnings of a system of belief that now included a faith in the goodness of neighborhood, playing fields, and Nature as a beneficent force, I found a way to say goodbye: to everyone who had come to our carefully planned birthday parties, to the three girls from the street who played hour after hour with our toddlers, to the friends we made at the Montessori school, to my work colleagues, to Horsebarn Hill, to the little chapel with the light streaming down and all the kind and quirky and just regular people who arrived there—who would continue to arrive there, without us.

When the bright orange-and-yellow play car that two-year-old Henry had just started to enjoy on our old driveway worked just as well in the slightly wider and longer new one, I let it carry me forth.

Chapter 19

Stopping By a Poet's House

Our priorities were, in a way, reversed. Rob was focused on trying to become the rector they called him to be in the new church, where a couple of hundred parishioners awaited his approach; I was pretty sure he saw our new house as mostly backdrop. In my own mental landscape, on the other hand, our new community, often called "Roadtown," was front and center, while the church sat a few rows back. But soon enough I saw that my thirst for connections could be partly quenched at the same trough where Rob drank. The act of worship itself was not a draw; the possibility of making new friends, though, certainly was.

On a September Sunday, just a few weeks after we had arrived, I joined other mothers with small children going through the front door where the church offices were, and found the toddler room—with a yellow plastic gate set across the doorway—just down on the left. It was cramped with toys and books and one presiding long-legged teenage girl. My older kids had already headed into their various Sunday school rooms. Henry was too squirmy at age two to accompany me into the main church service, and so I planned to leave him here just long enough for me to listen to Rob's sermon, the product of many hours of concentration, study, and rumination. Heading into the sanctuary still felt like offering a basic act of respect to my husband; for me, it was personal.

But I was carrying something else besides my son on this particular morning—grief. My childhood friend Lynn, who grew up across the street from me, had just lost her husband to cancer, out in Pittsburgh. All through the days when I was starting to unpack boxes up at our new home, I was also monitoring news through a website about his declining condition. Now, having always hoped to go there sometime for a happy visit, I needed to make plans to fly out for a funeral instead. I was keenly aware that, while I was a wife of a clergyman in a new parish dropping off a child for an hour of play, Lynn had become a widow with two kids who wouldn't have a father anymore. Our lives had been intertwined since we were five; she was now entering a cold new land, and I felt so far away.

As I took Henry's jacket off, tears started down my cheeks. I didn't yet know the teenager—now reading a board book to a kid cuddled in her lap—or really anyone else in the church.

A woman with curly dark hair who was on her way down the narrow hall with the creaky floor paused in the doorway to look over in my direction.

"Hi," she said softly, taking a step in. "I'm Edith and I think you must be new here. Do you need any help?" Had my emotion been that apparent?

"Oh, hi," I said, trying to rally. "I think your husband Don helped us with buying our house. So glad to meet you."

I had tried to be alert about who was married to whom, knowing that this was a good way to start making inroads. Just at this moment, though, she caught me being engulfed by waves from my past, creating a strangely altered present.

"Oh, so you must be the new rector's wife then! Welcome to Grace Church. But," she lowered her voice again, "do you need to talk a minute? Maybe in the next room?"

With Edith and a few others, I gained over time the most wonderful treasure: genuine female friendship. The fact that the relationships sprouted at church hardly made any difference. Gradually, our conversations roamed to realms well beyond whatever was happening on Sunday mornings. With some other female parishioners, however, I had to stay wary about dwelling on church topics. I learned the hard way that it is definitely *not* a good idea for me to be the conduit for messages to my husband about the ins and outs of the liturgy, for example. A casual statement like "so-and-so wonders why 'The Prayers of the People' aren't done in a slightly different format" wouldn't be welcome information conveyed over the kitchen counter. Other clergy spouses might be adept at becoming enmeshed with church politics, but that was not terrain I wanted to get mired in. My status as a kind of bystander disqualified me, anyway.

Now in the third church venue since our marriage, I wondered again how women in the congregation regarded me. Not that they were a unified group, but it's no secret that women generally are more interested than men in sizing one another up, and then, if we get over a certain hump of trust (big if), we can start offering compassion and understanding. Each time I walked through the mighty double doors I might as well have been wearing a sign that said, "I'm his other half" or, with a gloss of pride, "He's a parish priest here to everyone, but husband just to me." I felt that familiar sense of distinction and immediate inclusion, because some of the glow Rob started out with would surely rub right off onto me. But maybe the outer shape of *who they thought I was* would, as time went on, need to be colored in differently than they expected. Maybe my true identity as a woman, when fully revealed within the context of church life, would rub against a perception of me that served them well. Furthermore, Rob reminded me regularly that he didn't always enjoy the ecclesiastical glow I too often assumed; the clouds of discontent that sometimes formed within the congregation, over matters large or small, might cause rain to fall on me, too.

The fact is, the word "spouse" can sound unpleasantly like "mouse." I felt at once proud of my role and uneasy about it, too. While I sought, over time, to become closer with particular women whom I could trust, I remained aware that other women might continue to see me from afar as more of a stereotype than a real person. Any sense I had of being scrutinized was borne out one evening when Rob said, "Today, a parishioner you don't know pulled me aside after a meeting to express serious concern about you. She went on and on."

"Oh really?" I said, glad to hear amusement rather than anxiety in his voice.

"Yep. She's worried about the way you walk."

Now this was creepy. Apparently she had just completed a graduate degree in human mobility or something like it and had seen me as a perfect specimen of study. The fact that Rob was her priest apparently meant that I was fair game. I took offense partly because Granny, my mother's mother, had always prized good posture and I thought at least I was carrying on that tradition into church, apart from my iffy belief system.

"Isn't she an 8 A.M. service person? How has she even *seen* me walk?"

"Who knows." Rob shrugged, then continued, "How about we invite her over to the house sometime, and you come slithering to the door, like a snake, or you walk in like Quasimodo?" He was generally loyal to the eccentricities of his parishioners and didn't relish my own attempts at poking gentle fun, but occasionally he succumbed to seeing the humor in simple exchanges. These moments were like rays of sunshine to me. Maybe church didn't have to be sacrosanct every single minute, even when he was taking care of people.

Soon after we were reasonably settled into the rhythm of life in a new town, I began noticing that what I began to call "The Sunday Morning Factor" had an impact on my friendships, too. A group of women from Storrs invited me back for weekly all-female bike rides, in the most open time slot for all of them; same for the old book group. I yearned to go, as if I were a rock-climber clutching a rope that could pull me back to them, huddled in our cozy groupness. But no—Sunday morning was always out of the question; whether or not *I* wanted to attend a service during which I might or might not approach the rail, I still needed to get my kids there.

In my new town, too, Sunday morning was when the cool women I knew started training together for the triathlons they were signing up for. Now it was beginning to feel as if there were a conspiracy against athletic clergy wives. Instead of loping along with them, I passed the cluster in their multicolor jackets on the road down to church. "Heeeyy Polly!" they said, pausing in their laughter at each other's stories and waving energetically, wanting me to feel included. As I looked in the rearview mirror, I saw Henry in his car seat and Cora leaning over to offer entertainment. I recalled the premarital counseling sessions when I was asked whether I foresaw any problem with taking our kids to church regularly, the look of "Oh phew" on Rob's face when I readily agreed, even though I was then equipped with zero knowledge about how being a wife and then a mother would gel with being myself.

The women who gradually entered my life were all living and breathing beings, just about all with children of their own. One woman, however, was in a different category: childless, neither a churchgoer nor a runner, and furthermore, completely dead.

But, wow, could she ever write poetry.

Well before moving to Amherst, I had already begun a relationship with Emily Dickinson. In addition to the fact that, as an undergraduate English major and then again in graduate school, I had studied her poetry, there was also a strong family connection. My Uncle Harold, husband to my father's younger sister Winifred, was a self-made Emily Dickinson scholar. His early life was much like my own father's: born in Brooklyn the same year, attended the same high school where they were academic and athletic strivers both. Harold was a three-sport athlete—football, basketball, and baseball—and he lettered in all three at Amherst College. He had a gruff Brooklyn accent that made him sound like a tough guy and likely served him well as an attorney for the now defunct Trans World Airlines in Kansas City. But he also had a heart of gold, and that heart became smitten with Emily Dickinson's poetry once he arrived in her town as an eighteen-year-old. For the rest of his life, and he lived until a hundred, he was a devotee, reciting her lines whenever an occasion warranted her inclusion.

One Thanksgiving when I was home from college, about twenty of us gathered in my aunt and uncle's spacious finished basement a few towns away from ours. The weather was unusually balmy, presenting a perfect opportunity for Harold to offer this opening invocation—not quite the same as a blessing, but close in spirit. He needed no text as he began, with the turkey waiting to be served in front of him. "Some people," he instructed us, "like to call this poem 'Alumni Day,' and I think you'll see why." He smiled broadly. "But Emily Dickinson never gave titles to her poems; they speak for themselves, and they sure have always spoken to me."

These are the days when Birds come back—
A very few—a Bird or two,
To take a final look—

He took his time, savoring each word, looking around the table. We gave him our full attention, interested just as much in the person reciting as in what was being recited.

These are the days when skies put on
The old—old sophistries of June—
A blue and gold mistake.

He let "mistake" fall with a thud. And then, changing his demeanor, he became animated and adamant at once, cherishing every beat of his delivery.

Oh, fraud that cannot cheat the Bee,
Almost thy plausibility
Induces my belief.

Now, helped by that familiar Dickinsonian bee, I began to get that this was a poem about Autumn; it was also about the wisdom, in certain circumstances, of withholding belief. My brothers and I drank up the merging of our Uncle Harold with his heroine as if it were a kind of nectar—one of her favorite words.

Whichever poem Harold chose to recite, whatever the occasion, he would launch into the lines so naturally, with almost no distinction between his words and hers. But a seriousness of purpose would come over his usually smiling face and twinkling eyes, as if he needed to convey that we were now in sacred company. Almost, yes, as if we were in church together and her volume of poetry would be our prayer book. He saw her much as he saw Shakespeare: for just about any experience we either have already had or could imagine, she would have the right words. Once, at a dinner party, when a cousin's spouse casually mentioned that she never "got the hang of" Emily Dickinson, going further to make the claim that her lines had "no soul," Harold was stricken. To him, she was Soul personified.

The Soul selects her own Society—
Then—shuts the door—
To her divine Majority
Present no more.

This Soul is powerful, too; she knows exactly whom she wants and whom she doesn't need. One small person, going willingly behind a closed door, is anything but meek.

Back when I was ten years old, I went through a kind of psychological crisis. All of a sudden, I wasn't sure what "I" consisted of: was it mostly my physical self or more my internal self? Maybe the two were separate, even alien, making the unity I had been coasting along with really a fabrication. For a brief and scary time, I felt the distinct possibility that I was more in fragments than neatly tied up in a whole person. The peaceful, solitary hours that I had spent outside as an eight- and nine-year-old—climbing trees, exploring my grandfather's garden—shifted, temporarily, into a period of intense questioning. That summer, my parents, not knowing about my inner turmoil, treated me to a trip to spend a week with my older cousin and her husband out in Seattle. During a backpacking excursion, when we hiked through fields of bright red and blue wildflowers, with views to Mount Rainier, I confided in Mary that I was gripped by disturbing new questions about who I really was, about what a *self* was, exactly. Mary, a social worker by training, soothed me with something like, "I know what you mean. Try not to think too much about it, though; you're just *you* and that's OK! Let's go down to the barn and see the horses now." She was definitely my father's niece. Eventually, blanketed by enough comforting activities, the haunting feeling passed.

But I knew it would always be there in some form, retrievable and potentially explosive.

I didn't know Emily Dickinson's poetry then, but later on, when I encountered her eagerness to delve into fundamental questions about her own internal cataclysms, I was encouraged to think maybe I hadn't been cracking up as a child. The feeling I'd had was close to the one she had expressed in Poem 937:

I felt a Cleaving in my Mind—
As if my Brain had split—
I tried to match it—Seam by Seam—
But could not make them fit—
The thought behind, I strove to join
Unto the thoughts before—
But Sequence ravelled out of Sound—
Like Balls—opon a Floor—

So it was that I felt a rekindled kinship to the Belle of Amherst when I passed her scrupulously maintained, large house—at first brick, then painted ochre to bring back the color it had been originally—with picket fence nearly every day, often on the way to church. And my children gradually gained a cozy familiarity with it, too. Once, when Henry was a toddler in the backseat, seeing a car in the driveway, he piped up with, "Look, it's Emily A-Dickens house... and she's home!" Our friend Jane, an Episcopalian, happened to be the director of the Emily Dickinson Museum, a place that included The Homestead as well as The Evergreens next door, where the poet's brother Austin and his wife once lived. The museum was flourishing, offering a wide variety of programs to both passersby and a devoted Dickinson fan base from around the world, people who kept up their insatiable appetite for discussion about every aspect of the poet's world.

With resources conveniently at hand, I reacquainted myself with some of the key facts about her mid-nineteenth century, college town life. Her family members were Congregationalists and, in addition to attending church, there were probably daily services in their home. It's commonly known that, when she was at Holyoke Seminary as a schoolgirl, she witnessed many of her classmates giving themselves over to God, being saved. In New England, this was a period known as the Second Great Awakening. Teenage girls walked down the center aisle, swooning for the Lord left and right. But she couldn't bring herself to join them. The website of the museum devotes a whole page to this subject:

> Although she agonized over her relationship to God, Dickinson ultimately did not join the church—not out of defiance; but in order to remain true to herself.

Reading this from my home several miles up the hill, I felt an electric current of recognition. That was precisely the issue for me, too. More than one hundred and fifty years later, not as a teenager but as a midlife, married woman, I had essentially the same dilemma: trying to remain true to my own beliefs, trying to catch hold of what being true to myself *even meant*, but also embedded in a community with particular norms.

No doubt surprising and even vexing her family, Emily Dickinson took her stance, in some sense, apart from the Church. But she also wrote poem after poem about faith and God, life and death, heaven and hell. Her work is steeped in the language of Christianity because she was surrounded and influenced by it. She was also confident enough in her knowledge, apparently, that she could add her own spin. In the 2010 book *Dickinson, Selected Poems and Commentaries*, the critic Helen Vendler wrote:

> All of Dickinson's poems that resort to Christian imagery and language rework Christianity in some way—intellectually, blasphemously, or comically.

So, I ventured to think, if she could boldly leave her own imprint by owning up to her quirkiness, then maybe I could, too, from my different position as a clergy spouse. Then again, my pulls—husband and three children—were different and arguably stronger than hers. I kept trying to walk a kind of fine line, not completely part of exactly, but joining through marriage, through association. At best, I was fringe; at worst, actually a kind of fraud. Was I presenting myself as reliably *in* when I was actually more riskily *out*?

The following poem is Dickinson's best known on the subject of her take on formal religion, and it makes her skepticism plain. She doesn't need any team of like-minded people, so certain she is in the strength of her alliance with all of Nature. Arriving at it once more, twenty-five years after my first reading, I was floored by the jauntiness with which she approached a subject compelling others to maintain such sobriety:

Some keep the Sabbath going to Church—
I keep it, staying at Home—
With a Bobolink for a Chorister—
And an Orchard, for a Dome—

The lines bring me right back to my childhood self, perched in a tree, with binoculars around my neck and notepad on my knee. Then, it hadn't occurred to me that whatever I was doing was a kind of *parallel* to going to church; it was just what it was, no added meaning required. Now, though, more enlightened on just how central the concept of worship time was to my husband and his parishioners, I consider that maybe those hours of immersion in Nature, by myself, counted for more somehow.

Some keep the Sabbath in Surplice—
I, just wear my Wings—
And instead of tolling the Bell, for Church,
Our little Sexton—sings.

She's having a grand time here, substituting one thing for another, emphasizing the joy inherent in everyday occurrences in her own garden. And then comes an unleashing of her humor alongside a brazen claim:

God preaches, a noted Clergyman—
And the sermon is never long,
So instead of getting to Heaven, at last—
I'm going, all along.

Not only is her way of worship just as good as the church kind—it's better. She skips right over the clergy and has a direct link to God, confident that she's on the right path. A delighted renegade.

But Emily Dickinson had no husband to consider, when it came to going or not going to church. Indeed, her identity as a spinster had always been one of her most salient traits: she was a normally active teenager who went to all the parties but then gradually retreated to her chamber, greeting visitors there in a white dress. She fell in love more than once (exhaustively documented by scholars), was filled with erotic longing (right in the poems), but never became a wife.

On the subject of what it was actually like to be a devotee of Nature who was married to a preacher-man whose podium was indoors, I knew more.

If I were to write this kind of poem, it's unlikely I could bring myself to contrast God's sermons with Rob's; he is an especially gifted preacher, besides being the man I love. But the difference between Dickinson's status and mine is twofold: (1) I can't be sure that, wherever I am, God is there, too, because I don't understand God; and (2) since it is my spouse who perceives the constant presence of God, I would more likely feel any connection in that direction through *him*. This is in part how the magic of marriage works: you start out not having any idea about something; but then you get to glimpse it, not fully grasp it, via your beloved. If all goes well, expansion squelches discomfort.

Then there's the fact that, as Rob's wife, I got to know both his flaws and his inner struggles better than any member of the church did. This, too, complicated my thinking about whatever or whoever God was, or wasn't.

When Dickinson wrote about marriage, unlike when she wrote about being in her garden, she leaned heavily on her imagination. And sometimes the results included stating the elements of a typical union that she sorely lacked, as in this poem (#194):

Title divine—is mine!
The Wife—without the Sign!
Acute Degree—conferred on me—
Empress of Calvary!
Royal—all but the Crown!
Betrothed—without the swoon [...]

Here, as elsewhere, she presents herself as experiencing a degree of suffering that puts her on par with Jesus, and weirdly as if she were *his bride*. A status like that would doubtless bring even more expectation than my plain clergy wife one. But saying that she is missing "the swoon" is a way of expressing yearning for something no church service—outside or inside—could provide: sexual fulfillment, with a real live person. When it comes to this realm, in my experience anyway, the significance of either lover's type of occupation falls away.

On that Sunday morning when Henry leaned forward and piped up from the backseat, "Mom, it's Emily A-Dickens house, and look, she's home!" I found myself wishing she really *were* home, so I could go inside and have a good chat with her, as if her house were on my regular circuit of places where friends lived, where I could just drop in without calling ahead.

I imagine her peering out of her large bedroom window upstairs, pulling back the curtain just a bit. For neighborhood children, she often lowered treats in a basket, but because my toddler is coming in with me, and she and I have a well-established friendship already, she hurries downstairs to greet us at the back door before I knock.

"Well, good morning to you both," she says quietly, looking at me with intense eyes, auburn hair pulled back. "Please do come in. I'll get you some freshly made gingerbread! I was working very late last night, so please don't mind the mess." She doesn't rush to hug Henry, but gives a conspiratorial smile in his direction before heading down the hallway, knowing how he appreciates her baking.

"Only if it's no trouble," I say, walking inside. "We'll just stop for a few minutes, though, because I need to pick up the other kids at church soon. This morning, we decided to take some extra time at home and skip the service." Henry is gazing around, awaiting the inevitable arrival of Carlo, her dog.

"Oh yes, of course it's Sunday. My family is at church, too. I've already spent time out in the garden with my fellow parishioners—the bees, the flowers, the birds." We're in the kitchen now, and she's slicing up hunks of fragrant

cake. "Come to think of it," she says, "why don't you come earlier some Sunday morning and see if you like the kind of service I do? It's very much simpler than the one over there." She lifts her chin in the direction of Grace Church, a bit farther away than the Congregational one right across the street. Carlo is with us now, all wagging tail. "If you're lucky," she whispers, "I'll even try out a few of my poems on you. Last night was . . . well, my room was practically burning up."

Holding Henry on my lap, I say, "Fabulous!" We've talked before about the different ways ordinary rooms can catch fire. "I'd love to, but couldn't we do it some other midweek time? You know that most Sundays I really do like to hear Rob's sermons."

"Yes, of course," she says, blushing a little, then looking out the window. "Sometimes I forget what it must mean to be married to someone; to me, that's a faraway land teeming with mysteries." Henry is diving into his gingerbread now, crumbs everywhere.

"There are definitely mysteries all right," I say, knowing from past conversations that she has been gripped by desire and elated by love before; that she has also felt debilitating disappointment, too. "What's probably most interesting about it is figuring out how much of you can stay intact, how much of you needs to be ready to make shifts." Now, Henry is happily playing with a pile of blocks over in the corner, mostly used by her nephews who live next door.

"I can only imagine," she sighs. "But with the right person, I'd be so completely swept away, as if by the tide, that I'd probably lose track of knowing what 'intact' ever was."

With this, she reminds me that being overpowered by love, knocked off your feet by someone is not a fate to guard against so much as it is a triumph in itself. And when the other person can acknowledge being similarly overcome, then you can create a distinct kind of heaven.

Shaking my head from this fantasy, I kept my hands on the wheel and slowly cruised past her house with the white Subaru parked in the driveway, saying to Henry, "I know sweetie, it does look like she's home, doesn't it? But Emily Dickinson actually never drove a car; she didn't need to, really. So many places she went, right in her mind."

In just a couple of blocks, I would look for a parking place, scoop

Henry out of the car seat, slide the van door, and go in pursuit of my Sunday school–educated kids, hearing organ music emerge from the church service in session. I had friends inside, but I wouldn't mind not seeing them today. The poet who used to live nearby, who in a way still does, who called herself a little mouse without the church part, never failed to keep me company.

Chapter 20

In the Bedroom, Braiding Beliefs

In those early days in New Haven, after the initial adjustment to the fact that my husband was bringing God into our household, I wondered how, or if, this mysterious presence would change my everyday life, now our everyday life together. On his side, Rob must have wondered how amenable to God's presence I would be. Would I keep my doubt to myself, stash it away in a chest somewhere, and try to expand my horizons, seek to understand whomever or whatever it was that my husband turned to every single day for solace and strength? Perhaps, eventually, even move closer to join him in that cherished relationship? "It would be my dream come true if we could someday pray together," he acknowledged to me, not expecting any immediate coming over, but saying it nonetheless. Each time he said this, I was just as amazed by his willingness to be my husband as I was astounded by the very idea of me praying.

How could I start a new practice like this without becoming more like him? Or would that in fact be the goal?

Soon enough, as children began to be born and needed tending, there was less time or energy for existential debates. Those long discussions in which we strove to bring out deep elements of ourselves, almost as if we were hanging them on the clothesline for each of us to look over—"I believe this; what do you believe?"—were mostly in the past. The kind of gentle probing that came with dating was over; marriage became mostly about taking care of an array of daily tasks. What time was the evening service again? Who could get to the store for milk? Should we speak with Henry's teacher about what he told us happened yesterday?

Still, there were occasional times when we were alone together and in a certain mood not to grovel in the weeds of logistics but to float up higher, gain some elevation, approach the ethereal, even. We released ourselves, like winged creatures, to float on the breezes for a while. After all, besides the visceral, physical connection we felt from the start, the magnetic force that got everything started in the first place, we also shared a mutual affinity for the articulation of ideas.

Serenity reigned in these conversations. Something about the tender time of day, the desire to merge and gain sustenance from the contact, prevailed. But that didn't mean that after we'd had our fill of snuggling we couldn't also move each other's mental materials around and see what forms of life squirmed underneath. The fact was, I continued to be endlessly curious about the way Rob's brain worked, about how his synapses fired and connected to form his whole psychic landscape. One of the first things that attracted me to him was his mysteriousness of mind; he might explain a concept to me, a way of seeing God's connection to humanity, perhaps, but the explanation would always somehow leave pieces missing. I knew that there was a river running in him, and the waters flowed deep; still, when we ventured into some topics, I felt as if I stayed on the banks, watching him paddle. And then, soon enough, I would be prompted to wonder what kind of river was running in me, too; what the nature of it was, and whether my river and his were still in the gradual process of coming more fully together.

I recall one episode of bedroom lingering on a rare Saturday when we didn't have any scheduled activities until the afternoon. The light streamed in through our large windows, onto our pink walls. I was the one who got up to take Zeke out for a few minutes and then brought back two mugs of coffee. All three kids were still sleeping. When I returned, Rob was deep in his *Book of Common Prayer*, without even seeing the small leather-bound volume, I could tell what it was from the familiar sound of the thin pages rustling.

Deciding not to wait until he got done with his daily dose of Scripture, because that would mean I'd have to be too patient, I started with a question that I knew would get our pulses racing.

"How come it seems that you do so many more funerals than weddings?"

That sounded more abrupt than I intended, and Rob shook his head to mark the interruption, putting his finger down on the page to hold his place. But he was ready to talk; it was that kind of morning. "Hmmm ... Do I? Could be for a few reasons: mostly older congregation, young people getting married later. Also the fact that death is a constant we can count on; love is much harder to find, harder to guarantee." He was beginning to show his hand now, ready to reveal his particular combination of cards. We drew from the same deck, essentially, but our truths always came out looking slightly different—my diamonds to his clubs, as I saw it. Perhaps, to him, it was vice versa.

Grateful for the response, still I sighed. "There's that skepticism again."

"Skepticism? It's just the truth. And besides, you know I believe that ultimately love does always triumph over death. That's the story of Jesus." This was his trump card.

The kids were getting up now, running back and forth between each other's rooms, having their own conversations, padding downstairs for cereal. Zeke trotted out of our room to be part of their more interesting activity.

"OK, we'll get to him in a minute." I was confident we had some time to hash this out, letting the hands of the clock go past 8 A.M. "What was that your colleague Jonathan said about why he actually *prefers* doing a funeral to a wedding?" Jonathan, an older and single priest, quiet but with a droll sense of humor, preceded Rob at this church and had stayed on to be his assistant.

Rob was willing to keep going; I was in luck. "He said that, doing a funeral, clergy can at least be sure that the service 'takes.' With a wedding, the outcome is up for grabs. I've had that experience myself: doing the premarital counseling over some months with a couple, working with the family, learning the challenges they've had, writing as hopeful a wedding sermon as I can—and then hearing some months later that the whole thing crumbled. It's dispiriting, but it comes with the territory. Nothing is guaranteed."

We heard clattering in the kitchen, and knew the kids were getting bowls and spoons out of the dishwasher. The little television on the counter had been turned on. "Williiiieee! Let me watch my show!" Cora could be counted on to push against the dominance of her big brother.

I pressed forward. "Sure that's true, *some* marriages do fail, but what gets me is how that outlook goes against the kind of Shakespearean optimism that I stand by." The greatest playwright of all time, steeped in the King James Bible but not a *religious* writer exactly, was often my go-to guy. "I mean, when any of the comedies end with a group wedding, it's a sign that the society is renewing itself. There's a genuine spirit of celebration, of confidence in the power of love." My senior thesis in college about Rosalind and Orlando, Benedick and Beatrice fluttered in my memory; what I actually wrote at that mustard Corona typewriter had gone a bit foggy, but it was still accessible enough for the purpose of this debate.

"Sure, many couples do make it, but the fact is we all live in a fallen world and so must deal with each other's brokenness. The 'Happy Ever After' is really more of a coming-to-grips with one another's weaknesses, accepting one another despite the fact that we are all sinners, don't you think?" He turned to me at this point, giving me full recognition as someone whose opinion mattered. Almost above any other kind of sensual moment with Rob, I went on Cloud Nine when he asked me *what I thought*.

I grabbed the opportunity for all its worth, asserting myself. When we hit on certain topics in our conversations, my beliefs—oftentimes murky even to me, like amphibians slithering around in the bottom of a pond—started to come out, proclaiming themselves. "There you go, talking about brokenness again! Of course we all have flaws, but the way you describe it, we're hobbling around with casts on every limb. What about celebrating our capabilities, our natural tendencies to go toward the light, seek the good?" I was mixing metaphors, but my chirpy optimism wouldn't be contained. "Really, Rob, sometimes when I listen to you, I feel like I shouldn't even *try* to stand up straight because we're all walking around in a house with ceilings so low we might hit our heads at every turn." With this, I was also obliquely referencing the woman at church who had been concerned about my posture.

Brriiiing! went the kitchen phone, and then we heard the scraping of stool legs as one of the kids rushed to pick it up.

He absorbed my barrage quietly, then shrugged. "You see brokenness as a bad thing; I just don't." He looked right at me again, coffee mug in hand. "My faith teaches me that it's only through acknowledging our brokenness, not denying it, that we can achieve our full stature as human beings." He was as sure about this as he was about the Resurrection, and as he was about loving me.

"MOM!" Cora shouted up the stairs. "Can I go to Frannie's later?"

Neither view prevailed, again. What we had, though, felt like the opposite of an argument. There were no hurt feelings; we'd been like explorers in each other's terrain. We got up and started making the bed, pulling up the covers from our different sides. As he headed over to his dresser with his tousled dark hair, I put my arms around his waist just to feel his wholeness. And I sensed my own, too.

As best we could tell, the crux of the disagreement between our philosophies had to do with my instinctive confidence in the power of free will to determine much about the course of our lives and his equally firm belief that essentially we are all fallen and we constantly need forgiveness from God and from each other.

With the help of Rob's divinity school education, I learned that I was Pelagius to his St. Augustine.

Pelagius was a fourth-century British monk and theologian, a contemporary of Augustine of Hippo, a towering figure in the early years of Christianity. A very learned man, Pelagius was also considered a heretic by many because he was, apparently, largely misunderstood to believe that humans were not irrevocably wounded by Adam's sin and could in fact attain salvation *on their own*, without God's grace. He was propelled largely by a real worry over people not trying hard enough to attain a fully moral life because of a belief that it wasn't in their control. There's plenty of disagreement over how unorthodox Pelagianism actually was at the time, but it's fair to say he stirred things up with his assertion that we sometimes, in the quest of leading an ethical life, sell ourselves short. He made people wonder just where the line was between "Yes we can" and "Yes we can, with God's help."

Actually being Pelagius would, I knew, imply clothing me in religious garb that I didn't actually own. Still, Rob was the one who sensed that we had a certain kinship. I have always believed that we as individuals are responsible for making the best choices we can at any given moment, that the specter of Adam and Eve's fall need not haunt us, that we will always stumble but must recover as best we can, that no higher being can either rescue or punish us. For better or worse, we move through this world under our own power, and what befalls us must be endured under our own power also. We take what comfort we can from one another, because that—to me anyway—is the only game in town.

This way of seeing might seem limited and even harsh—as if we were forever standing as solitary beings on a windswept plain, open to all the elements and pathetically trying to make our way forward, in the face of endless threats, with no protector. But I see it as a reasonably optimistic view: we can accomplish a great deal; we can also be agents of kindness and good will and justice, every day, just by trying. This is not the same as believing we can blot out the darker aspects of life—failure, illness, cruelty in all its forms. These woes will always be with us and must be recognized for what they are. Unlike Rob, I just continue to believe that our own free will is not so much a liability, often bringing us to doom, but a means by which we can fly with our own wings, discovering new lands as well as the elements of our own beings.

Here's a statement from a nineteenth-century treatise called *Doctrine in the Church of England: The 1938 Report* that spells out Rob's view, more or less:

> Man is by nature capable of communion with God, and only through such communion can he become what he was created to be. "Original sin" stands for the fact that from a time apparently prior to any responsible act of choice man is lacking in this communion, and if left to his own resources and to

the influence of his natural environment cannot attain to his destiny as a child of God.

This is why, as I understand it, coming to the communion table each Sunday is so important for so many people. It is there that baptized Christians are reminded that they can, each week, reach for their "destiny as a child of God." There's this understanding that what the table offers is a kind of remedy for original sin; that the bread and the wine reestablish a kind of right relationship with the Almighty, which in turn will enable people to be more fully formed in their goodness.

Coming late to this as I have, through marriage, I still have difficulty accepting the concept that humanity is lacking. Lacking in what, exactly? Sure, we all screw up, some of us more than others, depending on our inherent natures; we make all kinds of mistakes, some more grievous than others. But this pattern of behavior, to me anyway, is not at all the same as being *actually deficient* in some kind of necessary material. And furthermore, is the influence of a natural environment always something to worry about? Does that imply that the world, as it is generally, pulls us down? I just do not believe this. It was, in fact, by *marrying Rob* and sharing a home with him that I began to clarify where I stood on some "big picture" issues; encountering his certainty often has helped me work to achieve my own, while sometimes taking in dabs of his philosophy, like a painter filling in cracks.

Although I never became a full-fledged Quaker, I prefer their emphasis on recognizing the "inner light" that each one of us can channel to guide us. The image provides a kind of hopefulness that rings true to me.

When, waking up in the morning, Rob and I tussled about original sin or free will or the reality of God, I wondered if our views provided any real indicators about how each of us would get on with our respective days. Did our "belief system" (mine was beginning to take shape) determine what kind of spirit we brought to the sidelines of a game, the supermarket, or the church office? If these beliefs were part of our internal fires, then did they actually come out in any perceptible way? People meeting us, for instance, would likely have no idea which one acted in an Episcopalian way and which one did not. And maybe the large areas of overlap that we have always had—our love of the outdoors and of books, our striving toward goals, our trying to demonstrate for our kids a sense of what "doing good" means—would be enough to make the areas where we were more like islands, waving to each other but staying put under our own palm trees, into a beautiful archipelago.

Chapter 21

I'll Be Kind of Worshiping over Here

However strong I imagined my friendship with Emily Dickinson to be, however the feeling of a bond between the two of us buoyed me, I also knew that her reclusiveness, separate from her hesitation about organized religion, would have made it nearly impossible for her to accompany me in a different type of out-in-public activity. Unlike church, which drew me in only because my husband's presence acted like a magnet for me and the kids both, this other activity, generating its own steady stream of events, was teeming with people other than Rob: our kids, lots of other kids, and parents galore.

In the early days after our move, I lay down my quilt of allegiance to kids' sports. With three able-bodied sneakered children—ages nine, seven, and two—we were entering a patch of years thick with schedules and practices and coaches and teammates and games.

The trick was how to make the sports part merge seamlessly with the church part, or the other way around. As soon as I let myself see the two entities in counterpoint, I got flummoxed. How silly, and in fact even *sacrilegious* to compare them! And yet, there was some truth to the conflict. Rob came to our marriage with his own blanket of allegiance, and he didn't just carry it under his arm like an accessory, as I saw myself doing; he was completely wrapped in his faith. Mine was more of a commitment to something—not a whole system of belief—that had gone dormant for a while but then was unfurled in full color once a whole new field of dreams opened up.

In the home movies that my mother made in the late 1950s, first stored on reels then cassettes and now digitized for the next generation, my older brothers play countless games outside with their friends. Sixty years later, the colors still come through with a hazy, beautiful lushness. The boys run obstacle courses in their rolled-up jeans—jumping over wheelbarrows and benches with frenetic steps; play soccer and football and baseball on our big front field near my mother's long laundry line; play basketball out back by the barns with a makeshift platform for jumping and my father doing chores in the background; ride go-carts around and around our driveway while waving excitedly; walk around on makeshift stilts, enjoying the feeling of power. There is plenty of strutting, arguing, laughing, and running, running, running. In winter scenes, they are sledding dangerously fast on our steep back hill, flaps covering ears; or throwing skates over their shoulders to hike through the woods with Clancy, our Irish Setter, to a place called The Cove, where, until the new power plant warmed the salt water, there was reliable ice for hockey. Kids converged there from all over the neighborhood called Crab Meadow. Most parents stayed home.

In these movies I am mostly seen toddling around near Clancy, my protector, gazing at my brothers in their nonstop activities. Occasionally one of them pauses to outstretch a hand and pay a little attention to me. When I got a little older, I would be able to join the games sometimes (with a minor role—say, blocking in football) but I spent more time with our horse and pony, having learned to ride from our father and an across-the-street neighbor named Sheila. When I was a teenager, with my brothers mostly gone and one black horse replaced by another chestnut one, my brother Sandy made me a series of fences for jumping in one of our fields. He also took some black-and-white pictures of me on horseback, but by then the thick-with-boys action had quieted.

My mother is silent—"I tried to just let the camera tell the story!" Movies are fascinating now, because so much has changed. While it's true that my family was particularly lucky to have had space to stretch out, the norm for everybody was fooling around with friends right from your neighborhood. Kids were dropped off or walked over to our place because we had the best location for lots of games. Adults were beside the point; they were around in a vague kind of way, rarely supervising or, please, no, judging our performances. When we did play team sports at school or at the community field, our parents weren't watching our every move.

In his essay "The Sweet Long Days," David Maraniss depicts this almost Eden-like existence. He says, "The essential wonder of the games we played is that we played them blessedly free from adults." It can't be just a coincidence that he borrows from religious language here; they *felt* blessed because of joy and freedom, even with no mention of God. He goes on to take a swipe at today's parents who see themselves as so positively involved in their kids' lives: "There were no soccer moms or Little League dads. For better or worse, we defined and lived in our own world." Pretty clearly, he's suggesting, it was better: kids got to be kids.

Now, though, in certain parent circles it's considered normal for adults—we who used to romp have turned into them—to give up *entire weekends* for our kids' games. Standard life maintenance tasks like mowing the lawn or cleaning the gutters now have to be wedged in between long distance drives to fields and rinks and courts. Something has become very compelling about putting our kids in the athletic performance spotlight many miles away from home. And, furthermore, all of this is happening in a time when the reality of global warming should have us questioning the need for more driving. We talk about carpooling bur rarely do it; for the most part we seem perfectly willing to spend hours in gas-guzzling vans with our kids to deliver them to their all-important contests.

We go. And very often we go on Sundays. It's happened gradually, and not necessarily with all sports, but playing official games on the Christian Sabbath is now standard operating procedure across the country. Orthodox Jews have had the Saturday challenge for longer. We succumb to the life of parents who drive their kids places where there will be other parents who have also done the same, leaving whatever the home projects are (or might have been) dormant so that they can stand around watching their kids, talking about their kids, and using their cellphones.

For us as a clergy family, the ante was upped. Beyond just the scheduling conflicts, enough of a headache, we had to take on a larger question. Would the underlying values of a ratcheted up sports culture—the messages it conveyed to kids about competition, about how to assess their own self-worth, about what really matters in the world—be discordant with the messages of Christian formation?

Just a scant few years back, I would have said that "formation" had to do primarily with how players line up on a field.

Since marrying Rob, I found that his whole way of seeing was seeping through my pores to my insides, and I wasn't sure what kind of chemical reaction was happening there. A kind of shift from innocence to experience was taking place. I became jittery as I sensed that *Good Old Sports* were being replaced by *Pumped Up Sports*, and then, morphing into *At What Cost Sports*. While living in Storrs, I felt the two pillars of Nature and Neighborhood holding me up; here a third was forming, taking on some of the weight from the other two. I began granting it more power, even while sensing that a new kind of wedge was forming between Rob and me. Maybe the signs were already there that sports, while pleasant enough most of the time, could never be something I could actually put anything like *faith* in. On the other hand, I was willing to try.

"You OK with me signing Willie up for travel soccer?" I asked Rob one morning in the kitchen, while I was checking to make sure that late summer bugs hadn't found their way into the cereal boxes. I didn't want my tone of voice to show any anxiety about the question as I pulled the plastic strip from the new Quaker Oats cylinder. "Tryouts start tomorrow. Well, actually, he missed the first round of tryouts everyone else did last spring, but they're willing to let him come on now, so long as he's got the skills."

"I guess so," he shrugged, not too interested yet. "But what kind of commitment will it mean? I'm fine with the kids playing on teams," he was now scanning for granola, "so long as they can still make it to church and so long as it's feeding them in some way, health-giving and not just hypercompetitive." Those words sounded solid to me, reasonable; but as I looked down at my bowl emerging from the microwave, all I saw was mush. I was pretty sure that only *one* of the stipulations after his "so long as" could be guaranteed by any team contract I was so eager to sign. The second one, about "feeding them," would be checked off, thanks to the many inherently positive qualities of the activity. It was the first one—"they can still make it to church"—that I had reason to be jittery about. No one thus far had specifically talked to me about Sunday morning games, and I had been avoiding asking that loaded question, but I had a feeling that we were heading into a problem. With a certain degree of cowardice, I decided to let it slide a little while longer. Maybe, I hoped, once Rob saw just how "health-giving" playing soccer was for this particular kid in this particular new town, he'd relent enough to allow Willie to skip an occasional Sunday in church. Maybe. We were heading into uncharted waters.

Never before did I have reason to be suspicious of athletics, my trusted ally. Now, though, I was trying to understand and respect Rob's point of view, and acknowledge what he considered to be some *negative* features of the youth sports world: the hypercompetitiveness, the pushy parents, the message that value came mostly through winning. I felt that I was trying to reach across the aisle, in a way; I wondered whether Rob, being wrapped in faith as he was, would allow himself to do something similar: accept the possibility that team play, with all the practices and games, could offer a bundle of positive elements to our kids, maybe even ones not generally available in church.

Just a few days after we moved into the new house, with many boxes still needing to be unpacked, I drove nine-year-old Willie to his first day of soccer practice with his new travel team. I was convinced that this would be just the right kind of entry—a kind of parallel one to the church—to a new community that we needed. With Henry strapped into his car seat, we made our winding way down the hill to arrive at the huge swath of fields behind the big cement football stadium at the University of Massachusetts. I immediately noticed a woman on the sidelines watching a toddler just the same age as mine. "Hello!" she said, "I'm Deb, the coach's wife. Are you Willie's mom?" She had a big smile and radiated warmth. Our younger sons needed no introduction to start tearing around with one another on the sidelines. They made their own team, effortlessly.

In short order I met Molly, who liked to sit quietly near the goal with her arms around her knees because that's where her son was playing, and Sam, her husband, who started offering to pick up and drop off our son for faraway games; Beth, a naturopathic doctor whose voice went amazingly high when she screamed, "Come on guys, get back on defense!" and her curly-haired husband, Josh, who often arrived at the field having just gotten off a plane from somewhere he had been teaching other up-and-coming naturopathic doctors; Linda, who had a constant glow that radiated to others nearby, and her husband, Wes, a longtime contractor in town with a wry sense of humor. David and Robin were an interfaith couple—he Jewish, she Episcopalian—and they gave me a sense that my not being cut from the same cloth as my husband wasn't all that weird.

All of these couples, these other families, gradually formed a new kind of large family; we awaited one another's arrival with chairs and blankets and coolers, knowing that whatever had happened in the intervening days, the ups and the downs, we could bring our tidings and share them. We watched our sons streak across the field, shouting, arms outstretched to show readiness, suddenly changing direction, trying to beat each other to the ball as if their lives depended on it.

When the schedule came out, showing—sure enough—at least several Sunday morning games, a couple of them at 8 A.M. in distant locations, I winced, but didn't waver. Then I got up my nerve and, choosing a morning when we weren't hurrying off and the rays of sun lit up the bedroom floor, casting everything in a positive light that prevented anything from becoming too big a problem, I broached the travel soccer subject with Rob again. It was wise, I knew, to begin by proposing a compromise.

"So I found out that there are *some* Sunday games, but how about if I let the coach know well in advance that he can only miss church once or twice, that we have a particular family need? And I'm sure I can get him rides for the games he does go to, so I will still be available for the other kids." Willie didn't sing in the same choir that his sister did, but he had recently started becoming an "acolyte," assisting the clergy with the service, on a rotating schedule. I waited, holding my breath.

The fact that Rob kept quiet for almost thirty seconds was definitely a good sign.

"I'm not happy about this, and I'm also not surprised. How important is it for him to be on this team? Would he really be missing all that much, by not playing?"

"I actually think he would, Rob. This is a really good group of guys for him to be with, and we're getting to know their families, too. Let me please talk to the coach; I'm sure he'll understand." I simply couldn't imagine pulling out of this now.

"Ok, then." He sighed. "But," he said, holding up his hand, "please just try to keep me out of it. You know how I feel, and my feelings won't change. But do what you need to do." His words weren't imbued with the same warmth that the floor had, at this point. I might have said, "Let's keep talking about this later, then—try to work it out more completely." But I opted to move along.

It took some convincing for the coach, Brent, to relent on the requirement of attending every single game—perhaps he'd never had a clergy kid on a team before—but he grudgingly did. Afterward, I felt drained, as if I'd sat at some kind of negotiations table.

One late afternoon, on our way down to practice, a cop pulled me over in a speed trap I hadn't yet learned about, for going forty in a thirty-mile-per-hour zone. After an interminable ten minutes, he sauntered back over to my car with a whopping two-hundred-dollar ticket. I considered saying to him, "Do you have any idea what it's like to be a mom new to an area and completely dedicated to getting a boy to his soccer team so that we might make a good start here?" But I held my tongue, partly in deference to the cleated kid in the back. I took the thin white slip, cringed, and crept along the road where the tall corn was lining both sides, moving slowly but steadily toward the promised land of the soccer field.

Life became a jumble of priorities. Sometimes, I was firmly in one place—making supper in the kitchen, driving the van, sitting quietly in a pew, or cheering on the sidelines—but just as clearly, in my head at least, in another.

Gradually, through all this activity, I got more glimpses of my own emerging belief system, because I was beginning to look for it with more interest. Was it ridiculous to think that Sports could join Neighborhood and Nature to form a kind of triumvirate that could stand up proudly next to—not against, but alongside—an entire religion? If I could discover, in conversation with Rob, that I *didn't* see most of us walking with difficulty, hobbled by our sins; that I *did* believe strongly in the inherent virtues of all kinds of games played on big fields, then maybe I could keep identifying other main truths I had always lived by but had barely noticed. All the while, I continued to wonder how important it was to find what I heard other people call a "spiritual home." I was still not sure there was such a place for me that could be entered through any set of doors, but I was willing to keep an open mind.

In the meantime, life clearly required one main thing from me now: become the best juggler I could be.

PART IV
CHURCH: THE FIRST HALF

Chapter 22

Getting to Church, Twice

We had lived in our house-up-the-hill for about two years and had settled into new routines for the five of us. On this particular Sunday morning, Rob had been gone an hour and I was still dozing. After hazily watching him tie his black shoes while sitting on the edge of the bed, put on his pants (always after the shoes), rummage around at his dresser for his collar stays, affix them at the back of his neck, then listen to his purposeful step descend the stairs, I'd drifted back to sleep. The phone jarred me awake at 8 A.M. I groped for the receiver on the bedside table, which was covered with a thin layer of dust where there was no reading material.

"Hello, Polly," said Allison, director of the Angel Choir and the Person Who Does Everything Cheerfully. "I wonder if there's any chance Cora could sing with us this morning? We really could use another voice! Might you be able to get her down here by quarter-to-nine?" Sounded like a plan, except that ten-year-old Cora was still asleep and the church was a solid twenty minutes away, maybe fifteen in a real hurry.

The sun streamed through the generously sized windows with gauzy curtains, and the pine trees outside glistened with a thin layer of ice; Zeke was stirring and needing to go out to investigate the new day. To him, it was just a morning like any other.

For a brief moment on the phone, I considered refusing, saying something like, "Oh, Allison, I wish I could, but I just think it would be too tough for me to get her up, walk the dog, and then put Willie and Henry in the car, too, making time for cereal, since I definitely won't want to come back home to get them later on." This would have been a rational explanation, in fact. But I didn't, partly because Allison was not generally a taskmaster but rather an energetic and kind woman, and partly because I frequently slipped into trying to compensate for what might be seen as my deficiencies as a clergy spouse. Never did I overhear anyone disparage me for my clear nonparticipation—I wasn't in the Altar Guild, not on the Welcoming Committee, not in the choir, not a Sunday school teacher—but if I couldn't at least get my children there when they were summoned by church ladies, I felt certain I'd risk Rob's disapproval. Maybe then he'd actually wonder why he had let those Episcopalian girlfriends (they were perceptible to me if never really named, in the foggy past) go. I was already unusual: I didn't want to move further toward weird.

Back when Rob and I were in premarital counseling sessions, those calm hours when little ones seemed in the distant future, the three of us had tossed around the question of my commitment to the cause. In one session, our counselor Gregory paused and let me stew in wondering about how every Sunday would feel. He shifted in his chair, stroked his beard, and said something like, "It's easy for me and Rob to think this would be no big deal; but for *you*, someone who has never been a churchgoer, maybe it really will be a big burden, not something you want to sign up for too readily." I looked right at him to make sure he knew I wasn't in avoidance mode. Then Rob, sensing a good opening, said, "I understand and respect that you, Polly, are not becoming Episcopalian; it's OK with me that you don't go to church. I do, however, feel strongly that our *kids*—when we have them—need to learn the traditions of my faith." There was nothing there to object to; I had no other distinct faith, no horse of a different color that needed to be recognized. Blankness was all.

"I give you my word that I will do whatever is in my power to start them out this way." Saying this then was a no-brainer; I wasn't giving up anything, was I? Unless he'd said I would need to hand my firstborn over *directly to God*, I was too swept up in love to let any future logistical details get in the way. Those were for later.

Now, with someone on the other end of the line waiting for my answer, *later* had turned into *now*.

So I said, "OK, Allison, I'll try my best to get her there." I decided that the only way I could succeed would be to focus on Cora, leaving the boys. Mothers who are also clergy wives must have exceptionally good transportation strategies.

Having unwisely not chosen a dress last night to wear today, I scrambled while shouting, "CORA! Angel Choir needs you! Willie and Henry—I'll be back for you in an hour. Can somebody please walk Zeke?!" The phone call had a domino effect, challenging me to see just how capable a church spouse/mother I could rally to be. Full throttle forward now, I was determined to play my part, pull my weight. I would deliver, in the form of a sweet, sleepy daughter, what had been requested of me.

So much of parenting is a hurry-up-and-wait operation. Get the children in the car, make sure they buckle, grab that van door handle, and give a commanding slide. Drive as fast as the speed limit allows, sometimes faster, with the single-minded goal of getting your passengers to the church door, the field, the teammate's father's car, the piano teacher's house, whoever is waiting to receive them. You watch them disappear, heave a sigh of relief, give yourself some credit, then wonder what your next stage direction will be.

On this particular morning, I had two other kids who still needed to get to *their* Sunday school classes, so after the almost silent ride—my girl was way in back, still a bit groggy—down the slippery roads to the drop-off, back up the hill I went, able to take only the slimmest satisfaction that, when Cora pranced into her rehearsal, Allison would breathe a sigh of relief and store away a little gratitude toward me. I would definitely need that on another day.

Chapter 23

On Time to the Diamond, Late to the Reception

My drives, however, were not always tinged in heroism. One late afternoon in June, I was alone in the car, on a mission that would take a few hours round-trip. Despite playing my favorite Motown music en route to picking up Willie from a Little League playoff game, the Toyota van felt bitingly lonely as I drove through the Berkshires, where I'd just attended a wedding where Rob had officiated. Marvin Gaye's "Ain't That Peculiar?" didn't have its usual bounce when I applied the question to my own predicament. Family life wasn't supposed to feel *fragmented* like this, with me charging off somewhere, for what I had thought was a legitimate mother's reason, causing me to be apart from my husband. I tried to be efficient in collecting Willie from one of the Mill River fields, sweaty and dirty and happy from the Giants' victory, high fives all around. Sandra, a teammate's mother, came over with a smile, "Oh, Polly, it was *sooo* great. Sorry you couldn't have been here!" I loved these postgame conversations; they were my bread and butter; but today I felt the minutes adding up, imagined the wedding guests heading to the buffet table and glasses clinking with toasts. The rest of my family was elsewhere; I hadn't made any arrangement for Willie to stay over after the game, thinking, as I often did, that it was possible to try to do everything, cover all the bases. Once I had collected my player, I needed to hit that highway—fast.

Our move to the Pioneer Valley of Massachusetts, primarily for a new church position, had also ushered in an era of deepening involvement in baseball for Willie. I was glad to have a reason to pick up a mitt again, and this time to have a more significant role to play than I ever had with my brothers: home practice coach. Throwing hard line drives to an eager ten-year-old, dribbling grounders and pop-ups after dinner—this was exactly where I wanted to be. Lasting until he was sixteen, Willie had years with Little League and then Babe Ruth as well as summer All-Star teams up through the high school JV team. His best friends were also on those teams, so the whole package was packed with nutrition. He steadily improved in all of the key skills—batting, fielding, baserunning—and, except for the inevitable strikeouts and bobbles in the field, it was all a pleasure, primarily for him, but also for me, too.

Rob, who had almost never played the game as a kid and occasionally recalled how getting hit by a ball was a hard to relinquish memory, supported the regular full plate of practices and games with a milder version of enthusiasm than my own. He was ever vigilant about watching to see whether the pure enjoyment the boys felt would ever be threatened by hypercompetitive, gruff middle-aged men who were, as Rob saw it, sometimes engaged in battles over what they may have already lost in their own youth. "Polly, don't tell me you *didn't notice* how unconcerned Coach T was when Willie got that terrible black eye from a ball he couldn't see coming down! He was all about getting on with practice." I hadn't been accustomed to harboring any suspicions about the *morality* of sports, but Rob began to usher them in, wanting to put me on alert.

Fortunately, unlike soccer games, baseball games almost never got in the way of Sunday church attendance. But occasionally we did have some conflicts with other kinds of special events, sometimes even involving another distant church, in a different denomination.

Back in March, a couple of months before my solo drive partway across the state, Rob let me know about a request he'd had from an old friend. "I've been asked to officiate at Keith and Amy's wedding in Lenox this June," he told me casually as he was pouring his morning coffee. "Great!" I said. "Which exact Saturday is it?" The Sierra Club calendar I had hung up on the kitchen wall by the phone already glowed with music lessons, school events, sports tryouts, community meetings, and the regular drumbeat of the church schedule. I tried to use different color pens in those days—bright colors for the kids' stuff, more sober black for Rob's. As if seeing the pleasant rainbow of commitments would lessen the strain of actually managing them.

Keith was one of Rob's best friends from college, a geology professor now in Utah, so just getting to meet his intended bride was a bonus; going to their actual wedding would be a thrilling prospect. "It's the 20th. We'll all go, right?" Rob wanted to make sure. On this point I got a little vague. "Hmm. I hope so." While tapping my finger on that particular weekend on the calendar, with a lovely picture of lush wildflowers above, I added, "We might have an issue with Willie, though, because that could be the start of baseball playoffs." Rob's face showed his displeasure; he wasn't appreciating this particular heads-up. "Oh, you're kidding me. Can't we just say that he's coming, no matter what?" I didn't answer, preferring to let fate takes its course. Maybe the Giants would be eliminated, or maybe I'd figure a way for *him* to stay and *me* to go. One thing, though, was never an option in my mind: relinquishing baseball.

Sure enough, a couple of months later, the collision happened. Having a head full of his wedding sermon, Rob left the arrangements to me. I talked myself into what I thought was a feasible compromise: leave Willie to play his game, get to the ceremony, then right after the wedding, drive the hour and half back to our town, bring him back to the reception to spend that night and the next day with us. Nobody would notice that I'd slipped out, I convinced myself. And I would have the satisfaction of knowing that my son had *been with his team*.

Mind at ease that my plan would allow me to juggle being wife and mother, I walked into the classic white New England Congregational church, and chose a sunlit pew near the front, the better to take in Rob's sermon.

After a few familiar statements, he turned to his main thesis. "Now I'm sure Keith and Amy will receive many lovely wedding presents," he began, "but mine will be a bit unusual."

He disappeared for a moment and returned with a large, green plastic composting bin.

"The longer I stay married," he explained, "the more I realize that living with a spouse is very much like making a compost pile together:

you toss everything organic and smelly in there—the rinds, the stuff scraped off your plates, the coffee grounds—and hope that chemical processes will bring forth new life. It isn't pretty, but it's real."

I felt my face start to flush and was convinced that, even though I was mostly among strangers, all heads must be turning in my direction. They were thinking, "So you're the wife he's suffering through life with?"

Rob was talking this way, I was certain, because of my loyalty to the playoff game. If I had been a reasonable wife who knew when to shun sports and stay with religion, or in this case the "Complete Church Wedding and Reception" package, he'd be comparing our relationship to twinkling stars in the sky or a magical carpet ride rather than a slimy pile of detritus.

Suspect as my absconding-for-the-field behavior was on this particular day, several years later I would do something arguably more outrageous, in the name of baseball. In a sermon, Rob would perfectly innocently mention something about fifteen-year-old Willie trying out for the "Mickey Mantle" league—a division for seventeen- to eighteen-year-olds in our town. Upon hearing the error, I would be unable to keep quiet from my pew and, as if we were sitting in the privacy of our own kitchen, actually shout out, "No—it's Babe Ruth!" Parishioners would hear me, maybe wince to themselves, but they would be too polite, or stunned, to stare. Now, more than a decade later, when I think back on this moment, I shudder with disbelief at my outburst. Who did I think I was, interrupting my husband's *sermon*? That was a potentially dangerous episode of crossing a line, insulting the Church, or maybe even God—third partner in this marriage.

Finally pulling into the grassy parking lot near the reception, I breathed a sigh of relief and walked over, with a hungry son. "Oh, you're back," Rob said when I reappeared at his side. It was now, in fact, well after the toasts and the cake cutting. Rob, never an enthusiastic dancer anyway, was already danced out. Suddenly I realized I had no idea with whom he may have danced. He didn't ask me to relate the jubilant scene I had witnessed back at the Mill River fields. "How was your dinner?" I asked, trying to be heard over the music. "Delicious," he said, not looking at me, "Not sure you'll find much left up there, though," nodding toward the depleted serving tables. Willie, fresh from victory, was glad to horse around with his brother and sister, forgetting his famishment momentarily. I went to get a drink and find some remnants of salmon and orzo salad, trying to recoup what I could, to dispel the chill in the warm and misty evening.

    I knew it wasn't baseball's fault at all. No, baseball remained solid. The sharp stab of betrayal that I felt came from right inside *me*. Accustomed to trying to juggle a bundle of activities in different locations, just about every day, and mostly succeeding, this time I had screwed up. The look on Rob's face made clear that I had dropped something that went clattering on the floor.

Chapter 24

My Angel Returns

Back down the hill and parked near the church, after my second run of the morning, I savored every minute of my slim slice of alone time in the van while my family members were doing four different things related to religion. Absorbing the rays of February sun that found me there, finishing the bowl of oatmeal that had gone cold, I was pleased that I had delivered my charges properly. I also wished for an extra fifteen minutes so I could talk to Jacquie, who would be just getting up out in Boulder, about almost anything at all: her dog walks in the canyon or mine in the woods; her efforts to get a new business started; my prodding for more and better science at the elementary school. Our words would have come tumbling out.

That conversation would have to wait, however. It was Sunday, and my family was missing a person.

The pealing of the bells coming from the very top of the steeple summoned me to meet my sons, occupants of my car on the second trip, at the back of the already filling up church. They emerged from their twelve-year-old and five-year-old Sunday school classes in another building, having engaged in tactile and conversational activities that prepared them for the main service in ways I murkily understood. Henry said, "Here, Mom, can you tell what this is?" On a piece of flimsy blue construction paper, I saw a picture done with magic markers of a big boat with animals about to enter. "Beautiful, Henry! It must be Noah's Ark!" I said excitedly, glad that this was one story I knew. Anything that he created, I loved immediately.

A smiling usher approached to hand us a bulletin with several pages of information. The bold headings were always the same; the content varied from week to week. This, I knew, was partly what people came for: a structure that they could rely on, an order of worship that held steadfast while so much else in life was erratic. You might be in your eighties and coping with a move out of your decades-long home, an adult stung by the loss of a job, a teenager who had been ostracized from a friend group—all of these mostly unmentioned pains and uncertainties had a chance of being subsumed, for a brief time at least, within the congregation's journey through the ancient liturgy. Here, there was stability.

Off to the left, in the doorway that connected the church to the aptly named "Connector," we saw a cluster of white-robed acolytes and clergy crowded together, some holding candles, awaiting their moment to move forward in the opening procession. Having on a previous Sunday made the mistake of getting in the midst of them, I knew not to try that again: it was like being surrounded by a flock of birds flapping their collective wings. In fact, the scene reminded me of tern nesting sites on a town beach I once helped to protect when I volunteered for the local Audubon chapter as a teenager. But, to be fair, those birds were downright dangerous—dive-bombing anyone who got too close to their eggs, driving you right out—while these church creatures were generally mild-mannered and kind, including the odd duck who looked away awkwardly when someone got close.

Although my status as a clergy spouse meant I got an automatic welcome anywhere in this place, something about how the people were so unified with common attire and a common purpose momentarily stabbed me with the consciousness that I was not part of this group. I did a quick inventory to check whether I could claim membership in any *other* group; nothing came quickly to mind except the clusters of parents on the sidelines, so I just made sure I had my fleece-jacketed sons with me.

Rob was at the back of the group in the Connector, and he would be the last person to walk down the center aisle. Right then, he was a kind of coiled spring, about to burst forth as a spiritual leader. We would be a family in our own particular Sunday morning kind of way, with our fifth member—our main breadwinner—set apart during the next hour and a half, longer when you count the recovery period. The boys and I chose a pew, never the same one, right in the middle, just in time to see the robes, in a range of heights, with golden tassels encircling all waists, walk in a measured gait past us, with each pair of eyes looking straight ahead toward their goal of the altar. Members of the choir went first, and the opening hymn rang out, "Praise to The Lord, the Almighty, the King of Salvation!"

This, I thought to myself, was one version of what "heeding a Higher Calling" looked like. Participants saw something invisible, something I did not see. I was a spectator, on the sidelines, yet in a distinctly different way than I was a spectator while watching a game. On a playing field, watching my kids, I wasn't asked to become more involved. Here, there was a standing invitation. One part of me wondered what it would feel like to be swept up in the drama unfolding around me, to let everything go for its sake, to jump in with abandon. But I continued to hold back, not knowing the version of me that could do that.

As I child playing in the sand on Asharoken Beach, I noticed graceful, silent sailboats on the horizon as well as, closer to shore, raucous motorboats pulling skiers who were waving their arms and shrieking. I looked up to watch but knew these activities belonged to families other than mine. I'd seen faded pictures of the sailboat my grandparents used to have, it was called "The Sonora," that had been moored right near here summer after summer, but as my father came into adulthood he gravitated to building fences and chopping wood. He also never spoke about *why* he thought we could do without any nautical life. An occasional ride on a cousin's boat or a chance to water ski with a friend was a treat, not a regular event. My brother Sandy got himself a little Sunfish when he was a teenager, just to try it out; but soon enough he, too, was more drawn to animals and fields. In church this morning, as I watched the procession move by me, I felt the odd mix of my *old* family and my *new* one. The white robes were, in a way, other people's boats chugging by as I watched from shore; but then there came my husband, my most intimate partner. He was sending out a long rope, across the choppy waves, for me to grab onto and then allow myself to skim over toward him.

I loved that he craved my closeness. I craved his, too. In here, though, it was always complicated.

For about the whole first half of the service, I went with the flow.

After some opening pronouncements at the altar, there was a pitter-patter of little feet, followed by a clomping of larger feet, behind us, as the Angel Choir entered, with overwhelming cuteness, in their own white robes. A handful of parents in the pews craned their necks, beaming. The angels lined up, poking each other and giggling. One rakish eight-year-old boy, nervous perhaps, twirled his tassel as Allison, the director, lifted her arms and waited for their attention. Cora, with saucer-like green eyes searching for her brothers, and looking proud in her wide headband, stood swaying back and forth, with hands clasped behind her back; she sang her heart out. "This little light of mine, I'm gonna let it shine!" Applause, usually considered unnecessary in church, came pouring out of the pews.

I was a wife, I was a mother; whatever *other* deep-seated part of me there had always been, aside from the pieces in these two roles, felt at once both almost imperceptible and also exaggerated, in bold, while I sat there. Maybe I was going through some kind of reintegration at this very minute.

After the performance, and a quick cast-off of the robe in back, Cora rushed to join us, saying, "excuse me" to our seatmates. She settled her blue-jeaned and sneakered self right next to me, sinking in with relief. We all rose for another hymn. A few minutes later, I leaned over and gently grabbed the finger that was making its way too often into her nose. Henry sat calmly on the other side of me, reading a picture book. Willie, looking handsome in his button-down shirt and khakis, stared intently at his bulletin, awaiting the readings that were to come.

I did not know a thing about heaven, doubted it existed, in fact; but this felt something like perfect harmony on earth.

Cora started playfully tilting her head from side to side next to me in the pew, as usual finding it hard to be fully attentive to whatever was being performed up at the front of the church, now that her part was done. Her legs jiggled; her eyes darted around. Just yesterday she had been all physicality, zooming down the ice in drills with her teammates, reaching for a puck with her stick, making crisp passes, shooting on goal. I had watched, oozing with pleasure and a certain degree of nostalgia as well as envy: for the flush of the cheeks, the exhilaration of movement and connection, the years still available ahead for getting better, even for the risk of falling.

Chapter 25

Hockey Is Definitely a Sport for Girls

My brothers and I got our first doses of hockey from our Canadian mother, who had played in high school during the 1930s. When I was a teenager, I came upon a team picture on the very first page of an old album stored on a shelf. All the girls were wearing kilts and holding sticks; Mom sat front and center, beaming, with cascades of red hair and her trademark, tilted head. As soon as I saw that expression, I got a jolt—a reminder that my father's staid Brooklyn ancestry had always been only half of our heritage. When I brought the photo to her, she brightened at first, but then with a crestfallen face said, "I could never lift the puck, though." While I knew something about the power of airborne pucks, this did not cancel out her prowess in my mind. Having heard only that she'd done a lot of skiing in her youth, I was eager for any additional clues about my mother's athletic zest.

Maintaining her love of hockey was one of the main ways Mom showed loyalty to her homeland. On any regular winter evening, sitting curled up on the couch in her earth-colored dressing gown, she'd gaze off into space and say, "Maybe tonight my brothers Ruston and Sid are with the crowds streaming down Atwater Avenue to the Forum." Voraciously following the Montreal Canadians was, for my mother's British non-church-going family surrounded by French Catholics, about as close to a religion as they got.

On the freshwater inlet where I learned to skate—with big kids tearing around me, and that wonderful carving sound their blades made—the ice was like a sheet of glass with no end in sight. During Long Island winters, the window of opportunity was always short. But it was glorious while it lasted. My brothers sometimes skipped school when conditions were right to go down to The Cove, an inlet on the Sound that was a couple of miles walk through our woods. After a snowfall, kids brought shovels and worked in unison to get their reward. Clancy went, too; his tail would start wagging as soon as he saw the boys go into the closet for their skates and sticks. They brought hardly any equipment—whatever football helmets and shin pads were available—but definitely no huge bags with last names embossed on them. Except for taking their own leisurely skates around the perimeter, adults had virtually no role at The Cove. When it was time for hockey, kids from nearby streets, kids in walking distance, and kids who'd been dropped off by their parents were in charge, together. They made the rules, picked teams, argued.

Older long-legged girls played in their figure skates, some of the same ones who came sometimes to ride our horses, but I was little, not confident enough yet to push my way in. And in those days, there were no teams for young female skaters.

My time came about a decade later, when I got a chance to be part of a newly formed women's club team at college. Not knowing how to skate backward yet, I believed I could continue to channel my mother's spirit. We were coached by a couple of Minnesotan frat boys, and we played in a beautiful, brightly lit arena, drawing a sprinkling of fans, some of whom guffawed more than cheered. Gradually, I could stop reliably on both sides; crossover, front and then back; pass the puck adequately and just enough ahead of my line-mates, and though my shot was more anemic than meteoric, I very occasionally found myself at the right place at the right time to score. It was empowering. On subzero evenings, as I made the long trek back to the dorm from practice, my nostrils stuck together and I noticed just about every part of my well-used body tingling.

Chapter 26

Listening to the Lessons

New England is no Bible Belt, but in every Episcopal service, everywhere in the country, you get a generous helping of the Good Book. First a section of the Old Testament, then a Psalm, then something from the New Testament, and finally—gussied up with a walk down the aisle and several people involved—the Gospel.

The term "lessons" was a little too didactic for my taste; maybe because I had already done so much carting around of the kids to cello and piano teachers during the week. I would have preferred something like "stories," because that's what they were to me, but then I remembered, again, that I was a kind of guest here. The first reader, a legal aid lawyer with plenty of common sense, ascended to the lectern and started reading about God making a deal with Noah. "Never again will all life be destroyed by the waters of a flood; never again will there be a flood to destroy the earth."

Every single Sunday, whatever wishy-washiness I might have carried in with me—being uncertain about so much, and so certain about the uncertainty—I would hear the bellowing voice of God, or of someone channeling God, and wonder whether this kind of thunderous authority had ever existed, existed now, or could ever exist in the future.

The reader concluded with "The Word of the Lord." We all dutifully responded with "Thanks be to God" and watched her head back to her pew.

Looking to my right, I spotted another woman of about the same age, never a reader, who always wore colorfully clashing clothes. On this day, along with a kind of perpetual tic that caused her to jerk her head slightly and frequently, she had a pocketbook with pictures of Marilyn Monroe all over it. Imagining the starlet's puckered up red lips and cleavage sitting through a church service made me start laughing, but I quickly squelched that.

Then we read the Psalm in a kind of interactive way, reciting and responding in half verses, one side of the aisle and then the other. The more than one hundred people in the church suddenly became compressed into two voices, in an intimate experience. Although I would have never said these words anywhere else, I joined the chorus of voices. If there is one thing I can claim, besides being a sports mom, it's my identity as a good reader. And the language of the Psalms always soothed and amazed me: a single person had the nerve to address the Almighty, whose identity remained a complete mystery to me. I did my own quiet responding to each segment, listening to the hum of the congregation, each person reading from the text printed in the bulletin.

At this point, in my mind, I was back on the ice in a give-and-go exercise, making sure my stick gave enough to prevent the black disc from careening off, trying to maintain control. After all, the point was trying to *do something* with the puck. Far too often, I lost it too quickly. With this Psalm, I tried to stay with each set of lines, make them my own as best I could.

> In you, Lord my God,
> I put my trust.

Can't beat the simplicity of that.

> I trust in you;
> do not let me be put to shame,
> nor let my enemies triumph over me.

Sounds like a bargain being wished for, or a plea.

> No one who hopes in you
> will ever be put to shame,

You hope so, anyway.

> but shame will come on those
> who are treacherous without cause.

Treacherous—a word we ought to bring back. We hope they feel shame, but the fact is, they don't always.

When it was time for the Gospel—something from the Big Four of Mark, John, Matthew, or Luke—we all stood in deference to the language we were about to hear. A teenage acolyte carried the weighty book above his head partway down the aisle, and then gradually lowered it in front of Rob's colleague to read. Today, it was Mark 1:9–13. Rob rose from his chair, where he'd been listening like the rest of us, or on a slightly higher plane of listening, and stood silently, hands clasped in front of him. The colleague's voice rang out, and my own inner track kept playing.

> In those days Jesus came from Nazareth of Galilee and was baptized by John the Baptist in the Jordan. And when he came up out of the water, immediately he saw the heavens being torn open and the Spirit descending on him like a dove. And a voice came from heaven, "You are my beloved Son; With you I am well pleased."

Watching Rob, I realized that yesterday, while we were seated on stools at our slate blue, kitchen counter, when I was launching into topic number five of that morning, something about a student of mine who had sworn at me in class, he had probably been deep in thought about *this moment, these words.* The magic of a voice coming from heaven with a message that bathed everything in Love must have felt exhilarating to him as he prepared his sermon, and now again, as he was about to deliver it to a congregation awaiting his words as a kind of centerpiece of the service.

Tales from my classroom in a high school where fights broke out regularly in the halls made Rob wince momentarily, out of sympathy and concern for me, but he couldn't fully enter into the experience. Fortunately, most of my classroom interactions were positive. Sometimes, say when a shy student volunteered to read a passage aloud or when one student benefited from the insight of another, there were moments as thrilling to me as words from the Gospel must have been, to him.

In all the time we've been married, except for once, several years ago, when I asked him to join me at an end-of-semester celebratory meal with Saudi Arabian students who wanted to share their dishes and even give me gifts, Rob has never come to either my high school or college classes. This has not been for lack of his own interest, but because it's just not done. Spouses aren't part of the classroom realm; having a husband or wife at the back of the room would be plain weird.

Sitting there in the pew, I wasn't wishing that Rob could see and hear how I managed an hour-long class; that would be too nerve-wracking. I also knew that he preferred I *not* refer to what he did as "work," believing that it was a "calling" or a whole way of life. Thinking of my own efforts during the week, I wondered whether teaching could in some ways qualify as a calling too, even though the class managing and paper grading was most definitely work. Seeing him gather himself for what was to come next in the service, I decided that the terminology didn't matter all that much. The fact that I witnessed firsthand his movements around the altar, heard the words he spoke to his congregation on a regular basis, while he relied on my accounts of my days to imagine me doing my job – well, that was just the way it was. And I had a fresh understanding, too, of why my expressions of support for his performance on any given Sunday would matter to him; it was because I mattered to him.

Chapter 27

Swimming Through the Sermon

Up until this point in the service, I had been more or less like any other middle-aged mother with school-aged children in the pews. When I glanced around, I saw about a dozen of us, most of them my friends. We were the same species, except that they were true Episcopalians. As Rob ascended to his perch, though, I felt my posture straightening, my identity shifting ever so slightly. I was not a full-fledged member of the flock, but I was still the preacher's wife, connected to him by an invisible line that had been strung across the spacious air above the pews. Whatever he was about to say, I felt somehow implicated through marriage. In a way, we would sink or swim together.

But years of experience out here, bobbing around in this Sea of Church, had shown me that I didn't need to have any qualms about my husband's capability as a captain. Preaching had always been his favorite part of the job; he steered the helm of a ship by also being a deep-sea diver in thought. During the week, he liked to explore the ocean floor, alone, bringing Scripture with him, to use as a kind of flashlight. It was a phenomenon we experienced at home: Where's Dad? Underwater. I knew that he saw beautiful, jagged coral reefs; sleek, silent creatures; and spiky, venomous plants there, and that he was most interested in the interactions between them all. Then, when he had collected a few specimens, seen enough, he'd head back up. After some gasps for air and a quick toweling off, he would be ready to share what he knew with his people, his passengers awaiting a new direction.

He began his sermon by repeating a line from the Gospel: "And a voice came from heaven: 'You are my beloved Son; with you I am well-pleased.'"

Saying this line again, I knew, was a way of showing that everything would launch from that dock. I settled into my wooden bench, put my arm around Henry, who had looked up from his picture book, turned my head to the rays of sun streaming in through the vivid yellows and blues and reds of the stained-glass windows, and prepared to soak in my husband's carefully crafted words.

This was the part when I opted to make a move, diving off the ship to swim rhythmically alongside it, with all the passengers up above, hearing Rob's voice all the while. I didn't want to separate myself so much as get a better vantage point, more personal, more active. And in truth, for a change, I wanted to be more than a spectator.

Each time my head turned up out of the water to gulp in air, I was following his woven words, but I was also going forward by my own power, one stroke at a time, encountering no obstacles except for small swells. Movement was all. I saw my children on board, listening to their dad and also peering out, making sure I was still there, buoyant and not submerged or drifting off. Sedentary in the pew only in one sense, I was also feeling what my four limbs could do in the fluidity all around me, while he stood still to speak.

In church, nobody is asked at any juncture in the sermon, "Do you agree?" or "Raise your hand if you think this is true!" In other denominations, and I know this because I've visited, there is more audience participation, or at least affirmation: "Can I hear an AMEN?!" Not Episcopalians, who have a long history of relative staidness. The sermon has been carefully prepared, like some kind of nutritional concoction, and the congregation's role is to absorb it through their pores, synthesizing their own personal responses quietly along the way.

Now Rob was really plunging into the material, and concurrently, I focused on how my arms, one at a time, could cut through the water, with heightened awareness for the contours of the surface. I tried, in my own way as a wife, to keep pace with him.

Rob: At this moment, when he is emerging from the water, fully baptized and apparently chosen by God, Jesus seems to be all set, on top of the world. He's like the golden boy or girl we all went to school with, the one who perpetually seems untouched by crisis.

This is always good, when he nudges us to dip back into our collective memories. I like recalling who used to walk the halls in my junior high, now that it's a safe distance back.

Rob: I remember someone like that in my eighth-grade class; Derek moved through the halls confidently, always smiling, acne-free, while I perpetually doubted myself. But very soon, Jesus will be in the wilderness, facing terrible trials and darkness.

Derek? Who's he? How come I never heard that name before?

It wasn't the first time, nor would it be the last, when he told a story, intimately, to the whole congregation—and from my wavy location I made a flash of a puzzled face as I treaded water for a moment and got my bearings, hoping my children weren't concerned by my reaction. I was the wife; wasn't *I* supposed to know everything important first? Was I not the most intimate partner? But then I resurrected the larger truth of the situation, that he did this talk for *everyone here*: anyone who took the time and effort to come to church would get, blanketed within an illumination of Scripture, a sprinkling of biographical anecdotes that would enable them to look beyond the priest's robes just enough to see him as a regular, flawed human, and thereby be moved.

Derek was really no big deal. At least Rob had the good sense not to sprinkle old girlfriends, the chipper but maybe also sultry Episcopalian ones I imagined, through his sermons. Those pop-ups would have really disrupted the rhythm of my stroke.

During the next few moments of collective stillness in the pews, I recovered from that slight bump, still alternating arms over my head, splashing, splashing. Once again, for the umpteenth time during the course of our marriage, I knew that Rob was providing people with plenty to turn over in their minds. And notwithstanding the fact that my childhood religious cupboards were bare, I *got it*, or at least most of it, too. Indeed, his sentences had a propulsive effect on me, giving me stamina to keep going.

> **Rob:** Jesus's baptism by John on this day sets him on a course that will first go uphill, and then down, down, down to the depths of what it means to be fully human. He will empty himself so that we all can live.

I could hear how the lessons, printed out in the Bulletin, provided the various strands that he braided skillfully together, with one generally being emphasized over the others. I heard how he built to a satisfying conclusion, I heard how much of what he had studied in divinity school, during those couple of years when we could barely keep our hands off one another, enabled him to move around from the Old Testament to the New, lighting candles as he went, giving off a glow.

He walked back to his chair and sat down. Tired now, too, I climbed the ladder back on board to give my body a rest.

Chapter 28

Not Jesus Exactly, but a Preacher Who Knows How to Frame

Instead of candles, Rob used a large spotlight to illuminate his work on the home ice rink. He would place the light up in a tree and run a thick orange extension cord to the outlet on the outside of the house. Watching him, I thought his actions were at least as heroic and inventive as when he worked a sermon.

After Cora started basic hockey skills clinics down at the University of Massachusetts rink, Rob and I found complete agreement in a big project for home sports. Encouraged by the example of my older brother Steve in upstate New York, who sent us pictures of his teenage sons taking slapshots on a modestly sized rectangle of ice next to a couple of feet of snow by his house, Rob took the lead on this project.

"We can do that right here," he said, game for a challenge.

My heart started pounding with excitement, but I expressed my usual caution. "I dunno . . . remember that Steve said that water is ruthless and will find any change in level."

"But our lawn is completely flat! That's how it was graded. It'll work."

Having gained acumen with tools from early teenage jobs, a trait that I admired and partly envied, Rob showed incredible devotion to the new project. He researched what would be the right kind of plastic to use for the base and ordered it in a huge roll that came on a special truck. He also went down to a lumber yard to buy the long planks for the boards and then spent an afternoon bolting them together, down on his blue-jeaned knees on the cold ground, gradually making his way around the huge rectangle taking shape, completely absorbed by the task. Willie happened to have a friend from Storrs visiting; they tossed around a football, occasionally being enlisted to help, mostly in holding the small pieces of hardware for the guy in charge.

Thoroughly engaged in this process, Rob was being his most sports-affirmative self. Free of any conflict with church, he was able to give 100 percent to the cause of creating a place for kids to play. I loved everything about this scene, this man, the promised rectangle of hockey.

"Can I do anything?" I popped my head out of the house occasionally, pausing from putting away the groceries, hoping that this might be something we could do together, especially since the mission had to do with a sport that I loved, but also anticipating that his greater expertise would make my help consist mostly of a lot of standing around. "If you want to keep me company, you can," came the reply, then more pounding.

Marriage presents many moments like this: Do you make the choice just to *be near* your partner, doing not much of anything while they do a lot, or do you opt for accomplishing some task on your own, especially one that might benefit them later, when they would notice that you prepared, for example, a good dinner, one they would thank you for?

Finally the time came to run the hose and start filling. One night, Rob even had to figure out how to position the long, green, snaking thing up in a tree, emitting a light spray, in order to fill a reluctant corner of the rink. It was the combo clergyman-handyman-father-provider versus the corner, and he was determined to win. Once successful, he was all in for getting a light strung up so we could have night skating. Neighbors dug out their skates or borrowed some, so they could enjoy it, too. To people who didn't know us well but drove by our house a lot, we became the family with the skating rink.

But, alas, it was short-lived. What started modestly enough as Saturday morning instructional time with blue boxes to push, orange cones to maneuver around, and the emptying of a bag of pucks on a college rink soon escalated, with some signing of forms and steeper fees, to a new relationship with the more intimidating and longer limbed creature of travel hockey. Soon, Cora's hockey commitments elsewhere would prevent her from taking more than a few occasional fast laps around our home ice. Reluctantly, Rob and I would decide that a short but beautiful era must come to an end.

PART V

CHURCH: THE SECOND HALF

Chapter 29

Getting to the Peace

Except for the troublesome details of getting everyone here, I have experienced no inner turbulence thus far in the service, and besides, I've had a nice refreshing dip. The listening has been easy—tranquil, even. I've gone with the flow. But it was about to get harder, much harder. I braced myself.

I also took a sideways glance at my three kids sitting next to me in the pew. Wasn't it just a moment ago that they were five, ten, and twelve? When Henry was sitting on the floor, turning backward to work with crayons in a coloring book; Cora was swaying back and forth, restlessly; Willie was listening as best a seventh-grader could. Now—though we were still in the same place, with another sermon once again ringing in our ears—they'd leaped forward in their lives. Practically overnight, it seemed to me, Willie and Cora had become high school students, gaining responsibilities and a greater degree of independence; Henry, at age nine, had just made us all proud by playing the role of Winthrop in a local production of *The Music Man*. Rob was still at this church, preaching and presiding, but probably he too had gone through some inner shifts. And me? I wasn't sure exactly how, or if, I had changed. The regular cadences of the church service, however, definitely had not.

Rob tells me that the reason the Nicene Creed follows the sermon is because the Church wants it to act as a kind of safeguard. A preacher is always a sort of wild card: you never really know if they might veer off somewhere odd. But wherever the congregation has just wandered, they're sure to be brought right back to the central core of the faith with the collective uttering of the Creed. It's almost a raison d'etre for the church service as a whole.

Originally called the Niceno-Constantinopolitan Creed, scholars take its origin way back to both the Council of Nicea in 325 and the Council of Constantinople in 381. In those days, apparently, early Christians were often getting together to toss around ideas and hammer out statements, in Greek, about what exactly their faith rested on, where they could all absolutely agree. I would love to have been a fly on the wall during any of those big meetings; the arguments must have been raucous, and perhaps those guys who look so sedate in the portraits actually came unhinged at certain moments when they weren't getting their way, even threw things or throttled people. It might have been a little bit like the process for writing the Declaration of Independence, centuries later. Someone with flowing white hair and a million buttons banged on the table and said, "Nobody is leaving here until we get this done!!"

In any case, the remarkable thing about this statement through the centuries is that it has remained, and continues to be spoken in both Catholic and Protestant services. It's a kind of common language, a way of expressing that yes, you belong here, you are part of the fabric. *We* are all in this together.

The problem I had is that elsewhere—at home, in a high school classroom, watching games, at the supermarket, visiting my kids' schools—I was accustomed to saying what I believed and believing what I said, in a low stakes kind of way. In here, though, I just wasn't sure. Once we got started with the opening line, we were *committing ourselves* to a whole chain of interlocking points:

> WE BELIEVE in one God,
> the Father, the Almighty
> maker of heaven and earth,
> of all that is, seen and unseen.
>
> We believe in one Lord, Jesus Christ,
> The only Son of God.

The congregation was now standing, heads bowed, their voices droning all around me. My kids joined the chorus, not paying any attention to my indecision. On the previous Sunday, I had plunged into the recitation with everyone else, much like I used to jump into a cold pool holding my nose when I was eight, but today I opted to remain quiet, looking straight ahead, hoping no one heard the silence emanating from my orb.

> For us and for our salvation, he came down from heaven.
> For our sake he was crucified under Pontius Pilate;
> he suffered death and was buried.
> On the third day he rose again.

When I was in seventh grade, I became swept up in the anti-Vietnam fervor. Two of my brothers had gotten high enough lottery numbers to miss being drafted, and the fact that the middle two were in college helped, but they watched friends who were not so lucky. For a while, during that time, I stopped saying the Pledge of Allegiance. My homeroom teacher, a cool guy with curly hair and narrow ties who taught social studies, let it pass. A few other friends followed me, glad for a cause. But soon I began catching random comments, such as, "I told my parents you don't say the pledge, and they thought that was pretty weird. Don't you love our country?" I responded with something highbrow: "It's actually *because* I care about what our country is doing!" Nonetheless, I was glad when somebody in the administration wised up to the fact that the pledge could quietly be dispensed with because: (1) preteens like to test requirements, (2) there was too much else to get done in homeroom, and (3) the war was clearly troubling.

I hadn't relished being a maverick then, I had just thought it was necessary. Now, thirty-five years later, some of that same stubborn spirit reemerged. *Just because you're here in this pew doesn't mean that you have agreed to check your real self at the door. If you care about the validity of words, then say only the words you can fully vouch for.*

> He will come again in glory to judge the living and dead,
> and his kingdom will have no end.

> We believe in the Holy Spirit, the Lord, the giver of life.
> We look for the resurrection of the dead,
> and the life of the world to come.
> Amen.

The last two full lines were so beautiful that I wanted to speak them for that reason alone, but I couldn't bring myself to say "the resurrection of the dead" because I'd never budged in my belief about the finality of our deaths. Since I liked both the imprecision and the expansiveness of "the life of the world to come," however, I joined in for that.

I looked at Cora and gave her shoulders a squeeze, as if we were greeting one another at some destination following a journey we'd taken on different roads.

As a reader approached the podium, the congregation reached for the indispensable little volume again, turned the thin pages that made a delicate sound, well aware that one bold yank could cause a frightful rip. The reader embarked upon a long list of statements, a string of concerns, each beginning, "For the [whoever it is] . . . let us pray to the Lord." We were pulling for the country, for the church, for the bishops and clergy, for the unemployed, for the sick. I wondered—would just speaking the words be enough? What portion of our minds needed to be focused on what we were saying? Was I being too literal here? Did there need to be some kind of majority of people who really *came through* in the pews for the prayers to be effective? Never having been taught as a child how to kneel down beside my bed with clasped hands to have a private tête-à-tête with God, only seeing this image in books of nursery rhymes, I really had no idea. I didn't trust myself to know how to achieve this connection any more than I would trust myself to know how to operate heavy machinery without instruction.

"Lord, have mercy," I said after each prayer, along with the rest of the congregation, hoping that everyone on the long list might be better off as a result of these few moments, and suspecting that the only real benefit could possibly be *within us*, the people standing quietly and listening to the reminders about so many other people needing whatever help we could actually give.

We moved into an introspective interlude, when we faced ourselves squarely and acknowledged how we have, yet again, fallen short. I watched my kids, still darling as can be, pull the red-cushioned bar toward us so we could all get on our knees, with heads shrouded by hands against foreheads. I was more interested in observing them than following suit, so I sat back just enough and took a sidelong glance at their devotion. Nobody goes to church to feel shame, exactly—or maybe they do—but because people are not exactly lining up the rest of the week to list their sins, this part of the service clearly provided that opportunity.

But the truth was, while the concept of *sin* was integral to the belief system here, I still had some trouble with it. Time spent in the classroom with Hawthorne's *The Scarlet Letter* hadn't made up for my first couple of decades spent mostly free of reminders about our "fallen" nature.

The most remarkable thing to me about the segment was that, no matter what kind of week you have actually had—whether you've destroyed your neighbor's brand new Mazda or heroically hauled him and his family out of their burning house—you still made the same admission when you came to church. "We have not loved you with our whole heart; we have not loved our neighbors as ourselves. We are truly sorry and we humbly repent." Thus far, life had shown me that being sorry is one thing, and truly repenting is a whole other step; but maybe by coupling them in a sentence, making it sound almost easy, we inch closer to shaving off some of our bad habits. Were bad habits sometimes the same as sins? I wasn't sure. *OK, this week I really will try harder not to blab so much during meals and let other family members' topics emerge gradually in the space I leave.*

Suddenly, Rob lifted his arms, and thus the mood, by pronouncing, in a bold and bright voice, "Almighty God have mercy on you; forgive you all your sins!" I was unnerved by this display of extraterrestrial powers in the man I slept with. How could he release everybody so optimistically, based on just those few moments of bowed heads? At home, in truth, he rarely showed this degree of looking on the bright side, often letting one bit of bad news start a long list of things that were generally wrong. And if people thought he really *could* do this, did they look at him as some kind of wizard, able to send them back to Kansas with a few clicks of the red heels? And then I caught myself: it need not matter *how* they looked at him if the goal of this whole service was for people to rededicate themselves to what was most essential in leading a good and moral life.

I had a little chat with myself at this point. *No, Polly, don't get carried away. People can't stay down on their knees all day, feeling bad; he is just moving them forward, helping them feel renewed, encouraging a fresh start. Just go ahead and take him up on his offer, or at least act as if you are. It's not as if you are without your own transgressions; if you don't buy that he can wash them away but prefer to think that this is your own row to hoe, well then, so be it.*

My kids pushed the cushioned bar back underneath the next pew, stood up, and stretched. Willie grabbed Henry in a mock headlock, Cora put her hands on her shoulders and twisted one way and then the other. Sins, whatever they amounted to in our particular family, were now officially in the rearview mirror.

The buoyant mood continued with the friendliest part of the service, the time when we could practice doing better in the upcoming week with our neighbors at home and colleagues at work, by greeting each other warmly, right here. Since I have always been a flaming extrovert, this minute or so of hand grasping and smiling came very easily to me. I was keen to make contact with everyone in a radius around me, and to show my very sunniest—albeit still not religious—self. The general rule here, unlike in some other denominations, was to keep the contact restrained—no jumping or laughing or hollering. A moment of simple eye contact with always the single word utterance of "peace" was all that was needed. Here's where I got a little hung up, though; going for the same unobjectionable goal was all well and good, but I liked a little individual zest in my greetings, instead of just offering the company line. So when I turned to the sixty-something woman I barely knew behind me, I said instead, "Peace—and that is some beautiful scarf you're wearing." To her husband, I offered, "Hello, nice to meet you," even though we weren't really fully meeting. It was my way of not following the rules exactly, giving myself a little breathing room. When I saw the involved-in-everything-church woman ahead of me leave her pew entirely to go seek out specific friends across the aisle, I wondered whether I should do the same—maybe go and plant a kiss on Rob's cheek, noticeably, up front. I quickly reeled that thought back in, staying with our children, where I belonged. He was in a unique orbit.

Chapter 30

Both Sides Now

"Good game, good game, good game, good game."

Two lines of sweaty, lanky, teenage boys walked past one another, speaking softly in the traditional way, hitting palms in a gesture of goodwill, or at least acceptance, at the end of the game. This, too, was a kind of ritual, an exchange of peace.

The fortresslike building where I worked as a school-to-career coordinator was one of the large public high schools in Springfield, sitting just a few blocks up from the heart of downtown. It took a full ten minutes to walk from the guidance office, where my office was, down long hallways and over a windowed bridge to get to the gym. In the huge parking lot in the back, I could see kids slamming car doors and shouting to each other, pumping themselves up for the game. When I arrived in the brightly lit gym to see the home team, almost all Black and Hispanic, take on my son's almost all-white team, the squads were warming up on both ends of the court to a loud R & B mix tape.

My loyalty was divided, and I didn't know whether to sit with a few of my colleagues, or my fellow parent friends. I had allies in both camps, and I knew most of the players on both teams. The fact that I had a son out there did not at all cancel out my cheering for the young men on the opposing side, some of whom had been knocking on my door asking for help finding an internship or a job, shyly unsure of which skills exactly they had accumulated during their sixteen years.

Though "my" school had traditionally been considered the stronger team based on experience from the past decade, as this game progressed the score teetered back and forth. Each time Willie knelt next to the scorers' table before entering the game, I beamed. Looking out over the whole scene, I understood that these were *all our kids*, and that this particular one had been mine, especially, since birth. He had worked hard for these chances, and now here they were. All that devoted reading of *Guard Play* on his bed, the dribbling drills, the looking up to the UConn players who had towered over him—it all came to a kind of fruition right here, whatever his stats might show. To stay right on his man, he needed to be as focused as he could be. Sometimes it wasn't enough—in a flash there was a turnover, or a missed shot and no offensive rebound—but sometimes, when he took a shot from the corner, *swish* was his sweet reward.

When I reached the small cluster of parents by climbing up the long planks, I enjoyed saying, "Hi everybody, nice to see you all here." With family members and friends dotting the bleachers on both sides, I felt a wave of Rob's "koinonia"—that divinity school term he explained to me after a UConn Huskies game some years before—sweep over me. We were partaking in something meaningful together. Though it wasn't exactly reverence, or worship, or prayer (I knew those things occurred in another league), it still felt like some kind of shared reaching for goodness, for unity. Despite being a spectator rather than a player, despite being on the margins, I felt fully involved, quaffing down the squeaking sneakers, the shouts for passes with long arms in the air, the sweaty mixing it up of races, the hoarse cheering.

It was almost as if the whole scene happened at a communion rail.

Chapter 31

Holy Communion for Almost Everyone

That part of the service (it came around every time) when I struggled most with how to behave, what to do, whether to fit in, was about to begin. Gym bleachers are not made for comfort, but for me, compared to church pews during communion, they might as well have plush, velvet cushions. This was the time when I felt most sharply the reality of being different from the rest of my family; the time when I wondered whether, years ago, I could have better anticipated this repeated rhythm, like a regular heartbeat just slightly outside of my own body, and made a better plan.

My husband has always relished this segment of the service perhaps more than any other. The setting of the table, followed by a meal of bread and wine shared with many others reminds him why he follows Jesus, and why he guides others to do the same.

Before my older brothers left home for college, we came together for supper at a big, round, oak table—a gift from former neighbors whom I had never known. Sitting cozily in the corner of the couch reading a book, I'd hear a singsong, "Polly, can you please set the table, and add one more place?" When my mother made spaghetti, there was always enough for a friend—Joe or Bill or Hank or Jeff—to sit down with us, often after a raucous game of basketball out by the shed. The extra kid, who often had to duck entering the kitchen, came in somewhat sheepishly, trying to tuck in a flannel shirt. Plates were quickly emptied and then filled again, and laughter and stories, often at someone's expense, filled the air. My brother Sandy would lean back riskily in his orange-cushioned chair, with hands pressed to the table, until he was admonished not to. I was mostly quiet, hoping that more experience out in the world, more escapades, maybe even some close scrapes with the law would eventually enable *me* to hold forth in the way that these big guys did. In our house, mealtime was far from reverential; it was a time when you got to entertain others and be entertained.

During the preparation of the church table, the congregation sang together a few lines that mysteriously swept me up every time: "Holy, holy, holy Lord, God of power and might, heaven and earth are full of your glory." A few people stood as if in a trance, hands out, and watching them I could believe that they were truly making contact with a higher power. I was not, but I was also not immune to the feeling, prompted by the music, that all of the goodness of the world was rushing in to buoy us, to soothe our ills at least temporarily, to provide a glimpse of a bright future, feelings akin to what I experienced when listening to Mozart—moved by beauty.

I changed my gaze, from the pews all around the church to the one the kids and I occupied. As if by magic, they'd grown once again. Willie was almost done with high school now, inching closer to leaving home and this pew; Cora was a sophomore, with longer hair, taller stature, an expanding social life and Drivers' Ed.; Henry had also shot up recently, beginning to shed his little boy look while gaining a fuller sense of who he wanted to be, distinct from each of his siblings.

The preamble to the moment when people line up for the wafer and wine is extensive, every single Sunday, with a summarized retelling of the ancient and miraculous story of Jesus's resurrection. I know that my husband never gets tired of retelling the story, never thinks anything such as, "This is getting a little repetitive; maybe I'll change it up a bit," because the drama, like some kind of mesmerizing fountain, provides a constant flow of sustenance and renewal to him. He has taught me the Greek word "anamnesis,"—describing how time collapses, with the ancient past merging with the present and on into the far future, and how this moment can provide a foretaste of the heavenly banquet, when people of all stripes will come together in unity.

Loving someone, really loving someone, I have come to understand, means trying to imagine what it feels like inside that person's skin; to have that person's same beating heart. To imagine why believing certain things makes life worth living.

"All baptized Christians are welcome to receive Communion," Rob said, standing behind the altar. But I am not a baptized Christian, first because my parents didn't make me one, and then, thirty-three years later, because I declined to become one despite Rob's urging in the months leading up to our wedding. Standing there on that morning, I was struck by this stark fact once again. Had the whole Charles Stuart drama not unfolded the way it did during that winter, giving me that one indelible nightmare, maybe I would have worked up the nerve, or the devotion, to make the leap into Rob's faith with something like conviction. But, more likely, that dream had served as a kind of *ping*, reminding me, even in its exaggerated way, that I—and we, ultimately, would be better off if I kept a firm hold of my genuine self.

I could still go up there and cross my arms for the blessing; some Sundays, I did. Today, however, something in me asked to stay put.

The ushers began to make their way up the aisles along the pews, pausing at each one to indicate that the occupants could rise and head to the altar. My kids waited patiently, knowing they were about to partake, glancing at me but not asking directly what I would do. For a brief moment, I wavered, thinking that my desire to stay with them would win out. Suddenly, Joe Strummer and the other four members of The Clash were pushing their way to get next to me, singing right in my ear one of Rob's favorite songs, about staying or going.

Lost in thought, I didn't notice the woman at the end of our pew, near the wall, needing to get out: "Are you going?" she asked me, point blank. "Oh no," I said, "but my children are!" as if this covered us all, made us a legitimate clergy family. They all four exited together, and I sank back, with the whole hard bench to myself now. I might as well have been wearing a sign that said, "Yep, that's right, I'm a little different!!" Nobody was staring at me, although I couldn't be positive in this large space, with my head down; but I felt my face flush anyway. I was exposed on a crag, and the wind was blowing all around me. I tested my foothold and it was secure; the grasp of one hand slipped momentarily, and I quickly caught the next available slight protrusion on the rock face, heart pounding. *Just hold on.*

I saw my kids make their way to the altar, kneel down in front of the rail, and await their father's approach. He leaned down to them, one by one. I was the absent parent, while they had an intimate moment together. I was in a kind of exile, but at the same time, I was also right in my own skin, fully present.

Miraculously, even from my distance away, I saw a toddler's sneakers light up, unbeknown to him or anyone else, at the very moment that he received his wafer. *No, couldn't be.*

When I let myself look around a bit, I noticed a handful of other people who also weren't rising. Some of them might have been one-time guests; I didn't know. And I also noticed no one at all looking at me. Then I realized that my kids' jackets were still spread out on both sides of me, promising that I wouldn't have to be alone for long.

When they did come back, we reached for our blue hymnals together and launched into "Lift High the Cross," a song with so much gusto that it could be a battle cry for weary soldiers or a sideline cheer for athletes' flagging spirits. Just like a satisfying book with a closing that circles back to its opening, the service concluded on the same robust note with which it began. If you go the way of Jesus, you cannot help but succeed in the way that most matters. Death will come, but death can be overcome!

I didn't know about that, but I'd go along with it for now. Why quibble when we were about to go back to our regular lives, when my kids would once again be in the car with me, poking each other and asking me to turn up the throbbing music? This other music, soon to surround us, would be only about the pressing urges of the living.

Willie leaned toward me during the final verse of the hymn. "Can we please skip coffee hour and just head home? I have a lot of homework." And Cora added, "Yes, please—I have to take a shower because it's *so dusty* in here, and Hannah's coming over." Henry, now a sixth-grader with several stage productions under his belt, belted out the hymn, with no earthly requests.

Chapter 32

He Isn't—Wait, He Is—Here at Lacrosse

The sun was beating down on the parched fields, and there wasn't even a wisp of a breeze to make spectating without a brimmed hat a reasonable option. The players had it worse, guzzling Gatorade each time a coach waved them in. Relieved from duty, they tossed sticks down on the ground, grabbed a drink, and then lay spread-eagle on their backs for a few moments of not even caring how their replacements would fare, before getting up to bark encouragement.

It was early July, about a month after the regular high school lacrosse season had ended. Cora, who was picking up skills quickly in this sport and discovering that she liked it just as much as ice hockey, had been recommended by her coach to join a Western Massachusetts team that provided *more* lacrosse. Rob had, again, reluctantly agreed; I knew the driving would fall on my plate. On this particular day, we were at a one-day tournament that took place at a boarding school campus, about an hour's drive from home. Henry, having no scheduled activities of his own and loving most any time he got with his sister, decided to ride along.

On the walk over to the fields—there were at least four of them, with half-hour games going on concurrently—we first had to pass a kind of marketplace. Sports equipment companies, sniffing profits, had set up white tents offering racks of Under Armour jerseys, and the latest model Brine sticks; at a separate table, they sold must-have T-shirts with the name of this tournament emblazoned in teal and pink on them; a playlist of Top 40 hits blasted from a set of tall speakers, providing an atmosphere of perpetual pump-up. It was an odd time of year to be strolling around the grounds of this elite private school, known more for its crisp fall days or blossoming spring ones, but most of the families here today were not new to this kind of scene; they had their credit cards at the ready, waving to people they'd met at past tournaments.

I was among them, part of this body of suburban adults with enough leisure time on this Saturday to stay all day, with my stash of Capri Suns and sandwiches and younger child in tow. But I was also relieved that my husband wasn't here, had no interest in being here, because I knew how much he would hate the hypercompetitive, consumerist bent. A hunk of me hated that part, too, resisted throwing my chips in with this crowd, this scene oozing privilege. But another part of me maintained that the *sport itself*—the running, the striving, the grabbing the balls out of the air and off the ground, the girl harmony—was still pure and beautiful, even unassailable. You couldn't separate it out easily, that's all.

Increasingly, this was how it was for me as a sports-mom-slash-clergy-spouse: I ran eagerly toward whatever the game was, seeing a promise there; when I arrived, sometimes the glow was as bright and bountiful as I'd hoped, and sometimes, like when the reception gets tangled on a television screen, it went fuzzy in my head. And I wasn't even sure anymore whether it was just me, or Rob's voice in me, or the whole blasted church, or maybe *part* of the church that was responsible.

What I knew for certain was that all the strands were getting more tangled inside me.

During a break in between games for Cora's team, when the girls got to flop down in clusters under the team tent, Henry and I headed over the endless green lawn to the empty tennis courts. That was *his* sport, and mine, and I made sure to bring our racquets and balls so we would not be completely beholden to the Lacrosse Machine all day. We played for a little while—he with the ease and grace he'd been gaining in weekly clinics, applying a topspin that still eluded me—until the heat began to assert its pounding quality, making running for the balls increasingly ridiculous.

It was too soon to go back to the field; we needed something else to pass the time.

I knew what. "C'mon Henry, let's go see the chapel."

If I'd spent decades with a guy who didn't spend much of his time in houses of worship, this plan probably wouldn't have occurred to me. Even as I said it, I was feeling again the merging quality of marriage, how elements of each individual gradually seep into the other, and vice versa. Especially when he wasn't physically with me, I felt the urge to do something *Rob-like*, anticipating the pleasure of telling him about the visit, partly; but also genuinely interested in entering the chapel myself, feeling a pull there, acknowledging the palpable effects of two decades of our union.

On this campus, the chapel was impossible to miss. Designed by the architect Henry Vaughan, who had among his credits the National Cathedral in Washington, DC, it was a perfect example of the Gothic Revival style that had its heyday in the late nineteenth century around New England. Reaching several stories high, the main tower of the chapel might as well have spelled out the words "highly distinguished," because it conjured all of the heft of the British Empire.

As we walked into the hushed space, I felt the air cool immediately. Referees' horns were still blasting in the distance, and an occasional shriek of "I'm open!" or "Oh YEAH!" reached my ears, but I was in a different arena now. Immediately ahead of us, carved in the stone, were a series of memorials commemorating alumni who had died in the two world wars. They, too, must have once played games right out there, whooping for joy and tackling each other. We walked slowly past each memorial, my son in his turquoise T-shirt and tan shorts that looked so bright against the unremittingly gray backdrop of deeply carved names, some including a "Henry" or a "Robert."

We moved past the rows of pews toward the altar in front, gazing up at the stained glass windows on either side as we went. The rood was a simple, restrained cross, without the suffering body of Jesus. The place exuded calmness. I heard Rob's voice gently reminding me what was being offered to us in this setting. "Rest in your own thoughts, whatever they are. Find refreshment here." Having arrived at the front, Henry had already taken his fill and was watching me to see how long I wanted to stay. "Done yet, Mom?" Although my lingering, aside from offering a reprieve from the glaring sun, didn't make sense, I felt myself being taken in. What was surrounding me here was definitely more *substantial* than anything happening on a lacrosse field. Here, there was history, heft. All that stuff for sale out there, the relentless focus on getting in the limelight, getting recruited, advancing—what did all of it amount to, anyway? It was embarrassing to be part of it. Sports had gone haywire, while church maintained its own decency, solidity.

Rob and what he stood for, *that* must be where I needed to be. There was still time, even for me, to learn how to pray, to study.

Almost immediately after floating here, though, I caught myself. It wasn't so simple. I knew that there really was no such stark dichotomy between the two realms; it was a false setup in my head. None of what I didn't like about this kind of summer exhibition day marred the whole legitimate experience of playing a sport. It was, for our daughter, all about developing skills, striving, bringing together a community with school spirit, learning how to lead, accepting defeat along with victory. We had lived it, and it was good. Standing in that chapel, I felt a beneficent aura, but the feeling didn't ensure that everything that had ever happened here, or in every other church, had always been so. I knew better. Just about nothing was completely pure, except maybe love.

I was carrying Rob's spirit with me; I was infused with it. I did not, however, need to become *exactly who he was*. That would be a kind of self-collapse.

A horn blew outside, signaling the end of another game. Cora and her teammates were probably getting up from their shady spots, refilling their water bottles, and moving toward their next assigned field.

"OK, Henry, I'm ready. They must be getting close to being done out there." We headed back outside. I asked Henry to stand in front of the towering edifice so I could snap one picture, eager to show Rob later. He groaned but then put his hands on his hips and struck a pose.

While I was disassembling dichotomies, there was one more that had to tumble. I realized that I didn't need sports to be my *alternative* religion. All the games I'd played, that my brothers had played, that my kids were now playing; all the horseback rides I'd taken; and toss in the rows and bike rides and cross-country ski excursions Rob had himself enjoyed—they didn't have to represent anything more than *what they actually were*. They didn't have to take on a solemn dimension of significance. Indeed, forcing sports to wear some cloak of meaning would be a surefire way to take the fun and grace and air itself right out of what had always been just part of the atmosphere I grew up breathing. Sports were no specific entity, personality; not a power to be obeyed or wrestled with; not a creed that we needed to buy into or reject. This was not an all-or-nothing proposition. No, the truth was that sports had always just *gone hand in hand* with the pleasures and pains of growing up and being human. This was enough; it was plenty.

Crossing the lawn again toward the games, I saw a few kids chasing each other and tumbling around on the grass, running freely and whooping it up. Some parents were packing up now, carrying their chairs and coolers, and scanning the area to spot the younger siblings whom they now needed to collect. They were dismissing themselves, after a long day of sidelines duty. Suddenly, I was so eager to find my daughter that I started trotting, wondering if I'd missed her last few rushes up the field.

Hey, Rob, you still here? I asked only myself, seeking reassurance that he was sticking with his family, making the shift in locations, jarring as it might feel. "C'mon—chapel was nice; I'm glad I had the idea to go over. But let's not miss watching our girl *play*. Lacrosse is just a game, sure, but it's a beautiful game, and she's so good out there."

I didn't wait to see whether or not he nodded; I hoped so, fervently.

Either way, though, I wasn't going to stop.

Chapter 33

The Dismissal

"Go in peace to love and serve the Lord," Rob said. "Let not everything that has just happened here evaporate when you walk out that door, lest you think that you're leaving God here in church, a common mistake. Remember that you're actually going to be God's servants all week long."

I imagined that, as we all walked out, each one of us had a kind of reminder bubble, like a giant Post-it, over our heads. I could imagine serving somebody, like Bob Dylan sang about, if the identity of this authority were not still cloaked in such mystery. The best I'd be able to do would be to sniff out what was just and right and true and try to heed it, hoping not to get in my own way in the process. If the Lord were to show up for real, say maybe on a late Tuesday afternoon when I'm walking Zeke and gazing at a salmon-colored sky, I hope I'd see the signs. But on every late Tuesday afternoon I've lived through so far, the salmon-colored sky has shone, from everything I could tell, all on its own.

"I'll just be a minute," I said to Willie. "I want to see Theresa and Edith quickly, because this is my only chance." He threw his head back and said, "With you, Mom, there's no seeing them quickly, but fine, I'll be in the car." Cora and Henry followed him, having had enough of church. After all, they did everything they were supposed to do. I had gotten through the hard part, the lonely part—now came my reward: schmoozing. Give me a roomful of people to work and no specific questions about faith, and I push the "flourish" button.

I headed for the Connector—now free of the flapping wings of the Chorus—and, not seeing my soul sisters right away, bided my time and started chatting with an older couple whose names I couldn't recall, their eyes twinkling in unison. "How are you, Polly? So nice to see you." Getting to the coffee urn and grabbing a raspberry square would have to wait.

Emily Dickinson, my friend perpetually around the corner, might be fine being "Nobody," but I believed, right then anyway, that I was actually "Somebody," and I strove to make the most of my time in this room. Jane and Bill—I saw the nametags now—most likely couldn't tell that I was split in half, with part of me in, part of me out. But once again church was over, and this little light of mine, I was gonna let it shine.

Rob appeared, having stood at the back of the church, shaking hands and conversing with each parishioner in the doorway. He was tired, but he would stay for a while longer, drawing on the stamina that an introvert must have for these weekly occasions. He glanced over to me, glad I was here now, and glad (I counted on this) that he'd see me later, alone. Suddenly I realized that, at certain times, I wanted to be *his* patch of shade and jug of Gatorade, and at certain other times, I wanted him to be *mine*. It was what we both had signed up for, with or without God as our witness.

Chapter 34

Into the Labyrinth

It wasn't unusual for us to get mail from the church, but this particular April letter was out of the ordinary. "The garden tour subcommittee met last week. We have made a number of decisions and have left some up to you. We hope that you will be willing to sell tickets at your garden on the day of the tour."

With a full-time job, three children, and a big dog, I still hadn't cleaned out my perennial beds from the winter, much less invited anyone over to see them. So I looked at Rob with suspicion; he mumbled something like "Oh that—don't worry about it; I've got it covered." He always kept much of his church business to himself, as befitted his profession, but this time I really wondered what he was up to because it apparently involved our home. Willie would be graduating from high school in early June, I was teaching an hour away; we were hosting something the next weekend. How on earth would we be readying our place for streams of people looking to admire flowers?

Pondering how best to prepare for the tour event, Rob didn't say anything like, "What would you think if I started making a labyrinth down below the stone wall?" He just started disappearing into our backwoods every evening with the tractor to clear brush and then haul rocks. And were there ever rocks. It was a little like the miracle of the loaves and fishes, with enough food appearing to feed all the masses. He kept finding just the rocks he needed, in a variety of piles that seemed to appear by magic, to make the twelve very large concentric circles. I happened to see a page he'd printed out from a Chartres Cathedral website that must have given him a guide for the overall design. It wasn't the usual picture of the famous soaring structure, but rather something looking more like coiled up intestines—almost circular—with a distinct center.

Once I got over the initial surprise, which in fact wasn't actually surprise because I had learned not to expect consultations about everything, I began to feel prideful. The innards of Chartres would soon be out my kitchen window! I hadn't made it there when I'd been in France years ago; now I was about to get another chance. He didn't ask me to lift a finger, preferring to do the whole thing himself. As the days went by, I could see that the project was giving him a new zest for life, a kind of post-Easter lift. Designing and building a labyrinth enabled him to do something multidimensional, perfectly suited to who he was. He could be alone in the woods working in the physical, spiritual, and artistic realms, all at the same time. Our aptly named German Shepherd mix, Rocky prowled around while Rob worked, chasing moles when they appeared. Doing the evening dishes, I could make out the two figures as the light faded.

Eventually, Rob did get some help, hiring a teenager (Willie was occupied) for a few days of rock hauling, followed by a friend from church who came to put in the final turns with him. On the evening before the garden tour, Rob was out there still moving stones. Meanwhile, I fretted about having a visitor book and maybe a vase of flowers in place for the people who were about to come, wanting us to be presentable for guests. That was who *I* was—caring most about being hospitable. My husband, on the other hand, told me it didn't even matter to him whether there were any visitors at all; the deadline of the tour really just gave him a reason to complete his chef d'oeuvre.

Because he had an all-day meeting on that Saturday, he had arranged for someone else to be an official greeter in the morning. As usual, I needed to drive our daughter to a lacrosse field an hour away for a summer team practice. By that afternoon, our combined way of life—one big part religion, another considerable chunk sports—was highlighted again. While I was back home welcoming walkers, my mind was partly on the logistics of getting to the state championship baseball game that our high school team was playing that same evening. It would be in a different direction from the lacrosse field from that morning. I had no time to go in circles; that was for sure.

Once the garden tour day was over, I got to thinking about the different kinds of trips people take and what they are seeking. Our new labyrinth provided an obvious metaphor: people who walked it were traveling spiritually, hoping for some kind of renewal without going geographically far at all. It provided an opportunity for an inward journey, for reaching a kind of center of the soul. When I went to the library to do some research, I found that anybody writing about labyrinths first establishes how they are different from mazes. While a maze confounds you with different choices, some of which will lead to dead ends, a labyrinth takes you gently around a middle place that you always keep in sight as a goal. And the going back *out* is just as important as the going *in*. Depending on the walker's state of mind, a maze can be exciting and challenging, or just claustrophobic; a labyrinth can be soothing and transforming, or just monotonous. Although it is often said that the Greek hero Theseus entered a labyrinth to find and kill the Minotaur, it really must have been a maze; otherwise he wouldn't have needed Ariadne's magic spool of thread to get out.

Willie had not been around to help during construction because of a good old-fashioned road trip. He and a friend headed south all the way to the Gulf of Mexico, taking our van; they were gone for two weeks. Their trip was perfect for two guys who had just collected their high school diplomas: they left with a sense of adventure and only some idea where they were going and who would take them in along the way. In one sense they were doing the opposite of walking through a series of rings—going, as they were, from point A to point B every day—but their easy self-confidence when they returned and pulled in the driveway left no doubt that the journey had lifted them up spiritually. They had done it all themselves. Instead of going in and then coming out again like labyrinth walkers, they had gone *out* and come back *in*. Our son's going off to college in the fall would just be a larger version of this, I realized, still not really wanting to confront his imminent departure.

And then there is the kind of traveling that young dogs like to do. Around the time that my husband was making the labyrinth, our Rocky had discovered the thrill of fetching a tennis ball—over and over and over again. When I looked out the window during construction, I saw Rob involved in a new ritual: place a rock, throw the ball; place a rock, throw the ball. If the labyrinth-maker was driven to create a spiritual oasis, the labyrinth-maker's dog was just as obsessed with his version of back-and-forth. What worked for *him* was a frantic "Got to get there!" dash; let others have their meditative one-foot-in-front-of-the-other walks.

As for me, I took my time approaching the labyrinth, as if it were a stranger I wasn't sure how to meet. I walked by it every day with Rocky and appreciated the serenity of the place, but I didn't see a pressing need to follow the path all the way in. Well acquainted with my own persistent uneasiness about religion, I was nervous that I wouldn't know how to *feel* when I reached the center bench. Was I supposed to pray there? What if I felt nothing? Would there be something wrong with me?

Finally, on one midsummer Sunday morning, I decided it was time to take the plunge. Before he went off to church, my husband left me *The Book of Common Prayer* with a bookmark at Psalm 139. So now I at least had something to read when I stopped walking. I thought of my friend Emily Dickinson, who proclaimed, "Some keep the Sabbath going to Church / I keep it, staying at Home / With a Bobolink for a Chorister / And an Orchard, for a Dome." The path in was very welcoming, and how lovely it was to find only one way to go. Having many choices can be wonderful, but also sometimes daunting. Just a walk down the cereal aisle in the grocery store could leave me flummoxed, and I was often my own worst enemy when I had the rare gift of free time at home—I started doing one thing and then immediately thought of something *else* that I was neglecting. So following a route laid out by someone else felt like being on vacation. I thought of my mother, who used to say, "I'm just on a conveyer belt!" And finally, I could fully appreciate what my husband had done; it was intricate and huge at the same time. How he managed to make the whole thing flow in every which way, I'll never know. I did see why the older people from church had been concerned about the roots underfoot, because there were plenty of them, but they added to the labyrinth's natural beauty. In fact, the whole area was thoroughly *earthy*, with just a suggestion of the celestial.

When I reached the bench and read the psalm, about the constancy of God's presence, I tried not to judge myself as a labyrinth-walker too much. This time, it was enough just to have made it into the center to join the part of my husband that he had left for me there.

PART VI
SPUTTERING, THEN RIDING

Chapter 35

It's a Calling, Again

One October day, I came downstairs early to see, along with the usual spread of kids' homework from the night before on the dining room table, a glossy publication featuring a cathedral with soaring towers; the print identified a West Coast location. Without even asking I knew: Rob was being wooed. The sunlight that filtered through the canopy of trees down into the labyrinth gave a beautiful, mottled look. Rob was upstairs reading *The Daily Office*, crinkling the pages, with a mug of coffee beside him. I was about to glance at the calendar that helped me preside over the kids' multicolored schedules; Rocky went out and came back in, just as usual. But change was afoot. The entire Church was out there, like a multilimbed animal—watching, breathing, praying, and creating niches all along its sinews for clergy who were contemplating moving on.

One of them was right upstairs, his motionlessness at that moment only a mirage.

Filling my coffee cup and noticing how the fluttering leaves had taken a serious turn to orange, I brought the colorful brochure back upstairs with me, Rocky padding behind. I didn't need to say anything for Rob to notice what I was holding. "Oh, I thought you'd be interested in that—it just came yesterday. I didn't request it or anything. They sent it to me because I guess they must have seen my profile."

He tried to keep his attention on the little black book, turning another crinkly page, but he could see that I was still standing there, wanting more explanation.

Feeling the cool wood floor under my bare feet, I remembered that he had in fact told me some weeks before how he wanted to spruce up whatever it was I'd never seen in the computer called a "profile" so that he might be ready to at least consider other positions. The topic had started coming up the closer we got to Willie heading to college, especially since my run with the public schools in Springfield was coming to a close. "I really need to *advance*," I'd heard him say, almost under his breath, as he was putting the clips in the back of his collar. He felt the weight of supporting the family like a winter cloak over his shoulders, and I couldn't exactly argue that it was, instead, a light summer jacket. Supporting a family was serious business, and I'd been a kind of in-and-out breadwinner. He also needed me to understand how his motivation to make another change, a geographical change, sprang from a place of wanting to be a better provider, not from a different psychic place of wanting to attain a higher ecclesiastical status for himself.

We both knew, however, that these outcomes would go hand in hand. Just as he had experienced, in the last place, an outgrowing that pinched him, nudged him on toward a larger congregation, here he was feeling a similar thing, except this time the next step would more likely take us to a substantially different realm, a higher perch with a wider panorama.

He was taking off his glasses now, putting down the book, looking right at me. "So maybe it's a good time to talk about the difference between being a dean of a cathedral and being a bishop of a diocese."

I felt a little bit like a recipient of a lesson on the game of chess, a game I had never really tackled, preferring to stick to placing the smooth letter tiles on the Scrabble board as my grandmothers had done.

"OK, hit me up on that."

I learned that a cathedral is often a kind of megachurch and that, along with the spire reaching high and higher, it can house a wide variety of programs that broaden the religious mission enough to have a significant impact on many areas of life in the region. A dean, chosen by a search committee, is often in charge of a large staff who work in one place. A bishop, on the other hand, presides over all the Episcopal churches in a certain geographical area, often a whole state. A bit like a school superintendent supervises a cluster of schools, except with many more branches. The bishop oversees what goes on in churches, and how the clergy are doing—both supporting them and, when necessary, disciplining them. The second part would be harder, presumably, than the first. Bishops are not appointed but are elected by a combination of clergy and lay people (also called "the laity," a slightly more graceful term that nonetheless still can bring to my mind a group of hens).

"Which one would you rather be?" I asked, trying to imagine what it would feel like to believe that either position was within reach. While Rob's career path had been like an escalator, moving steadily upward, mine had resembled a jagged line on a graph: have a child, stay at home, move, venture out part time in a grant-funded job that ends as second child is born, seek new child care and new job, move, and so forth. I wasn't exactly knocking it out of the park in the building-a-resume (not a profile) department. Was I also *sacrificing* something? The familiar question buzzed around me like a bee, then disappeared.

"I like aspects of both," he said, willing to expand on this topic. "I'd like to put my name in for this position, if you're willing to consider moving across the country. It would be a plum job, definitely. The idea of living in a city really appeals to me, too. But it's probably a long shot. On the other hand, there are a couple of bishop openings right here in New England, and the decade I've spent at a big church might give me a pretty good chance at getting my name on a ballot for either of those."

He paused to read my expression. This was, twenty years into the marriage now, a familiar kind of moment. My insides were in a turbulent state as I tried to distinguish the strands of my various devotions: to him, to the kids, to our community, to the elements that most made me sing. But what was most salient, most illuminated in that moment, was my husband's desire to keep moving, exploring, and, yes, expanding within this other (to me) particular world he called home. And he still wanted, even needed, me to accompany him. Later, surely, there would be time for my own emotions to catch up. At this moment, there was a *whoosh* sensation.

"Wow, sounds like you—I mean we—should go for it and see what options we might have." I was reaching out to grab onto his arm now, not wanting to be left behind.

In the coming weeks, I was amazed both by the ease with which Rob was able to get excited about uprooting all of us and by the corresponding reluctance I felt about the prospect of another big change. Hadn't we been living in the same place? Raising the same children? Caring about the same people? How could he be propelled by so much forward momentum, making him fully obedient to the Holy Spirit? Or, contrarily, was there something askew inside *me*, something that drearily expected life to go on just as it always had, allowing for zero growth? I'd hesitated the last time before a move, fearing loss, but the gains eventually compensated.

The difference, more marked this time, was that he felt that he was moving *toward* something definite: thousands of Episcopalians, sprinkled throughout a whole city or maybe even a whole state, who needed a spiritual leader. He knew he could be that person, and he also knew that by assuming the role, he could support his family in a new place.

I did not want to hold him back. What kind of wife would do that? A drag of a wife, that's what kind. But, once again, I would be moving not to the definite but to the unknown. I knew who my friends were—a whole hard-earned second set since we'd left Connecticut—and they wouldn't be coming with me, wherever we were going. Furthermore, even though Cora would soon finish high school, Henry hadn't started that key chapter yet. How would the move affect *him*?

The truth was, no one knew. If my parents had told *me* when I was thirteen that we would be packing up, leaving our hilltop with the ring of pine trees and my best friend across the street, I would have thought that some kind of bewitching had gone on, that my real parents had been whisked away. Henry, however, somehow sensed that clinging to the familiar was not a wise response, no doubt partly because his siblings were already headed out. He would begin to chart his own course, too, knowing that whatever new destination his parents chose wouldn't affect him quite as much anymore.

Eventually, when the idea of a bold thrust toward a soaring steeple near the Pacific Ocean fizzled—"Do we really want to be that far away from family?"—opportunities for advancement elsewhere in New England began to appear. Rob and Henry got to hash out the possibilities of which bishop election to pursue, on a trip they took together to the rain forest of Costa Rica, made possible by the offer of a house by a quasi-parishioner. There, with monkeys swinging and screeching from the trees that touched the clouds, Henry was a sounding board for his father's deliberations. Why not New Hampshire? It wasn't far at all from where we lived now, but it would be different enough to seem like a new frontier. Plus, Rob had some family ties in the state. His father and sister had both gone to the University of New Hampshire, and his brother, Mike—now his only sibling—was firmly established at a boarding school there. As father and son took their zip-line rides through the fog, it was all becoming clearer.

When they returned and I heard the news, knowing that I just needed to give a simple thumbs-up for Rob's enthusiasm to maintain its healthy level, I felt no alarm bells going off, no reason to say, "But wait! How do we know what our quality of life will be like there? Whether we'll gain as much as we lose?" Though *I myself* felt no compelling reason to change everything, *his* drive was strong enough to send us both forward. We were a team, weren't we? Last time, I had dragged my feet some; this time, I could show him how I could rally, let go of my risk-averse self, be a believer in positive change.

"I'll put my name in, and we'll see what happens. This could be very exciting for both of us." He was so sure, or at least he wanted to sound that way.

Having spent much more time in Vermont than in New Hampshire in recent years, I checked in with my main associations with the state. The White Mountains—rugged and beautiful, were definitely a plus. The proximity of my alma mater was more of a mixed bag; I didn't see myself trotting back there all the time since my good college friends lived far away from campus. And it sure would help if I could stop hearing a certain segment of "Men of Dartmouth," the original before-coeducation version, playing in my head, over and over:

> They have the still North in their hearts
> The hill winds in their veins
> And the granite of New Hampshire
> In their muscles and their brains
> And the granite of New Hampshire
> In their muscles and their brains

The image was peculiar then, several years into coeducation, and it still felt peculiar now. Since when has anybody's mental capability been enhanced by rocks?

Before the actual bishop election took place, there would be a series of "Meet and Greets" around the state. At these, the three candidates would be on display for the local parishioners. The candidates would make some introductory remarks, and then there would be a question-and-answer period. Spouses were welcome to sit up front, near their partners, and be available for inquiries, should any arise.

This fact alone suggested that a spouse could tip the scale one way or the other. I wasn't sure if this was a compliment or an invitation to screw things up.

My now well-established stance on the edge of church life would surely come under scrutiny, and it probably wouldn't give my husband a boost, unless there were plenty of people out there who felt strongly that only the candidate themselves was in the running for the job. I supposed it was possible that some people hoped spouses would steer clear, or at least be firmly established in their own careers.

My own current teaching job made attending these sessions in another state logistically challenging, but I managed to make a few of them, often driving unfamiliar roads back to my school early the next morning. Given an opportunity to demonstrate support for my man, I would be foolish not to accept it even though I also knew I couldn't pretend to be someone I wasn't.

So instead of focusing on how I would *behave*, or the kind of aura I wanted to project, I focused more on what my outfits would be and how I would *look*. I might be a nonreligious clergy wife, but I sure as heck wanted to be adequately stylish. It was easier to work with my outside than my inside.

One of my dresses—bold yellow linen—ended up being a tad too short, requiring me to tug at it too much during the course of one particular evening. We were in an enormous, newly constructed classroom, with full-length windows, in a boarding school science building. Fortunately, Rob provided beautiful answers to all the questions asked him, moving easily from talking about the national condition of the Church ("We need to get beyond those sleep-inducing downward graphs") to showing his knowledge about the various regions of the state ("I really look forward to learning more about the particular issues facing the North Country"). He was emanating leadership qualities: humble, but demonstrating breadth of experience.

Toward the end of the session, when I was relaxing my posture a bit, a middle-aged woman stood up and directed a question my way: "I'd like to ask Reverend Hirschfeld's wife, 'How do *you* feel about the prospect of him becoming bishop, about uprooting your family and coming here?'" Suddenly, all eyes were on me, awaiting a read on the level of my enthusiasm. Everyone I saw was smiling, trusting that I knew how to put icing on this kind of cake. In my mind, I heard another woman say: *Oh, I can't wait! We are really excited about moving (again) and I just have a feeling this is the perfect diocese for my husband.* But I was not another woman, so something like this came out of my mouth: "Well, I'm not really sure yet, actually. Moving is not likely to be easy, especially since I have many good friends where we are. But I definitely think Rob will become a wonderful bishop and I support him in this venture completely."

In Jackson Hole, when Rob proposed, my words hadn't communicated an effusive "all in" spirit, and I was doing that same thing again now. It was as if I felt the need to guard something, not toss everything in the ring.

I sat back down, not positive if I was seeing the smiles persist or fade just a little bit. Afterward, I felt the words ringing in my ears, hoping fervently that my truth hadn't undercut his presentation, hadn't made anyone in that room see me as a liability in a slightly too short yellow linen dress.

Chapter 36

At the Consecration

I am ten years old, lying in a huge open field, feeling the scratchy grass beneath me, gazing up at a calm sky, drinking in the endless possibilities, all of them beneficent. It's delicious that no one knows where I am or what I'm doing. I take off my sneakers and wriggle my bare feet, spread my hair out behind me, extending my arms. Then, without warning, crows are swooping everywhere, squawking and making a ruckus. They're trying to zero in on something, creating a disturbance, causing alarm. It's not me they're after, but they mean to upset a balance that's been, after all, a kind of hoax. Clouds skirt across the sun, the sky darkens momentarily, and I realize that I need to absorb a new reality. It's not enough to just lie there, trustingly: I have to pay attention and guard what I hold most dear.

Never was there a moment when I was more keenly conscious of my identity as a clergy spouse than when I officially became a bishop's wife; to be precise, wife of the bishop who was assigned Number 1067 in the American Succession, going back to Samuel Seabury in 1784. In the state of New Hampshire, Rob's number is considerably smaller, and nice and neat: Ten. That's what his predecessor started calling him right away, with laughing eyes. But I would never know him by either of those numbers. In my life, he held another spot: one and only. And that,

I believe, is why his consecration on a humid day in August affected me differently than it did everyone else.

I wish I could say, as many attendees did, that the occasion was stunning in every way, but the truth of the matter was that almost precisely because it was made to be glorious for the attending public, it was something different for me, the wife. I was bathed in light, but at the same time, I felt in a shadowy place. No one handed me fear, but that's what I was holding.

Since the beginning of our marriage, I had attended a number of these transformational ceremonies in churches, bearing my special status awkwardly. I acquired the vocabulary all along the way, little by little, as if I were a grade school student. First Rob had been brought into "the diaconate" and then "the priesthood." Those were both called "ordinations." Moving forward in his post-ordained life, Rob needed to be "instituted" at each church where he'd served. That term struck me as particularly rich, suggesting that he became a kind of appliance, like an oven. In a way, I saw the parallel: he promised to provide sustenance, warmth, and meals to all of his congregants. His role was to be something like a hearth to others, forever giving.

Through all those previous ceremonies—in Hartford, New Haven, Storrs, Amherst—I was calm if not fully at ease; each one represented a major change in my husband's life with ripple effects out to me. For continuity's sake, or more likely because I didn't plan much ahead, I wore the same long, dark blue and lilac flowered dress with a belt repeatedly. It never needed ironing, and there was no risk of it clinging inappropriately, so it felt like my ally. Since the installations went in tandem with geographic moves, those services definitely helped to mark the beginning of each new chapter. In both cases, though, we were already unpacking boxes and meeting neighbors; the ceremony capped off the process rather than began it.

The "consecration," though, was on another scale. The name, first of all, indicated weeks, even months, beforehand that something big was coming down the ecclesiastical highway. Was it just a coincidence, I wondered along with the non-Episcopal friends I confided in, that it sounded so close to "coronation"? For just a moment when you hear the word, your mind might whisk you back to the days of Henry VIII, since he was in fact the bearded guy with the barrel chest and fancy clothes whose marital troubles caused the break with the Catholic Church in the first place. If my husband were to suddenly turn royal or even have some close new allegiance with the Crown, it would definitely cast a new aura over my life, too. But no, it wasn't quite that. Still, learning this new word with roots far back in history, being able to *really say it*, took me some practice. I was glad I wasn't alone in trying to look through the mist and make out the outline of whatever a "consecration" was.

I took some comfort in the fact that relatives and friends who weren't Episcopalian tried out other terms as they sought to congratulate us both before and afterward: inauguration, conflagration, Episcopal extravaganza. Whatever the event would turn out to be, "simple" would not be the way to describe it. The consecration committee met over the course of some months, zeroing in on every detail—readings, hymns, processions, dances, pronouncements, and more—for this culminating day.

New Hampshire Episcopalians from all over the state, some descending on Interstate 93 from tiny towns almost three hours away in the North Country, flocked to the Capitol Center for the Arts on the steamy Saturday afternoon. There's no cathedral in Concord, a mixed blessing according to my husband, so this big entertainment venue, where touring shows like "Salute to Leonard Cohen" and "Cabaret" fulfill their marquee billing, was the next best choice.

Our three kids had gone ahead of me, with Rob's parents, and after fussing with my appearance more than usual, I was just on the verge of being late. I drove myself downtown, feeling my heart beating at every stoplight.

Banging the car door shut and putting the strap of my purse over my head so it stayed securely in place, I started trotting down the cobblestone sidewalk in my heeled sandals, getting in a rhythm and convincing myself this was a perfectly appropriate way for an athletic, about-to-be-bishop's wife to conduct herself. Passing people I didn't know, keeping my head down, I came upon Kate, a dear college friend of mine who had traveled a couple of hours with her family to get here. She was gripping the hand of her middle child and looked up, moving aside so I could pass, and gave me a big smile. "Hey Pol—we made it! And you'd better get in there, right?" Apparently, she was not at all surprised that I was clickety-clackety hurrying rather than sedately walking.

Wow, Kate must be here partly because of her strong Catholic upbringing and partly out of loyalty to me, since she has barely had a chance to know Rob. She looked so calm, walking with her husband and kids, and here I was trying to get to mine, on the verge of screwing up even before the ceremony started. Right now, I continued in my head, she might really be wondering if I'm up to this whole challenge, fit and ready to walk through the portal to a new kind of life requiring me to conduct myself with more aplomb, to wear a greater sense of ease about all things Church.

Downstairs, I found clutches of clergy milling around on the spacious carpeted floor, gathering before the start of the procession that would head upstairs—adjusting each other's collars and robes, exchanging quips, and plainly glad to see one another. They were, at this point, still strangers to me. For them it must have felt something like the locker room before a game. Then a female voice over a microphone said, "OK, everybody, time to line up!" I knew this meant I'd better find my three kids, since they were the only category I belonged to here. There they were, across the room, in thick with a few adult friends who were parishioners from our old church.

"Oh, Polly, Henry has gotten so tall, I almost didn't recognize him!" one of them said when I approached.

I looked at Bob and Allison and Ray, and then at all the clergy I hadn't yet met—my husband's new flock, who didn't know our kids at all—and wondered how possible it was in life to keep hold of what you already had while reaching forward to grasp what was now being offered to you. Standing there, knowing that Rob was in this building and yet psychically somewhere very different at this same moment, his heart no doubt pounding with excitement, I felt like I was in a dream. I was being initiated into some kind of next chapter of spouse-land, crossing the border into a new country where I would need to make inroads somehow, find a path through the thicket.

Fortunately, I stood next to Willie while walking into the auditorium, and gained some strength from taking his arm. As we progressed down the aisle, everyone already in their seats smiled up at us. We must have looked wholesome to them, but I couldn't help wonder who exactly they were hoping we would be. Would they accept me no matter who I was, what I believed or didn't believe? Were we entering into some kind of contract that I hadn't actually signed? Not knowing yet, I tried to beam back. I'd had this feeling before, but this time it was intensified. The lights felt so bright and hot on my neck, and I wasn't sure whether to look restrained or ebullient.

And then, contrary to what I expected, there was my husband—taking a seat in the front row, right next to me and the kids, with his parents on the other side of him. He looked warmly at me and asked, "How're you doing?" I can't recall my answer. He held my hand for a time, in a way that was more about reassurance than about you-are-mine-and-I-am-yours. For a while, it felt as if we were almost at a regular church service, with lessons from the Gospel and hymns. Except that I wasn't used to Rob being next to me for those.

All of the other bishops—they were *already* bishops from other states—were lined up soberly on the stage, awaiting their turn to play an important part. They looked so established, in their long cassocks and special hats, called "mitres." They gazed down at us, clearly certain about what was to come and how our lives would change as a result. Their wives, meanwhile, sat behind us. These women smiled and gave me knowing glances. One or two had already taken me aside and said, "You'll likely feel overwhelmed, but I'll be here for you." They were kind in their reaching out, eager to share what they had learned. But I wasn't at all sure that I would fully become one of them, attending national meetings and traveling with my husband to other consecrations. I had gained a spot on their team; would I play?

At a certain point, Rob was summoned to the stage. He released my hand, looked tenderly at me, and then departed to walk up some steps. In a few moments, a man with an elaborate camera claimed the empty seat; he barely looked at me and said only, "Hello, I'll be here a while because I need to get the best view." He starting clicking, and I suddenly felt woozy. I wasn't sure if I was just witnessing this drama as a spectator or—yes, this was much more likely—if it would affect key elements of my life, such as the identity of the man who would be next to me, as long as we both would live.

On the stage, I saw Rob kneeling. He took solemn vows before a select group of bishops, and then many more bishops surrounded him until he emerged, apparently a bishop himself. If there were ever an illustration of being both the humble supplicant and the center of attention, this was surely it. "The presiding bishop presents to the people their new bishop!" There was thunderous applause. Whatever had happened in that huddle, the people believed that Rob was now anointed. The choreography was unmistakably ancient; there was a precise rulebook to follow and it was the very link to past generations that made the process so meaningful.

Joyful as the collective response was, I was acutely aware that mine was colored with something different. Indeed, as Rob disappeared underneath the robes of his new colleagues, who themselves looked like a flock of enormous birds, I felt him being seized by a tremendous and mysterious force. Perhaps I had lost him forever to something greater than whoever I was. This was not just my imagination; it was a real possibility.

What I was experiencing in that auditorium was no more important than what anyone else felt. They all had a perfect right to be thrilled by their new bishop; he would become their spiritual leader and serve them to his full capacity. I knew he had what it would surely take to help steer a buffeted Church through tumultuous times, to provide support and wisdom to clergy who often felt their own inner resources drained as they sought to help parishioners in need. Indeed, looking back on these moments, I feel some sense of shame. Why couldn't I, the person who had loved and lived with this man for all those years, feel only pride and joy oozing out of all of my pores? Was it flat-out selfish of me to feel also something akin to terror? When I lost sight of him completely, as he knelt down on the floor encircled by other bishops, I realized I didn't have any idea what this would mean for him and me, even how much *we* would still matter.

And then, instead of just spectating with my private turmoil, I was asked to enter into the proceedings. Late in the service, the kids and I each took a turn on stage to present the new bishop with various accoutrements, his tools of the trade: a crosier (shepherd's hook), a bishop's ring (he would wear this on his right hand), a prayer book, a cope (cape for a procession), and a chasuble (vestment to wear at the altar). Completing my walk to the front of the stage with two thousand pairs of eyes watching me, I gave Rob the bright red chasuble. Later, I would learn that it had oxblood orphreys (stripes)—symbolizing the juxtaposition of spiritual elation and suffering. I hadn't fully known this before, but by this point in our journey, I might have guessed.

When asked to greet us as a whole family, the audience provided enthusiastic and lengthy applause. How could they not love watching each of us demonstrate our support in this very tangible way, by helping him, piece by piece, before their very eyes, *become* their spiritual leader? We were put there to be an important part of the whole magic; but in some way, I also felt like a kind of prop. As I walked toward him and our kids under the bright lights with my offering, I tried to keep my balance. Surrounded by well-wishers, I had no obvious reason to be anxious about the future; everyone was pulling for us. But pulling where exactly?

At that moment, I felt a vibrating string of connection with spouses, mostly wives, throughout history who had joined their husbands on a stage or a podium or even an adjoining throne, and wondered silently how this public ascension would, going forward, affect their own intimate world together. It was similar to what I had felt in the car, about fifteen years earlier, on my way to meet the church ladies. People I'd never much considered before—Winnie Mandela, Barbara Bush, Prince Philip, Coretta King, Yoko Ono—they swooped into my head now. Surely they didn't like *all* of the limelight; they must have had pangs about fulfilling their roles, about sharing their spouses, about trying to preserve the strength of the original bond of marriage, which started out as inherently private. The neatly coiffed astronaut wives from the movie *The Right Stuff*, for instance, were thrust into the media spotlight because of the enormous risks their husbands took by heading up into space. Suddenly everyone wanted to know what they were thinking, how they were responding, how deep was their support for their men. Maybe there were correct answers. Annie Glenn and Betty Grissom each had their own emotional trajectories, but they needed to choose their words carefully, not let too much of their real selves shine through.

That could be risky.

After this climactic part of the ceremony was done, Rob stayed on the stage and the kids and I returned to our seats. The eager photographer was still there, snapping away. After the next, most solemn part of the service was over—the vows and the laying on of hands—and before the communion, the mood in the place shifted. An enormous blue curtain opened to reveal a group of about a half-dozen drummers, all Black men in colorful African garb. They sat, loose-limbed, pounding on their instruments and creating what sounded like the very pulse of life. Mixed in with them were an equal number of brightly clad Black women clapping their hands, waving their arms, and dancing without any rules. They radiated joy and abundance, providing a kind of antidote to the sober proceedings that we had just been through. If this was still New Hampshire, the land of gray granite rock faces, you'd hardly know it. Restraint was tossed away, and the stage reclaimed its identity as a center for the arts. Afterward, glancing at our programs again, we all sang a hymn in alternating English and South African verses: "We are marching in the light of God . . ." Faith had returned, with its own Christian solidity, but the strength and confidence of the verses had been won through the celebration of everything that was natural and good and free.

I gazed up at Rob in his seat of honor, imagining that his heart was close to bursting. He sang vigorously, looking down, but it was hard to tell what he was thinking. Part of me was soaring out into space; the performance had released something powerful at my core and now that was zooming on its own velocity. Another part of me, though, was weak, wobbly, and still feeling the residue of fear from the drama a few minutes before.

The life of a marriage, and the life of a family that grows from that marriage, is its own small universe. The Shakespeare comedies that I had written a thesis about in college portrayed this, over and over. How it all works can be about as mysterious as the world of ancient rituals.

In contrast to the sacred items that we gave Rob one at a time, the key elements of a union between two people remain intangible, and the dynamic is ever shifting. To maintain harmony, both individuals must pay attention to their partner as well as to the skies all around. Even though there may be no controlling outside weather, each person can practice tenderness where it most counts—in close.

After the service was over, we visited with the gaggle of good friends and relatives who came to the reception held on the ground floor of the house where we were staying, on a nearby campus. I busied myself with introductions: "David, this is my big brother Mike—he was a few years ahead of you at Wesleyan!" "Oh, Ben, have you and Tony already met? I forget." The thick, hot air together with the concentration of people I loved plus the absorption of the ceremony made for a potent mix, and soon I felt limp. After everyone left, Rob and I knew that we needed to be alone together for a while. Leaving our kids to have their own kind of rest, we put on our bathing suits, took our towels, and hiked down to a sparkling and mostly deserted pond for a swim.

As we walked in sandals down the dirt road, we kept mostly quiet, both sensing that the air was filled with the desire for reconnection. The trees were thick on either side of us, offering green-leaved relief and a quiet suggestion that not everything would change at once.

"That was pretty overwhelming, wasn't it?" I asked.

"Sure was," he said. "How're you doing?"

"Better now," I said, honestly. Then, trying to rally, I added, "Congratulations, Bishop! I hope it's OK to say how glad I am to have you back as regular Rob right now."

Seeing him dive off the dock with sinewy muscles and the shoulders I'd always craved was way better for me than watching him sit on a stage acquiring all those things with unfamiliar names.

Both of us knew that important things *would* in fact change. We were about to start a year living apart, for one thing, since we still needed to sell our home in Massachusetts and find a new one in New Hampshire. I would continue my teaching job while also making forays up north to house search, stay with him in his temporary abode, and occasionally dip into church services—each one with a different congregation—on weekends. There would inevitably be sources of stress, including the question mark around whether my *nonbeliever* status might bring some new scrutiny, as well as how and where we would manage to spend whatever hunks of time we would have together. Our joined life had always been the two of us plus the Church; now that same Church would be claiming more of him, sending him farther afield. We would need to be creative in finding ways to feed our own flame, or it might get snuffed out.

On this afternoon at least, we didn't want to dwell on those challenges. After such a ceremony, we needed to recognize that there had also been, some years back, a rite of marriage. And that, too, was sacred. When we got back to a silent house with the kids apparently conked out in their rooms, we made love as if our lives depended upon it. And in a way, they did.

Some years later, Rob told me that as we walked silently along that dirt road, he'd seen a snake slithering into the brush. Accustomed to them in his woodpiles, he still must have startled at the sight. "Why didn't you tell me?" I asked. He shrugged. "I didn't want to worry you," he said. Even I knew about the Garden of Eden.

The next day, the front-page photograph in the newspaper showed my husband, fully bedecked with that new tall cone hat soaring way above his head, reaching tenderly for my hand, with several smiling and clapping bishops behind us. It is painful for me to admit it, still, but in that photo I looked both timid and uncertain. This was the same woman who had responded to a *marriage proposal* from that same wonderful man, now bearing a distinguished title, with the ridiculously bland and thoroughly unromantic, "We'll take it in stages." Maybe she still needed to unleash more of her own passion, see where it could fly.

Chapter 37

The Last Time There

There wasn't anyone to talk to as I stood in the kitchen, looking over the slate blue countertops in the bare room. If I ventured to speak, though, or perhaps make one last call on the phone that I was about to unplug from the wall, my voice would have echoed through the empty house, an anachronism now that everyone was gone.

It was early June, the azaleas outside were bursting in color, the spring air was light and fresh; inside me, though, there was tumult.

The enormous moving truck had left for New Hampshire earlier that afternoon, and up at the light green Colonial on a quiet street—the fortieth place we'd looked at after the election—Rob and the kids were hauling in boxes, setting up beds, putting books on shelves, and reserving a room to be my new study. They sensed that it would be better for me to enter when the first visible steps toward creating a new home had already been taken. With each of their own transitions made smoother by one big new job and three different schools, they knew that I would be the one arriving with many question marks still fluttering around my heart.

Taking up temporary residence in an apartment close to his new office the previous September, Rob had physically and mentally moved months before; he was impatiently awaiting the house sale. I stayed in Shutesbury, carrying out a teaching job and returning to a dog with wagging tail each day. Carefully staged for viewing, the brick red, squared-up place with a wide, inviting driveway stood like a neatly dressed and polite kid awaiting guests.

Rob and I strained to stay connected over the course of the year. He was meeting Episcopalians each day, getting his legs in his new position, shedding the old because he didn't have space for it. He was, now in the new place, like the telephone cord I now saw stretched across the empty floor: plugged in. I, on the other hand, was lingering here but in the process of being disconnected. While my reasons for remaining were compelling to me—the teaching job, plus Henry was now living by choice at a boarding school nearby, close enough for me to dash over repeatedly—and Rob had gone along with the plan, he also felt let down, too, as if I were dragging my heels.

When I would drive the two hours up to see him during the pre- or postchurch part of his weekends, the tension would hang thickly in the air between us. Over a meal at a restaurant, he'd go quiet and then blurt out, "I don't understand why you're not here with me already." Once, when I gamely drove *just* to attend a church service close to the Massachusetts border, knowing we could share only a few private minutes after the coffee hour, I felt subsumed by the congregation and their smiles, how they all knew one another. Whatever those perfectly nice people wanted to talk to him about over treats on a tray, didn't they understand that the vehicle that was our marriage needed refueling, right away? Instead of being lifted up by being once again in his presence, I felt the opposite; bleakness was my only companion on the drive back. No internal jabbering voices with suggestions this time; no energy really, at all. The conviction that *he* was probably feeling excited about all the newness while I was treading water stung.

On the one hand, I loved that Rob clearly needed me; his life overseeing dozens of new churches was not on its own sufficient. But like a plant with a tangle of roots stretching deep into the soil, my leave-taking needed to be a gentle, gradual extraction. I felt a hollowness about moving, not knowing what I was going toward but keenly conscious of what I would be leaving behind.

And today would be the final tug. Rob had even suggested that I be the last to close up. "Take as much time as you want," he'd said that morning, the last one in our sun-soaked bedroom with the same gauzy curtains that had been there a dozen years ago. "The kids and I will have already set up a few rooms by the time you get there."

There I was, taking myself smack into the core of the sentimentality I already inhabited, doing the final run-through, walking room by room to absorb the full impact of a dozen child-rearing years.

Pushing my body against the cabinets next to the dishwasher, I reached my hands across the smooth counter surface as if to dole out three last bowls of pasta-with-veggies to the kids perched on their raspberry pink stools. In the language of *The Book of Common Prayer*, Rob "kept the feast" over and over again at church by presiding at the communion rail. My rail, insofar as the comparison went, had always been right here, at this counter with edges partially peeling off, amid bubbling conversation and pokes and silliness on the other side.

As I stood in the near-silence, though, with only the humming of the refrigerator, and the twittering of birds and trickling of the water in the little pond outside, I breathed in fullness.

Lifting my gaze through the windows to the back porch, I saw Cora twirling and singing "I feel pretty! I feel pretty!" during a spontaneous performance of *West Side Story*; Willie's high school friends sitting coolly with their burgers and outstretched legs on the green metal-latticed chairs; Rob setting up the pop-up screened gazebo that provided a refuge from mosquitoes for a few larger parties before self-destructing in an ice storm; Henry clomping around in big rubber boots. I saw myself whacking away with a scythe at the weeds by the stone wall and then dragging an Adirondack chair into the sun on the deck to lean back into idleness. We were all here together once, but now, with this move, we were about to disperse, with Rob and I trying to hold the center.

I checked the wire shelves of the walk-in pantry, off the mudroom. No more boxes of granola bars to grab on the way to a game, spilled rice to sweep up, or crinkly lunchboxes needing washing. It was here that once, in a harried before-school moment, I had been pleased to discover a tall glass container of pistachio nuts and rapidly put a bunch of the slightly opened shells and their green treasures in a plastic bag, certain that my third-grader would earn some credit from an unusual snack. As soon as the string of bells on the back door clanged at the end of the school day, however, and the backpack was plunked down, I was met with, "Mom, those nuts had WORMS in them!" Cringing at the memory, I recalled Rob's many sermons featuring some version of how it is best to embrace our failures, because God does.

Walking into the empty study where I used to sit at a clunky desk computer to write newsletters for the Science Alliance at the elementary school down the road, I scanned the highest shelf of the built-in bookcases for stray puzzle pieces or algebra workbooks and then made my way to the front entrance of the house, right across from the bottom of the staircase. The evergreen-colored screen door allowed the soft spring air to drift inside. I sat on the granite front stoop that was big enough for three friends to occupy, the stone cool against my bare legs, and looked at the steep bank that formed a barrier between the lush and level lawn and the mostly quiet road on the other side. Pine trees, still oddly similar to the ones my grandfather once planted at my childhood home, stood sentinel all along the top of the bank, ready to dance with the wind.

About eight springs ago, Cora and Henry invented a game in which they each claimed a spot to set up a house. Home base consisted of a piece of plywood or maybe an old chair, and then they would make forays to the garage or toolshed to gather items—a scrap of rug, a plastic recycling bin—to add to their décor. In the heart of the game, I could see them tending their spaces or shouting across to one another to arrange best visiting times. Cora had already staked out the woods in back of our house as an entire territory called "Kid Town," with elaborate stations requiring significant furniture that needed hauling out from wherever it wouldn't be immediately missed. Years later, walking Rocky, I would come upon a broken lamp or cache of clementine boxes, wood gone limp from many downpours. Her most important rule: no grown-ups allowed. Glancing out of her bedroom window while putting away clothes, I'd see her ten-year-old self at a full run, light brown hair flying, on a mission.

Right then, watching to see whether I'd recognize the occasional cars that went by, I felt a twinge of unexpected envy for Rob, how his affiliation with a church—the Church—could provide both an immediate and a perpetual sense of connectedness. A few months before, in an effort to bolster my spirits, he had offered a compliment: "You create community wherever you go, so I know you'll be fine." But creating community is not an abracadabra thing, not a simple plugging in. For me, building an authentic sense of *true belonging* has happened in tiny increments, never with just entering a certain building where particular people are sure to go and read from the same book, but more slowly, more organically, with the kind of falling in step together that happens over time and with regular proximity. Friendships with Mary Jo and Jeff, Josie and Ed, Martha and Jerry—they felt as solid as the tree trunks surrounding our property, and yet, at first we had intermingled as seedlings.

Getting up from the stoop, with the backs of my legs now imprinted, I went back inside and climbed the stairs one last time, slowly passing the little nook under the eaves where for a while we had put my brother Sandy's old catcher's mask for decoration. I headed into our bedroom, completely bare and showing not a trace of the sensual joy, the exchange of impressions about our growing kids, or the heavy, stagnant air that sometimes settled around us when we sank into conflict.

I slid the closet doors open, first one way and then the other, checking corners and looking for wayward shoes. Nothing left, just my one lone overnight bag. There was no point staying here anymore; it was getting spooky in the broad daylight. "C'mon, Polly," I heard myself say, gathering up my bag, "your time here is up; everyone else in the family knows it. And besides, weren't you on board with this from the beginning? I mean, it's not like someone pulled a fast one on you or anything." I glanced into each kid's room as if to lock their configurations into my brain, then headed down the stairs. In the kitchen, I grabbed the disconnected beige phone with its sticky long cord and headed for my car.

Being married means, in part, being willing to move on *in order to* stay together. For me at this moment, as I turned left out of the driveway, it was all jumbled up with the silent power of a rail at the front of a church. In fact, there would be many more rails in front of many more churches.

Chapter 38

Running with Rocky

I hear only the steady chorus of late summer insects, the crunch of the leaves underfoot, and, when we go on a certain stretch of trail uphill by a stream, the gurgling of water. My companion is faster than I am, but he pauses frequently to drink, to investigate anything fascinating, to chase creatures scuttling and chirping in the brush. Nothing is happening, and everything is happening, all at once.

These runs take place on a Sunday morning, with church bells calling people to services once again, or perhaps on a late Thursday afternoon, with the shadows lengthening.

When Rocky and I are running alone on a trail, I feel that most everything is right. We are in motion, we are exploring, and we are free from everything else. Here, it doesn't matter what we believe or don't believe. No one asks; we don't say. All that counts is being fully alive. We let our limbs carry us and open our senses so that we can imbibe as much as possible about our very real surroundings. On his four feet, my dog rarely stumbles; on my two, I sometimes trip on a protruding root or stone and lose my balance, go down. If I do, Rocky comes right over, concerned in a dog kind of way, trusting that we will go on together shortly.

I still don't know if I can convincingly use the term *spiritual experience* to describe these times, because I'm still not positive I know what a spiritual experience is. In truth, it often seems to me that people are eager to affix this label to feel better about whatever they're doing, to give themselves some heft, or perhaps to be let off the hook for not showing up in church regularly. For all I know, the times I run in the woods with my dog may be only physical and, as my tennis coach likes to say when he teaches us about the subtleties of net play, "nothing more than that." It's not as if I have any grand thoughts or revelations or "Aha!" moments; I'm just running, watching my steps, pushing forward, breathing.

But it is enough. It is my cup overflowing. I am far from any altar, but I am drawing sustenance from the gifts offered here. They are indeed gifts, but with no clear identity of a *giver* beyond Nature itself.

There's also no real sense of community, unless you count the combination of us two, dog and human. But what there is, unmistakably, is a sense of rightness, of *I'd-rather-be-nowhere-elseness*. The sound of cars on the nearby interstate compounds my feeling of relief in my own good fortune. People whizzing by, enclosed in steel, are shut off from the elements, maybe grudgingly exchanging pleasantries with their fellow car occupants. I get to be here, with the breeze, on a mossy path that absorbs my mind's meanderings.

No matter the trail, Rocky forgets that every single previous time he has chased a chipmunk, he's failed. Hope springs eternal in my big black dog with the tall ears, so he goes for each tantalizing chirp with every fiber of his being, ending the chase by stretching his neck to peer up a tree toward the disappearance. I say to him, "Come on, Rock, you know how this is gonna end, so why bother?" And if he could, he would rightly say, "What kind of vapid view of life is that?" On the last stretch of our runs, he searches for a big stick to carry. Once the stick is lodged in his mouth, his white teeth showing, a kind of fire in his eye, he prances proudly by, unconcerned about scratching me with it. He knows how to live in the moment. When the day comes that finds him drooping instead of exulting along a path, that's when I'll need to check my own vitality, too, make sure the well within me is still pumping.

In dog years, he is a bit past his prime; I'm at about the same exact stage, maybe a bit farther on. Everything in my body works, my mind functions adequately, I have ideas bubbling up that feel worthy of sharing, I am not burdened by my sins or anyone else's, I have loved ones to listen to and care for. Perhaps there is some aspect, some corner or crevice, of my soul that is going untended. But the woods, streams, and fields will find it eventually, revealing to me wordlessly how to bring about new growth in stubborn old places.

I've come far enough now, first in my years as a single person and then in the course of my marriage, to be able to discern a number of key signposts that provide something like direction in my life. They have not been written down anywhere, have rarely been spoken aloud, were not tested in any formal way. I sense them best when looking up at tree branches waving in the sky, similar to when I felt the spirit of my father there, after he died. It doesn't really matter where we live, just that I have access to the sky. I keep trotting along, following the bits of guidance that I can decipher. Perhaps they resemble principles more than beliefs. Whatever they are, they keep me company, helping me feel that I'm not just groping in the dark. I hesitate to make anything like a conclusive list, knowing that a fresh addition could take shape at any time. Since our move to New Hampshire, I can identify five that have stayed put:

1. Where there is life, there is always goodness and joy.
2. Pain will come, and it will hurt, inescapably, so it is best to develop resilience.
3. Do what you can to honor someone else's grief, need for support, as well as their happiness.
4. Be who you *really* are, while being porous enough to heed suggestions that might result in greater flourishing.
5. Each of us can choose to cultivate love—do what we love, be with people we love, generate more love.

In my thirty years of marriage, through plenty of wear and tear, these have held up.

Chapter 39

There's One Kind of Service, and Then There's Another

Alerted by a welcome text message on Saturday evening—"9:00 tomorrow, you in?"—the next morning I made the half-hour drive past barns, apple orchards, and hayfields to get to the court. Pulling into the town park, I saw the familiar figures watching for my car. Immediately, I felt a sense of belonging, of fitting in. They needed me to be a fourth, and in a way, I needed them, too.

Rob was at St. So-and-So's, wherever the calendar put him. Right then he was maybe getting a short breather after the 8:00 service, which was attended by a small group of mostly elderly worshippers, who have likely been coming every Sunday for years. Perhaps, although it's not likely, he was getting to eat that hardly-anything granola bar he grabbed at 6:30 in our kitchen. The pews, bathed in light streaming through the stained glass windows, were about to fill up again with the substantial 10:30 crowd. The opening hymn would be rousing, and many women around my age would have given some careful attention to their clothes, their scarves, and their makeup. If they remembered over their first cup of coffee at home that this was going to be the bishop's visiting day, perhaps they took a little extra time choosing this swirling skirt or that pendant, glancing in the mirror. I would, too, if I were heading to an occasion taken up a notch from the ordinary. Also at this moment, slightly younger women, with only the beginning of gray, were tousling their children's hair as they made their way down the sidewalk, over-the-shoulder bags full of coloring books and toys at the ready.

I would not be among them, not be in position to receive the glances of various people who might whisper to their pew-mates, "I think that's the bishop's wife over there." I was elsewhere, in scuffed sneakers.

"C'mon—it's gettin' dark!" said Mac, our tennis coach, wanting us to stop dawdling and chatting out on the court bathed in light on a summer morning. He was short in stature, with a combative nature but a ready laugh once you earned his trust.

The sun was still on its way up, we were able to use every part of our bodies and each of our five senses, but my coach's reminder was not out of order. Play when you can, he meant, because soon enough, you never know. My own experience in church has shown me that essentially this same message gets imparted there with some regularity, too. The Book of John, for instance, has Jesus saying: "For a little while longer, the Light will be among you. Walk while you have the Light, so that darkness will not overtake you" (12:35). It's good, solid advice in any context, and I have taken it to mean that *running* in the sunshine to swing at balls would get the nod, too.

As the leaves begin to turn and the days get shorter, my May to September tennis group will fade out once again, but we will also, like squirrels urgently storing up acorns for the winter, take with us sustenance, both physical and spiritual, from these times.

I might have gotten up earlier, walked the dog quickly, grabbed the dress that I had chosen the night before, then joined my husband in the car for the journey toward his "visitation" on this particular Sunday. If I drove, he could even grab some precious minutes to sip his coffee, read over his sermon, and gather his thoughts before the deluge. Other bishop's wives have recommended the practice, even saying it provided them with quality time together. Maybe, if you like being near your husband when he is wrapped up in a kind of cocoon and if you fancy being a personal assistant in addition to being a wife.

He hadn't asked me to do this, although I was sure he would have appreciated it if I had volunteered. Once, perhaps, I actually *did* mention, in an airy kind of way, that we could consider this strategy. But in truth, my heart really wasn't in it, because then it would be someone else driving, not the Polly I have always been. It wasn't just that I would be in his shadow for the whole event, a person of interest almost completely due to being a spouse; it was also that what transpired during the whole church morning would not be of particular interest to me.

Blasphemous? Not exactly, and this far into the marriage, I knew I didn't need to be afraid of incurring anyone's wrath, either. But I still had a voice on my shoulder saying, *You know you're going against the grain.* The fact was, now that I no longer needed to transport kids to services conducted by their dad, I'd rather be outside, playing tennis in the sunshine.

"It's about time!" somebody said good-naturedly as I approached. Sandy, Lydia, and Byron were already rallying while our coach stood nearby, with arms crossed. "OK, Polly, you jump in here on this side, and let's get this thing started."

As we lined up for some drills, with him feeding us balls, we each hit our share of spectacular (or at least decent) shots, and also plenty of duds. When we screwed up, our coach confirmed the mistake with, "That was SOO ugly!" But when we got on a bit of a roll, sending the balls deep to the baseline, he said, "Now we're talkin'!"

We may or may not have been improving, but we were living totally in the moment, striving together, hoping that our forehands and our backhands would bring us some degree of pride in ourselves, boost our optimism for the future. We were, indeed, a privileged little band, gathering for the sheer fun of it. We were not strangers to degrees of success in other areas; nor were we strangers to setbacks and some terrible losses. It was only after playing with him for several months, during a water break at the net, that I had learned how Byron, who immigrated to New Hampshire from Australia, lost his wife to an aneurism when she was just in her forties. Retired now, with no children, he relied partly on seeing musicals and working on his tennis game to assuage his grief. For me, dogged by a feeling of still not being fully at home in this state, the act of arriving at a court where others were expecting me, needing me, even, gave me a surge of adrenaline.

Mac's wire basket was empty now, so we moved around the court to gather in dozens of fluorescent balls. It was about 10:15. In a town across the state, the parking lot was filling up at church, with some people hurrying in with their trays of chips and hummus, cheese and crackers, slices of banana bread; others came slowly, with walkers;

children were shepherded into their Sunday school classes. The choir finished practicing; the organist readied the music for the morning; while donning vestments in the sacristy, the rector of the congregation filled the bishop in on how many were to be confirmed that day. All around the building, people were glad to be together again, sharing a common purpose.

Our much smaller group on the green hard courts was not a church—not at all. But we were getting to be a community, in a kind of backhanded way. As our banter, sometimes enlivened with our attempts at trash talk, continued week after week, our bonds to one another grew a little stronger. At first just there to play, we soon discovered a mutual willingness to broach off-the-court life when we took breaks up at the net. Staying away from heavy topics worked best in these moments; we kept our words light, like balls floating through the air. "You won't *believe* what happened to me yesterday when I tried to get a new phone!" or "This weekend I need to move my daughter's stuff down to New York City—anybody want to come?" or "What'd your class say about your writing, anyway?" We had as many problems as anyone else out there, and sometimes they appeared on the court in the form of a downcast or hungover or just distracted disposition. Usually, though, we knew that during tennis we were in a kind of parenthesis. Problems could wait.

Eventually, Sandy and I would cross over that threshold between don't-go-there-here decorum on the court and let's-actually-talk-for-real off the court. Once we began meeting for movies and meals, we were deciding to open up more, to become friends. Tennis was like a starter dough that produced loaves on top of which we could slather on layers of rich peanut butter. She's moved farther away now, and our get-togethers take more effort, but we are still nourished by our bond.

At church, too, parishioners gradually become accustomed to one another, opening up little by little during coffee hour and committee meetings. Generally they come for the service itself—the language of the prayer book, the confession of sins, the peace, the communion—but rubbing shoulders with others becomes an integral part of the experience also. In this setting, and while uttering lines like, "Lead us not into temptation, and deliver us from evil," you can't easily escape the fact that everyone, sooner or later, will need some healing. Building up the resources on your team, nurturing a support network—this makes sense, in any context. With the growth of enough trust, people will want to peel back their outer coverings a little, so long as others do the same. In many ways, it's like a gradual disrobing, a process of getting closer to one another's more intimate truths.

At the same time as I was insisting on seeing parallels between my tennis life and my husband's church life—valid, to a degree—I also went one step further in a flight of fancy to bring about a temporary kind of reembodiment of my husband *himself* with a professional tennis player. Fortunately, no harm was done, but I'm still trying to figure out what, if anything, this might show about our marriage.

You know those displays, often at museums and fairs, that let you put your head through a hole in a colorfully painted wooden structure and then suddenly, to people looking at you anyway, the rest of you becomes someone else entirely? The appeal lies in the juxtaposition: viewers laugh at the world of difference between you and the costume that surrounds you. You'll never in a million years become Derek Jeter or a maiden in eighteenth-century Sturbridge Village, but the momentary merging is intriguing.

A few years back, prompted by a flurry of media coverage of the US Tennis Open in Queens, I started constructing these tableaux in my mind. Absurd as it was, I put my husband's head in the body of a tennis player.

This is a guy with *zero* interest in tennis; he even has had the gall to say, more than once, that it's "pointless."

Now there's an adjective that spouses might disagree on, any number of ways.

When he made this breathtaking accusation the first time, I maturely resisted the urge to retaliate by calling him out on a few of his favorite activities. Pulling up boulders just for the sake of exerting himself? Sitting on an ergometer at the Y, going nowhere? Uttering a prayer for almost every occasion of regular life?

It was a rare moment on one particular evening when, pausing on his walk from his desk full of theology toward the kitchen, he watched the fiery Rafael Nadal for a few minutes, expressionless, until he got bored. It was then that I realized that, in fact, my husband—or a younger version of my husband, from a picture of him rowing shirtless with a bandanna around his head in high school, to be precise—actually bears some resemblance to the Spanish tennis player.

That in turn made me feel a little woozy with a combined kind of longing. OK, so the present-day Nadal on the TV set drew me in, viscerally, as he leaped off his feet to pound a ball, yes; but the reason he *did* this at all had more to do with the fact that I had *already been drawn in* by Rob, also on a visceral level, just not pounding a ball, years before. And that feeling was still there, pulsing.

Funny thing is, even though Rob never goes anywhere near a court with me, I often feel his presence as I play, or when I read about the pros.

I'm sure I'm not alone in doing this kind of thing: inserting my own life into the more famous lives I read about. Teachers talk about how students naturally bring "background knowledge" into the study of literature; this can either go smoothly and add to understanding, or it can be like putting a head into an opening and seeing how silly the picture can get.

Right around this time of Rob/Rafael confluence, the *New York Times* ran a story in the Styles section about the high interest in the wives and girlfriends—dubbed "WAGS"—of professional tennis players. Television cameras take us over to these stylish creatures in the stands frequently, presumably because that's what many viewers want.

Reading this, I suddenly wasn't sure if I felt a tad envious, wishing that the WAGS of bishops, especially the ones who have shed whatever plainness they might have once had, would also get more of the spotlight; or if it served as a kind of reminder to me that I could still get more of the spotlight (albeit muted, due to lower numbers in the stands plus the religion factor) if I got myself to church more often.

"There's something about tennis that may explain fans' fascination with the romantic companions of their favorite players." Not surprisingly, we don't get as many shots of the husbands and boyfriends (they would be "HABS") of the women players. In both cases, however, glimpsing them is supposed to give more depth to the drama unfolding on the court.

I resonate, or I imagine resonating, with these women in their designer glasses. How many times has that camera in church (when I used to go more often) swung over in my direction, catching me just as I'm finding the right hymn, or showing concern about my husband pulling off yet another sermon? I also sympathize with their need to identify themselves as more than just appendages. As one girlfriend in the article put it: "it's very important for me to build myself, and I want people to know about me, that I am doing modeling, and that I do something, and I don't want people to know me because of my boyfriend." *You tell it, sister!* I decided this would be a little gem I could put in my bag when I took a break from my own modeling career to go to the New Bishops and Spouses conference later that same month.

Another article on the same day, this one in the Sports section (Stuart Miller's "If It Works, Tennis Players Stick With I, Whatever It Is," in the August 31, 2013 issue of the *New York Times*) also brought my non-tennis-playing husband to mind. It was about the high incidence of ritualistic activity among these same pros. Other athletes have their little routines, too (my nephew does a great imitation of particular baseball players before stepping to the plate). Some of it, like eating and sleeping properly, doesn't really count; but what about Tim Mayotte saying that each day he used to "eat three-quarters of a pint of chocolate chip ice cream and throw out the rest"? Or Goran Ivanisevic, who had to watch an episode of *Teletubbies* each morning in June 2001 before playing at Wimbledon? According to the article, Nadal "is the king of routine and ritual. He is well known for carefully positioning his water bottles and drinking from them in a certain order."

There! I felt vindicated in my seeing Rafael and Rob as two peas in a pod. My husband can also be seen filling and arranging drinking vessels in a very particular way, although there are a number of significant differences, including the fact that other people will be doing most of the partaking. Still, it was he who reminded me that the words we commonly associate with magic—such as "hocus pocus"—have their origin in the Latin version of "this is my body." Going further, he said that back in the Middle Ages, there was indeed a belief that the transfiguration happening in communion was something akin to sorcery. And that some people *still* hold to the "magic cookie" theory: the priest, abracadabra, transforms wine and wafer into blood and body. Rob, on the other hand, believes that the prayers of the whole congregation, led by the priest, provide the living presence of the Holy Spirit.

This was the kind of ruminating I was accustomed to doing as a clergy spouse, forever keen on understanding why people do the things they do. Like someone with a pointer in front of a huge tapestry with both secular and religious scenes, I was trying to make connections, see parallels. Tennis, with its distinct pleasures and challenges of keeping a ball within certain lines, is in a completely different realm from church: I know that. But as long as I keep playing and watching the game, with a steady infusion of worship life coming to me through my companion at home, I will probably continue to meld the two together mercilessly in my mind.

Chapter 40

Everything's Closed

"Mom, NO! You can't go to the tennis club tonight; it's too risky." Cora widened her green eyes as she spoke. She had just gotten home, having cleared out of Boston where the spike in COVID-19 cases was more marked than it was in New Hampshire. She could do her nonprofit job from her computer, and so she would take refuge with us. Henry, who hadn't gone back to college when his February break ended, also chimed in while getting his laundry out of the dryer. His tone was calmer but still firm. "It's really not safe, Mom. Who knows what you'd bring back here?" This odd feeling of being almost parented by my own twenty-something kids had preceded the pandemic, in spurts, with an uptick of their offering unsolicited advice about my daily habits, but with a couple of them now in residence, it was becoming more marked, and was not entirely welcome.

It was the Monday after schools had been shut down for an indefinite period of time. That previous Friday, in the hallways of the Massachusetts high school where I taught, there had been speculation about when we'd hear from the superintendent. Finally, during the last several minutes of Block 7, when my students were already gathering at the door for release, the email came. I stood at the computer and started conveying some of the contents of it to them, but the words didn't matter; they were gone. A great whoosh of teenagers moved through the hall, some with raised arms or pounding the walls. My close colleague, Doug, popped his head in. "Got the word?" he asked. A week or so before, we'd been instructed to start wiping down surfaces in our classrooms, sharing spray bottles and pieces of white cloth from dubious origin. This seemed like a slippery slope, not to mention another thing to do in the course of already packed days. A decision from the governor clarified everything: everybody must go home, until further notice. I made the long walk out to the parking lot, carrying no more than the usual heavy sack of papers, feeling like my own share of responsibility had just been sliced; certain things had been taken out of my hands. The thick patch of woods behind the huge, curving, triple layers of asphalt looked no different this afternoon. I broke up the hour-long drive north with a stop at a grocery store, more crowded than usual. A feeling just a notch below frenzy prevailed there, with people remembering to say "excuse me" behind carts piled high with whatever paper goods they could find; family members conferring about who was going over to a grandmother's house to deliver *her* stuff first; cashiers the same age as my students ringing, ringing, ringing.

Still, that weekend felt more like "wait and see" than "it's all over now." Maybe we'd have a week away from school while the worst of the virus ran its course. Like a hurricane coming up the coast, this could either gather force or peter out, getting us back to business as usual.

I wasn't really surprised when the Monday email exchange about indoor tennis practice for that evening included some who were bowing out and others still willing to show up. One teammate wrote, "Maybe need to cancel the next two weeks. Just for safety reasons." Before consulting with my kids, I first replied, "I don't want to mess up the numbers, so I'll come if you need me." A few minutes later, though, sounding like a person relinquishing autonomy for the sake of the greater good, I wrote, "My family wants me to stay home." And so it started.

Four women did show up to play that evening, but the urgency of the official announcement from the US Tennis Association, with an umbrella over all programs like ours, was unmistakable: "We are immediately cancelling all events through March 31st." School was cancelled for at least a week, now tennis until the end of the month. What next?

Well, church, of course. That bastion of solidity (and for me, mystery) in our marriage was also losing its mooring. All the buildings that used to throw open their doors to people, at almost any time, without question, were now closed. The Church itself was entering uncharted waters.

Rob, the man I knew to be a deep-sea diver as well as captain, head navigator of his vessel, which consisted now of a fleet of vessels, needed to find a new way forward, and fast. And he would do it from his basement studio. No longer would I see him affixing his collar in the early Sunday bedroom light, or hear the garage door open up and then the car purring as he plugged in that morning's destination while I was still drifting. Now he had time for a bowl of cereal in the kitchen, with the rest of us circulating around, before passing through his new gateway—the door to the basement stairs—first walking through the main space filled with boxes from our moves that I had yet to sort through and then, shutting the door to his chamber, with a cross and one of his own large, deep-hued paintings set up behind him, bringing God to worshippers who were scattered all over the state and beyond.

Church may have once been characterized by its antiquity, but, almost overnight, it went through a reincarnation into complete modernity, with Zoom links taking the place of steps up to wide wooden doors.

As Rob adjusted to the new normal, saying very little about it, I could tell that his brain was whirring a million miles a minute. Even though he needed to carry out his responsibilities as bishop differently, would the bedrock of his being—his faith—preserve itself despite not having the usual means of demonstration? In all the years that I'd known him, the rhythm of going to and returning from church was a given, like breathing in and breathing out. I'd grown accustomed to his pace.

"I've got to get down to the church."

"I'm not sure when I'll be home from church, probably around midafternoon."

"Today I've got three services."

"Are you bringing the kids to church this morning?"

"I now feel as if I've really been to church."

While much of it—the spoken word part, and some of the music—could still go on, one of the centerpieces of an Episcopal service, the piece that had always presented a clear conundrum to me, now was impossible to perform: communion. The coronavirus had made this ritual history, at least for the time being. No matter what level of divinity a presiding clergy person had, putting a morsel of *anything* in someone's palm or offering a cup from which others had already sipped became completely out of the question—precisely what *not to* do, in fact. Now the whole practice, even though it had gone on for centuries unchanged and indispensable, felt like part of a defunct culture.

And yet, by April, there were already rumblings among worshippers who wanted what some Catholic churches were doing: either allow people in their homes to experience a kind of communion by using something other than wine and wafer, or have the priest take communion themselves on screen, thereby offering watchers a kind of vicarious fulfillment.

Rob held the line: there would be no substitutes for the real thing. They would have to make do without communion, and that other part of the service inviting close physical contact—the peace—would also be put aside. No choir either. Heavens, no! Early on, the evening news brought us a nightmarish story of a church choir somewhere that ignored warnings about the danger of water droplets from wide open mouths in close proximity and went ahead with rehearsals, resulting in the falling of dozens of singers and their family members. Rob shook his head, saying, "We cannot allow anything like this to happen here."

With a few segments lopped off, services were definitely shorter now.

I understood that this was all a big administrative challenge for Rob: *this* we'll still do; *that* we won't. But I also wanted to understand how the changes affected him personally, trying yet again, as always, to get a clear look at what made him tick, the heart of it all.

One Sunday afternoon I asked, "How's this new way of doing things going for you? I mean, is it giving you what you need, spiritually?" It was a clumsily worded question, but I did my best to convey that I was trying to put myself in his shoes.

"It's hard," he shrugged. "I miss everything about what we used to do, all the ways we expressed being in community together. We are in a kind of exile now."

For one of the Easter services, he asked Cora and Henry to help him do some singing, perched next to him in the basement, but otherwise we were upstairs, either tuning in with plates of scrambled eggs on our laps, or with some sheepishness, just carrying on with our own tasks, so long as they were quiet. Because I was required to post an overview of the week's schoolwork on each of my online classroom websites early on Sunday morning, a task that took its own kind of scrambling, when 10 A.M. rolled around, I was ready to sit on a couch with my kids, differently than how we used to sit on pews, and relax. Whereas before my *not* accompanying Rob to his services, in the flesh, might have been noteworthy to some, now it became a moot point. For the first time ever in our marriage, my arrival or departure—once through those big wooden doors, now miniaturized into a blue link on the screen—was completely anonymous.

I was free to notice a different kind of miracle than those described in the Bible—fishes and loaves multiplying, for example. When the screen shifted from one person's study or living room to someone else's, miles away, or when a singer finished a hymn and just continued looking at us with a smile—these moments were sometimes awkward but also in their own way magnificent, showing as they did how wondrous this whole new way of cobbling together a service was. Even without being a full participant, I could still be momentarily transfixed. And, after a few times, I decided that my favorite part of the service was not so much the sermon but when Rob read, from a corner of his screen, "The Prayers of the People." He did it with just the right tone, the right level of compassion in his voice. I could see him up close. "And we pray for the recovery of Sue Harrison's nephew, who is in the hospital after being in an accident last evening." Pause. Then a bit of a smile broke with, "We give thanksgiving for the birth of Mary Tyler's granddaughter." Something about the straightforward way he said it let me zoom right into Mary Tyler's very being, celebrating with her.

The Easter Vigil, always the most momentous service in the church calendar, included a segment this time when he walked outside to our garden, in flowing purple cassock, to read ancient liturgy over a makeshift paschal fire with logs from our firewood pile. As I watched from inside, seeing him wave his hands at certain intervals, I had a mix of feelings: the old one, that he was a million miles away in a place I couldn't reach; also a newer one, that the way we do this daily life—him holding fast to his one strong faith through each and every minute, exercising it over and over again; me finding comfort in an array of other—other *what* was still hard to pinpoint, but my powers of deciphering were growing—that *this* situation right here, he and I, me and him, the two of us, was itself a kind of marvel.

Not on par with the *Resurrection*, exactly, which must be considered by believers a true miracle, but still an earthly kind of marvel, nonetheless.

He looked past me, out the window to the bird feeder, pointing. "That's the bird I was telling you about—right there! Do you recognize it?" We didn't often sit at breakfast together, but today was an exception. It was Monday morning; I had just finished posting new assignments on my classroom websites, and Rob hadn't yet gone down to his lair and was munching on a poached egg and dry toast. He'd asked me if I wanted a poached egg, too, but I've never understood those, preferring fried, scrambled, or even, when I have more patience than usual and want to replicate how my mother used to prefer them, boiled.

The bird was mottled, fairly small, with a mostly red head, darting around energetically by the feeder and twittering softly. I didn't recognize it immediately, which did not please me. After all, I was the one in the family with the most ornithological experience.

"Hmm . . . I'm not sure actually. It's not a rose-breasted grosbeak, and it's not quite a sparrow—the size of a warbler, but I don't recognize the species." Now Rob was poring through the Audubon bird guide, studying it as if it were *The Book of Common Prayer*. "Not that one, no definitely not." He was willing to pick up whatever tidbits of knowledge

I might offer on this subject, recognizing that while my Bible muscle remains weak, my natural world muscle has always been quite well developed; but so far I was coming up empty.

Maybe it was because our dining table had been moved right next to a large window with the recent just-before-coronavirus kitchen renovation, that Rob had decided to keep on filling the bird feeders into April this year. This seemed odd to me, against the rules, since we'd always heeded the local warnings about asking for trouble with bears. Furthermore, in past years it seemed to me that he tended to bird feeders mostly to *please me*, because he knew it would help me feel more at home, make a link with my girlhood, my great-aunts with simple brooches and sensible shoes who had binoculars always at the ready. For him, it was all a kind of curiosity—something like religion still was for me.

But this spring, along with everything else that had shifted, my husband was adding new tones to his personality palette: he was finding contentment, maybe even moments of true joy bursting inside his soul, in simply watching the cardinals, jays, woodpeckers, and goldfinches that were almost close enough to touch. As much as he was watching them, I was watching *him*. For so many years I had been trying to accompany him, in a way, by intermittently going to church; too often, though, it felt more like *trailing* him, without ever being fully caught up. Now, it was as if he were arriving at a place where I had already been.

We parted ways after breakfast with a nagging uncertainty about the identity of that one sweet little creature at the feeder. I told myself all would be revealed later somehow, not pausing to pick up the bird guide myself because teacher duties awaited my attention. Rob, though, did not abandon the search. He headed downstairs for a time, then returned with a gleeful pronouncement: "I've got it! It's the common redpoll." He showed me the picture, and there was no doubt about it. How did I miss this—a name that, oddly enough, was a combination of my own name, what Dad used to call me, with that of my beloved pony from years ago? Maybe this hadn't been a common species on Long Island during my childhood, being more Northern, and I was getting a first chance to get acquainted with these birds right now, instead. And maybe the fact that Rob had made the discovery and was so eager to come back upstairs to share it with me was a small thing to celebrate.

In any case, I believe that marriage brought these birds to us both, together.

Chapter 41

On the Motorcycle

He has the bike all revved up and waiting when I get outside. I grab my helmet—a big, heavy bubble with a shield of scratched plexiglass. Plexiglass! Pre-COVID-19, this material hadn't yet vaulted to its current status of much-in-demand, back-ordered, just the thing for installing as barriers in offices. Some grocery store workers are peering through neat sheets of it now as they calmly replenish peppers in the vegetable area; their contraptions, open at the bottom, are less encumbering than the one I am about to put on. I fiddle with the straps to make sure they're secure, and swing my leg over the seat behind Rob, who has been waiting for me, looking straight ahead, hands outstretched on the controls of the machine. It's a 1985 BMW K100, a bike sometimes referred to by motorcycle buffs as "the flying brick" because of the rectangular engine slung beneath the frame.

"Could you move back a little?" he turns to ask, once I nestle in. Closeness is good, but leave a little space, too.

I have never been able to stay inside on a beautiful summer evening when everything is ripe and the mists are beginning to drift in. Throughout my life, the sheer abundance of outdoor activities that beckon during the long light of June, July, and August has made me almost physically dizzy. I didn't grow up on a farm exactly, but we did get something like a farm mentality. There was always something needing doing, or just needing to be enjoyed, outdoors: mowing, getting in the hay, going for a run then a swim, taking a hike with the dog, being in the garden, going for a horseback ride. The list has shifted some through the years, but it has always had a burgeoning quality to it. To me, the only wrong—even *sacrilegious*—choice is being inside and sedentary. And during the present COVID-19 era, the imperative to stay outside as much as possible has taken on more heft.

Darkness will descend, and when it does you'll be glad you got every slice of light.

Rob and I agree on this. While he's never complained about needing to be at an early evening meeting or a service that takes him inside a church during that magic hour when the light outside has a soft, perfect quality and the leaves on the trees are gently rustling, when he's free at home and the weather is good, he's outside. Many evenings, we're glad to be doing our different tasks in the same vicinity, but more and more, we see the wisdom of getting on the motorcycle to take a spin.

I'm well aware that the words "wisdom" and "motorcycle" don't generally appear in the same sentence. But in our case, they most definitely belong together. On the back of his bike, I'm right behind those shoulders that first drew me in. Plus, the roar of the machine makes conversation unnecessary—a blessing sometimes, especially when you're dealing with a raging extrovert and a determined introvert who recharges his own battery with stretches of silence.

We head out of the driveway, bike purring. I'm staring at the blank whiteness of the back of his helmet, noticing how, without fanfare, he has removed the sticker that had been there at the end of last summer. It was the blue, red, and green insignia of the Episcopal Diocese of New Hampshire, meant to represent the theme of "Tending the Vine." A perfectly fine design, expressing both the affiliation with the Church as a whole as well as the more particular mission of churches in the Granite State, it went through numerous iterations before being agreed upon and then put on the website and on all kinds of items from stationery to signs to water bottles. There is absolutely nothing wrong with it, unless you choose to raise an eyebrow about the possible choking features of vines themselves. With coaching, I got over that part, and thought instead about the heady sweetness emanating from the grape trellis outside my oldest friend Clare's house. There, dappled sunlight fell through the openings of the slats amid the laughter of her family members.

But then I acknowledged to myself that staring straight at that sticker for an entire ride made me feel that Rob and I weren't entirely alone; that once again religion had seeped into our own private world, and this feeling diminished the other feeling of exhilaration with the whole experience. I got up my nerve one day when we were both in the garage doing the recycling, and said to him while gesturing over to the helmet, as lightly as possible, not wanting to appear kvetchy, "Just wondering, did you want me to have greater awareness of being a few inches away from your diocese than being a few inches away from *you*?" He looked momentarily startled, almost wanting to say something but not wanting to take on the whole history of our relationship in that moment. Over the long winter, when the bike went into his downstairs study, I hadn't checked back; but now here we are, just the two of us, with no vines to tend.

I feel vaguely guilty, imagining all those times when he rides solo, proud to show his faith to any passers-by. But then I rise up to claim my spot as the only person who regularly occupies this space. It's all milky whiteness in front of me, except for the small, black "D.O.T." imprint. Yes, Department of Transportation, you can come along.

He picks up speed out on the main road, and we fly by the yards and houses I've come to know from my regular runs. It's taken a half-dozen years here, but I can now count some almost-friends among the owners of these places. There's Sarah, who walks her golden retriever; Kristen, who keeps a stunning garden in front of her compact, neat house; Jess and Drew, who park the family cars so that their four young kids can play safely in their driveway; the man who has a little ironworks shop connected to his house. Some go to a church on Sundays, many do not; the subject doesn't come up during the moments when we wave and share a few words, gradually getting acquainted, peeling back the layers of ourselves over time. Right now though, on the bike, is not about getting acquainted; it's about holding on.

Rob first sprung for a motorcycle when he was a curate in New Haven. He may not own up to this consciously, but I believe that the purchase had something to do with the nature of working in a "high" church: the solemnity, the sacredness, maybe even the preponderance of older people. Whatever the pull was, I was absorbed in caring for our infant son and can only recall his telling me about taking the motorcycle test at the DMV and having the evaluator put him through the paces, deferentially asking him to, "Take the turn right there, Father." That guy had something to tell his wife about at supper, for sure: "Had my first clergyman come through on a Kawasaki today!"

There wasn't much bombing around on a motorcycle during the years when our kids were young, although Rob did use it quite often to go back and forth to church. It was perfect for that, really, since we lived so close. Plus, it was always easy to park right out in front. And he cut quite a figure with his black shirt and white collar. When that first bike gave out, he went back for a used BMW, a mellow machine compared to the more brazen Harley Davidsons that arguably form a kind of religious group of their own. Once in a while he would give short rides, often just around the lawn, to kids' friends, and occasionally he and I would spring free for a real date, heading up to a favorite café in the fading sunlight and returning in the deep night. I liked wearing my leather jacket for the wind and holding on for dear life, and the fact that only two of us could fit.

Then one year he had pangs, suddenly seeing it as a frivolous expense, and told me, "I'd really better sell the bike." Back to the dealer it went. At around the same time, the unicycle—one he learned how to ride as a teenager—also disappeared from our garage. "What's going on?" I demanded to know. "Don't you get to have any fun?" He mumbled something about having more responsibilities now, little kids.

Soon enough, though, he discovered that, apart from whatever I thought, he actually missed the bike and so, abracadabra, it was back. *Vroom, vroom*, and thank goodness. It would take more than another decade for him to order another unicycle. Impressive as it was this spring to watch him ride it around the New Hampshire State House, with arms outstretched for balance, bishop's mitre on top of his head, COVID mask across his face, reporters nearby, I prefer the two of us on a motorcycle out on the open road.

With few cars on the roads he chooses, we make tracks, slowing down to traverse one village center at a time. Each time another biker, often helmetless and on a Harley, approaches in the opposite lane, Rob's left arm extends downward, in the standard subtle greeting; most of the time the other driver responds in kind. When we're out here, Rob is temporarily part of a different tribe. His tan shirt, sleeves rolled up, billows in the wind, and my thighs are against his. I can't help communicating inessential things like: "It's amazing to see what some people do with their sheds, isn't it?" He turns briefly to say, "I can't hear anything you're saying." Here, I don't mind.

I'm not a particularly brave person; I've heard the statistics about motorcycle accidents. But the riding we do doesn't feel dangerous; it feels necessary. We do not claim to be essential workers this spring, as we pass the newly installed signs with tributes to these neighbors of ours, not knowing exactly where they live. But this kind of riding together is work, or play, that is essential to our particular marriage. What we need most is to share the same vantage point for a while, take the same turns, pass the same barns, breathe the same air, feel the same chill. And not think about churches thriving or churches struggling or about my distance from either kind. We're moving through some kind of Presence in the universe that is greater than each of our own individual presences. There's precariousness, too: we're always a hair's breadth away from death, and yet we also feel secure, leaning one way, then the other, together.

All we really have is the quality of each of our days—and twilights, and evenings. I have come to seek more and more that magical sense of motion combined with just the right amount of thought, like the opening of *Zen and the Art of Motorcycle Maintenance* says: "without being hurried and without a feeling you're losing time."

Once addressing the Corinthians well before the time of motorcycles, Paul gave a compelling list of reasons and rules for how men and women could live in harmony, with the possibility of an unbelieving spouse being made holy through the power and faith of their believing spouse. I wouldn't object to tagging along to heaven—or wherever you go once you're saved—with Rob driving us both in that direction; maybe that's how this trip will end. But I believe there's more truth in seeing us as equal partners, each one offering, thousands of times over as we spend our days together, distinct value to the communion that is created by a marriage. We generate energy, in concert with one another, to fuel everything else we do in the outside world.

Riding on the back of a bike, I feel the open air, my husband's back, and no rail whatsoever.

Afterword

As I write this, in mid-March of 2025, it's been five years since the COVID-19 lockdowns began, which means it has been almost five years since I gazed out the back window and watched Rob performing those ancient rites for the Easter Vigil service, holding the Paschal candle. It was that same spring when we left the bird feeders up longer partly because he loved seeing and learning to identify the colorful little creatures, darting and swooping, oblivious to the pandemic.

In the summer of 2022, I joined him in August for the tail end of the Lambeth Conference in England. Bishops, and many of their spouses, from everywhere in the Anglican Communion traditionally gather at the University of Kent, near Canterbury Cathedral, for this two-week session, every ten years. This time, of course, it had been postponed for two years. Walking around that enormous campus amidst all those clerics, at least half of them African, listening to addresses under an enormous tent, reporting also to the designated "spouse building" for mornings of Bible study—all of it served to remind me that the Church lumbers along on many legs, faces many challenges, and tries to stay devoted to serving the needs of millions of people. It was an honor to be there. Still, my favorite part of the trip was taking a train ride to walk the White Cliffs of Dover, alone with Rob, on a brilliant, breezy day.

In his book, *Good Spousekeeping*, Dave Meurer writes: "A great marriage is not when the 'perfect couple' comes together. It is when an imperfect couple learns to enjoy their differences." With each year that goes by, this truth gleams brighter, as both differences and imperfections show no sign of disappearing. The concurrent truth, though, is that appreciating our similarities as well as our strengths is pretty wonderful, too.

Now in the busiest season for my own job at a high school—planning Spring Career Fair #4—while Rob approaches the build-up to another Easter in a time of national political turmoil, I'm struck by the beauty of the regular "kitchen moments" that happen most every evening. These occur when, whatever our days have been like, however religious or secular, we meet again, just the two of us, there for one another.

References

Chapman, Gary D. 2014. *The 5 Love Languages: The Secret to Love That Lasts.* Chicago: Northfield Publishing.

Church of England. 1982. *Doctrine in the Church of England*: The 1938 Report. London: SPCK Publishing.

Emily Dickinson Museum. 2009. "Emily Dickinson and the Church." Emilydickinsonmuseum.org. 2009.

Douglas, William. 1964. *Ministers' Wives.* New York: Harper & Row

Johnson, Thomas H. ed. 1980. *Final Harvest: Emily Dickinson's Poems.* Boston: Little, Brown and Company.

Maraniss, David. 2001. "The Sweet Long Days." *In The Games We Played: A Celebration of Childhood and Imagination*, edited by Steven A. Cohen, 23-31, New York: Simon and Schuster.

Meurer, Dave. 2004. *Good Spousekeeping.* Life Journey.

Miller, Stuart. 2013. "If It Works, Tennis Players Stick with It, Whatever It Is." *The New York Times*, August 31, 2013.

Pirsig, Robert M. 1974. *Zen and the Art of Motorcycle Maintenance.* New York: Bantam Books.

Putnam, Robert D. and David E. Campbell. 2010. *American Grace: How Religion Divides and Unites Us*. New York: Simon & Schuster.

Vendler, Helen. 2010. Dickinson: *Selected Poems and Commentaries.* Cambridge: The Belknap Press of Harvard University Press.

Whitman, Walt. 2002. *Leaves of Grass and Other Writings* (Norton Critical Edition). Edited by Michael Moon. New York: W.W. Norton & Company.

About the Author

A graduate of Dartmouth and the Bread Loaf School of English, Polly Merritt Ingraham has published essays in *The Hampshire Gazette*, *The Concord Monitor*, *Tikkun*, the *Boston Sunday Globe* magazine, and *Dartmouth Alumni Magazine*, among other outlets. A pre-election essay with the title "Hockey Moms Are More than Pitbulls with Lipstick" aired on National Public Radio in October 2008.

Her work is included in the anthology *Concord Writers' Night Out* (New Hampshire Writers Project, 2018) and in the flash nonfiction anthology *Fast Fierce Women* (Woodhall Press, 2022). In September 2023, a short excerpt of her memoir was published in *Unleash Lit* and was nominated for a Pushcart Prize.

In 2011, Ingraham launched a blog, "The Panorama of a Pastor's Wife," choosing juxtaposition as its theme: the way that two things, or people, can live side-by-side with a glaring difference between them but somehow manage to harmonize too. If we were all the same, how boring life would be!

She attended workshops at the Iowa Writers Conference, Wesleyan Writers Conference, New York State Writers Institute, and the Madeline Island School of the Arts. In 2017, she was accepted into Grub Street's Memoir Incubator program.

In her regular work life, she has toggled between classroom English teaching and administering job readiness and internship programs for adults and youth. Currently, Ingraham is the school-to-career coordinator at a New Hampshire high school. Follow her Substack called "Side by Side" for more writing on juxtapositions, adjacencies, and border lines on life and love.

Acknowledgments

This book and I have been on a long road together. It was almost as if I started nurturing a fourth child just as our youngest pushed off for college, eight years ago. Along the way many individuals have held up lanterns, encouraged me to keep going, and offered me nutritious morsels.

To my loyal cadre of "The Panorama of a Pastor's Wife" blog subscribers: I can't thank you enough for your patience. I've had more than enough time to "find my voice," don't you think?

Terry Miller, Vermont alpaca farmer and web designer extraordinaire, has been with me ever since I launched that site. She is an extraordinary human being: highly skilled, so helpful to her clients, and also grounded in what's most important.

I'm grateful to the good people at Rootstock Publishing who accepted my manuscript and then guided me through everything that needed to be done through the past year. It's been a great honor to join this mutually supportive community of writers. My enthusiastic appreciation goes to Deborah Heimann for her sharp editing work; what a relief it was when she dug in!

A couple of decades ago, as I started trying to discern broad topics from the ragtag material in my "clergy wife journal"—a blue, three-ring binder—I found my way (thanks, Margaret Bullitt-Jonas) to a wonderful first editor. Jeanne Braham provided just the kind of encouragement and guidance I needed in that early stage. She allowed me to wonder, "Should I keep going even if I'm not at all sure *where* I'm really going?"

At the Wesleyan Writers Conference, one of my instructors was Honor Moore—accomplished poet, nonfiction writer, and daughter of the late Bishop Paul Moore. She used the word "fierce" to describe one of my essays. I had never thought of myself as anything close to that, but she helped me to try on the adjective. Thanks to my classmates in a memorable two-week summer session at the New York Writers Institute at Skidmore when our teacher was Phillip Lopate. I'll never forget the reception there when I found myself having a casual conversation with the amazing Joyce Carol Oates, a frequent visitor to the program. She actually looked right at me with her unforgettable eyes and said, "Tell me about your blog, Polly."

Several autumns ago, I was very fortunate to spend a week on an island in Lake Superior at the Madeline Island School of the Arts in a class taught by Mary Carroll Moore, whom I'd first met at a compelling session about book structure, thanks to the New Hampshire Writers Project's annual conference. Riding a bike around that island, hugging the shoreline and hearing the slosh of the waves against the rocks, peering into mossy woods that resembled fairyland, I imbibed a kind of wildness that was freeing.

Enrolling in Grub Street's Memoir Incubator course was a big step, but it was the right one. Once a week, I made the long drive down to Boston; nine of us shared our drafts, offered feedback to one another, and pushed forward. Thanks to all of you, and to our teacher, Garrard Conley, who brought just the right mix of seriousness, empathy and humor to our sessions.

Thanks also to Alysia Abbott (the next M.I. instructor) for taking the initiative to bring Grub alumni together. Kristen Paulsen-Nyguen, Linda Button, and Molly Howes, as well as Michele Cubelli-Harris, have all provided valuable support. Robin Taylor, whom I met at a Grub event, and I clicked immediately; it's a good thing that Zoom works well from Scotland!

Profound thanks to Diane Les Becquets, who was the first to edit the whole manuscript when I thought it might be "done" (a term easier to apply in cooking, than in writing). She has also stayed supportive through the final stretch. I am also indebted to Ethan Gilsdorf, a nonfiction pro who teaches at Grub, for editing and coaching me through another wave of revising.

I'm grateful to the amazing and hilarious Gina Barreca, whose generous spirit benefited me when I was in the throes of working on this book. Thanks for inviting me to contribute twice to your *Fast Women* series and for reading my whole manuscript.

Thanks to Concord friends Laura Knoy and Margaret Porter for reading the manuscript and offering feedback, also to Wendy Jensen and Ian Rogers for becoming writing allies through the New Hampshire Writers Project.

To David and Barbara Webb: if you two hadn't slyly suggested that Rob and I might hit it off, this marriage never would have happened. Then where would we be?

To my cousin Mary Ann: thanks for asking me to be your flower girl when I was five, and thanks for believing in this project, as well as carrying the torch for Emily Dickinson. Thanks also to my cousins Barbara and Brenda, for cheering me on in the last few years.

My parents have been gone for years, but I think of them each every day. I'm so lucky to have been their youngest child, and just as lucky to have grown up with four spectacular brothers. Mike, Steve, Rob and I now miss our irreplaceable brother Sandy tremendously. Thanks also to each of their wives—Sally, Sheila, June, and Amy—for being a strong sister group. And special gratitude to Amy, accomplished author and editor, for her steady wisdom and for helping me finally land on a title.

To my vibrant mother-in-law, Marie: your optimism, generosity, love of reading, expert cooking skill, and excellent sense of style enhance all of our lives. To my three now adult children—Willie, Cora, and Henry: how proud I am of each one of you, and how wonderful it is to see you care for one another. I wouldn't trade all those Sunday mornings in the pews with you for anything.

And, finally, my unending gratitude to my heartthrob Rob: for falling for and with me in the first place, for tending to our home fires with such attentiveness, for sharing at least some of what's in your fascinating mind, for listening to my musings. I love you and look forward to the ribbon of road ahead.

🍃 **We Grow Our Books in Montpelier, Vermont**
Learn more about our titles in Fiction, Nonfiction, Poetry
and Children's Literature at the QR code below or visit www.
rootstockpublishing.com.

www.ingramcontent.com/pod-product-compliance
Lightning Source LLC
Chambersburg PA
CBHW060516080526
44586CB00012B/503